INTEGRATING LANGUAGE AND LEARNING FOR INCLUSION

AN ASIAN/PACIFIC FOCUS

D1417671

CULTURE, REHABILITATION, AND EDUCATION SERIES
SERIES EDITOR
Orlando L. Taylor, Ph.D.

Bilingual Speech-Language Pathology:
An Hispanic Focus
Edited by Hortencia Kayser, Ph.D.

Integrating Language and Learning for
Inclusion: An Asian/Pacific Focus
Edited by Li-Rong Lilly Cheng, Ph.D.

INTEGRATING LANGUAGE AND LEARNING FOR INCLUSION

AN ASIAN/PACIFIC FOCUS

EDITED BY

LI-RONG LILLY CHENG, PH.D.
SAN DIEGO STATE UNIVERSITY
SAN DIEGO, CALIFORNIA

SINGULAR PUBLISHING GROUP, INC.
SAN DIEGO · LONDON

Singular Publishing Group, Inc.
4284 41st Street
San Diego, California 92105-1197

19 Compton Terrace
London, N1 2UN, UK

Typeset in 10/12 Palatino by So Cal Graphics
Printed in the United States of America by McNaughton & Gunn

Library of Congress Cataloging-in-Publication Data

Integrating language and learning for inclusion: an Asian/Pacific
   Focus / edited by Li-Rong Lilly Cheng.
     p.   cm. — (Culture, rehabilitation, and education series)
   ISBN 1-56593-451-2
   1. Asian Americans—Education.   2. Asian Americans—Educa-
tion—Language arts.   3. English language—Study and teaching—
Oriental speakers.   I. Cheng, Li-Rong Lilly.   II. Series.
LC2632. I58 1995
371.97'073—dc20   95–7517
                                                             CIP

CONTENTS

Foreword by Orlando L. Taylor, Ph.D.   **VII**

Preface   **XI**

Contributors   **XV**

Acknowledgments   **XVII**

PART I   **1**

1   Asian/Pacific Islander Students in Need of   **3**
Effective Services
Li-Rong Lilly Cheng, Ph.D., and
Ji-Mei Chang, Ph.D.

2   LEP, LD, Poor and Missed Learning Opportunities: **31**
A Case of Inner-City Chinese-American Children
Ji-Mei Chang, Ph.D.

PART II   **61**

3   The Pacific Islander Population and the Challenges   **63**
They Face
Li-Rong Lilly Cheng, Ph.D.,
Jean Nakasato, M.S., and
Gloria Jean Wallace, Ph.D

4   Understanding Southeast Asian Students   **107**
Huynh Dinh Te, Ph.D.

5   India: Its People, Culture, and Languages   **125**
         Chandra Shekar, Ph.D., and
         M. N. Hegde, Ph.D.

6   "The Crying Father" and "My Father Doesn't Love Me":   **149**
         Selected Observations and Reflections on
         Southeast Asians and Special Education
         Kenji Ima, Ph.D., and
         Phinga-Evelyn Kheo, M.S.

PART III   **179**

7   ESL Strategies for API Populations   **181**
         Li-Rong Lilly Cheng, Ph.D.

8   Assessing Asian Students for Special Services: **213**
         A Pre-Assessment Consideration
         Li-Rong Lilly Cheng, Ph.D.

9   LEP Parents As Resources: Generating Opportunity to   **265**
         Learn Beyond Schools Through Parental Involvement
         Ji-Mei Chang, Ph.D.,
         Anna Y. Lai, M.A., and
         Ward Shimizu, M.A.

10   Reframing the Structure   **291**
         Li-Rong Lilly Cheng, Ph.D.

APPENDIX

         Hawaiian Demographics   **325**

         Index   **327**

FOREWORD

This book is the second in a series of books on "Culture, Rehabilitation, and Education in Culturally and Linguistically Diverse Populations." The series represents the first major effort to present, in a comprehensive, interdisciplinary manner, the state of the literature on culture and its impact on rehabilitation in a variety of fields, especially the field of communication disorder.

The series focuses on this rather broad array of disciplines in response to the changing environment in which health care, rehabilitation, and education are offered, particularly in the United States. It is increasingly the rule that speech-language clinicians, teachers, social workers, psychologists, nurses, physical therapists, and others work in collaboration to provide services for the **whole** person. For school-age individuals, one cannot readily divorce the services provided to individuals who are disabled in clinics and hospitals from those provided in schools. Thus, the eclectic approach of this series will enable readers to see how culture affects the full range of services offered to individuals who are disabled in a variety of settings and from a variety of disciplines.

At the dawn of the 21st century, the topic of cultural diversity has permeated virtually all disciplines within the social, behavioral, and rehabilitation sciences, as well as the field of education. Beginning in the late 1960s and continuing to the present, research, theory, and clinical practice have increasingly considered topics pertaining to culture as they relate to the nature and acquisition of "normal" behavior and function, and to issues pertaining to the nature, assessment, and management of various disorders and disabilities.

Scholars and practitioners have advanced several reasons for increased interest in cultural considerations in understanding normal behavior and disabilities. Some of these reasons have focused on the rapid demographic changes that have occurred in the United States.

Others have focused on the establishment of increased ethical and legal requirements for gender, race, and disability equity. Still others have focused on theoretical requirements for considering cultural issues in addressing topics of development (acquisition), assessment, and intervention.

The demographic issue cannot be overemphasized. According to the 1990 census, for example, people of color (African Americans, Hispanics, Asian Americans, Native Americans, Aleuts, Eskimos, Pacific Islanders, and others) comprised almost 28% of the American population. Moreover, they comprised more than 35% of the school-age children and were the majority of the population in most of America's urban centers. If current birth rates and immigration patterns continue, they will comprise a majority of the American population by the middle of the 21st century. This is true already in the state of California, and will become so in Texas by the turn of the century. More importantly, these rapidly growing populations will continue to comprise a substantial portion of the pool of individuals seeking services from professionals in the rehabilitation and educational fields.

To assure that these professionals are prepared to provide such services, it is important—indeed imperative—that they are well informed on the nature of culture and its effect on normal behavior and disability. In the field of communication disorders, for example, clinicians must be fully informed on the nature of the family and community environments in which speech and language behavior are acquired. They must know how to infuse notions pertaining to cultural diversity into assessment, diagnostic, and intervention strategies.

A good case also can be made to use legal issues and legislative mandates to validate the notion of cultural considerations in the rehabilitation fields and education. In addition to the presence of such laws as the Americans with Disabilities Act, federal law, for example, requires nondiscrimination in the assessment, diagnosis, educational placement, and provision of rehabilitation services to children with communicative disorders and other special needs in public school settings. Clearly, the intention and substance of these laws and mandates cannot be achieved unless the professional workforce is well informed on the nature of culture and its effect on education and rehabilitation.

More important than demographic and legal issues, for purely theoretical reasons the topic of culture and cultural diversity should permeate every aspect of the disciplines that provide services to the disabled. Even without the legal, ethical, or demographic factors, we are required to address the nature of culture if we are to have valid notions about the nature of normal and disabled behavior and function. The reasons for such a claim are obvious.

First, all behavior—and especially communicative behavior—is acquired within a family/community context. With respect to communication, for example, culture determines everything from the language/dialect to be acquired, and their cognitive underpinnings, to how communication is used as a function of purpose, audience, and meaning.

Second, the determination of what is and is not "normal"—and what to do about "abnormal" behavior and function—is culturally determined. Also, certain culturally based genetic, social, physical, and nutritional issues can result in differences in prevalence and etiology considerations for some disorders in different groups (e.g., sickle cell anemia in African Americans).

Finally, intervention issues in all disciplines should be culturally driven if they are to be effective. Everything from the instruments employed to assess behavior and the interactions with the client and family members to the underlying intervention strategies and the materials used in intervention settings should be culturally driven.

The focus on a sub-set of the Asian American population for one of the early books in this series is not accidental. Persons of Asian background, who represent the largest cohort of individuals on the planet Earth, are one of the most internally diverse groups in the United States. In 1990, they represented almost 4% of the population. Perhaps more impressive is the fact that the Asian population was among the fastest growing groups in the United States during this period. Between 1980 and 1990, the Asian American population increased by about 80%. Compared to relatively flat population growth for whites and more modest gains by African Americans, this rate of growth is both phenomenal and a powerful indicator of the evolving character of the American population.

In this book, Lilly Cheng and her collaborators deploy their vast knowledge and professional experiences to present a comprehensive and interdisciplinary view of the relevant educational, special educational, and communication disorder issues and topics that have relevance to Asian and Pacific Island peoples. They provide a historical, geographical, and demographic context for their discussions, which are presented from the vantage points of a wide range of populations—many of which are typically omitted from the literature, for example, East Indians and Vietnamese.

The special feature of this book is that it looks at the "whole person" and not just an individual who may have a communication disorder or an educational need. By presenting information from such diverse fields as education, special education, communication disorders, psychology, counseling, multicultural studies, sociology, political science, and others, Cheng and her co-authors provide the reader with a glimpse of how issues of culture and culture diversity are best discussed in the fields of education, rehabilitation, and health.

A new America—a multicultural America—is just over the horizon. As a result, rehabilitation workers, communication disorders specialists, and educators will face new challenges—and opportunities—in the years ahead. However, the emergence of new basic and applied data and theory pertaining to culture, behavior, disability, and intervention will permit us to meet these challenges and opportunities with unprecedented success.

Orlando L. Taylor, Ph.D.

PREFACE

We can not change history, but we can change the future.
BUTLER, 1994

So, what does our future look like? The population will be more diverse in age, ethnicity, culture, language, and social-economic status. We will be driven by new technologies that will become rapidly obsolete, and there will be more demands on education and services from our clients. Furthermore, we will need to be globalized (Johnson, 1994). A major shift has taken place in globalization from north to south, from west to east, the so called "Asia-Pacific era" (Gaddala, 1989).

Asia-Pacific will play a pivotal role in unfolding this future that we share. Asia, the largest continent, contains nearly 50 countries as well as portions of several others. It encompasses one third of the world's land mass and is home to two thirds of the world's population. Asia has the largest concentration of the world's consumers and producers. Culturally, its diverse heritage reaches back many millennia, representing a valuable resource for enriching world culture. The Pacific Islanders are separated by the Pacific Ocean and at the same time linked by this body of water. They bring common heritages and different stories.

East Asia, Southeast Asia, and South Asia form the main immigrant groups of recent immigrants to the United States. These areas encompass the People's Republic of China and India, Japan, South Korea, Taiwan, Hong Kong, and Singapore and North Korea, Kampuchea, Pakistan and Bangladesh (political hot spots) and emerging market forces in Vietnam and the Philippines (Asian and Pacific Horizons, 1994).

According to the Statistical Abstract of the United States (1994), the seven countries sending the most immigrants to the United States in 1992 were Mexico, Vietnam, the Philippines, the Dominican Republic, China, India, and Korea. Five of the seven are Asian Pacific countries. These people come to the United States to seek a better life and employ-ment opportunities. Many of their children will not be able to use English during their first few years in the United States. The Asian Pacific populations are concentrated mostly on the east and west coasts of the continental United States.

The dramatic demographic changes that have taken place in the last two decades in the United States have been reported by many researchers (Fong, 1994; Ong, 1994). Their works provide specific data on the status of Asia Pacific America. It is important for us to have correct and current information on immigration, because there has been misinformation and misunderstanding about newcomers in the United States causing racial tension and friction.

Although China's economy is growing rapidly, legal as well as illegal aliens continue to enter the United States representing the largest Chinese-speaking immigrant population. China is a country with an authoritarian and often brutal regime presiding over an explosion in living standards for its 1.2 billion people. It is a country where dissidents are punished and incarcerated while entrepreneurs prosper and flourish. Besides the influx of Chinese immigrants, poverty and internal unrest have driven many Indians and Filipinos to migrate to the United States. In addition, there has been a continuous flow of Southeast Asian immigrants to the United States since 1975. This trend is projected to continue. How we can provide equitable services to such a diverse population remains a challenge to all of us.

In terms of education, the 1994 California Department of Education data indicated that 14.4% of limited English proficient (LEP) students received only English language development (ELD), while another 12.5% received ELD and specially designed academic instruction in English (SDAIE). This means that 26.9% of LEP students received special instruction, but only in English. Another 18.4% of LEP students received these English services and some communicative support in non-English language (ELD+SDAIE+PLS). Only 28.1% received academic support in primary language (ELD+ASPL). Another 26.6% received no special language instructional services at all (University of California Linguistic Minority Research Institute, 1994).

This book attempts to fill the information gaps relating to the social, economic, and linguistic dimensions of Asian Pacific populations for service providers. The first part of the book focuses on the theoretical and philosophical underpinnings of service delivery to the linguistically and culturally diverse Asian/Pacific populations.

The second part of the book presents demographic, cultural, and linguistic data about the following focused groups: India, Samoa, Vietnam, Hawaii, Chamorro, and other Pacific Islands. There is a lot of information available about the Chinese, Korean, and Japanese (Cheng, 1991) because they have been in the United States much longer. However, the other groups are less known, and they form the core group of our discussion. The most visible recent immigrants are the refugees from Southeast Asia in which the Vietnamese form the largest group. Although immigrants from India have been coming to the United States at a steady pace in recent years, little is known about them. Finally, the Pacific Islanders are the "invisible" group, and they bring diversity and challenges. In this second part, both traditional culture and contemporary trends are addressed, with a major emphasis on social, cultural, linguistic, and educational issues.

The final part of this book addresses current paradigms in pre-assessment, assessment, and intervention as well as suggested practices. Case studies are presented to provide a more cohesive and comprehensive understanding of the challenges that children, their teachers, service providers, and parents face.

"The future will be much brighter if we enhance our educational efforts by teaching respect for each other's dignity and humanity, and we work to make our differences our strength" (Castro, 1994).

REFERENCES

Asian and Pacific Horizons. (1994). Fall Newsletter (Vol. 1, No. 1). San Diego: Asian Studies Institute, San Diego State University.

Butler, D. (October, 1994). Honoree Remarks. Second Annual Awards Luncheon. Minority Health Professions Education Foundation: "A Golden Opportunity," Sacramento, CA.

Castro, D. (October, 1994). Honoree Remarks. Second Annual Awards Luncheon. Minority Health Professions Education Foundation: "A Golden Opportunity," Sacramento, CA.

Cheng, L. (1991). *Assessing Asian language performance.* Oceanside, CA: Academic Communication Associate.

Fong, M. (1994). *The first suburban Chinatown.* Philadelphia, PA: Temple University Press.

Gaddala, S. (1989). Lecture series on globalization. San Diego: San Diego State University.

Johnson, P. D. (October, 1994). Keynote speech. Second Annual Awards Luncheon. Minority Health Professions Education Foundation: "A Golden Opportunity," Sacramento, CA.

Ong, P. (1994). *The state of Asian Pacific America: Economic, diversity, issues & policies*. Los Angeles: LEAP Asian Pacific American Public Policy Institute and UCLA Asian American Studies Center.

Statistical Abstract of the United States. (1994).

University of California Linguistic Minority Research Institute. (October, 1994). Vol. 4, No. 2.

CONTRIBUTORS

Ji-Mei Chang, Ph.D.
Division of Special Education
and Rehabilitative Services
San Jose State University
San Jose, California

Li-Rong Lilly Cheng, Ph.D.
College of Health and
Human Services
San Diego State University
San Diego, California

M. N. Hegde, Ph.D.
Department of Communicative
Sciences and Disorders
California State University
at Fresno
Fresno, California

Dr. Kenji Ima, Ph.D.
Department of Sociology
San Diego State University
San Diego, California

Phinga-Evelyn Kheo, M.S.
Head Counselor
Wilson Academy of
International Studies
San Diego, California

Anna Y. Lai, M.A.
School Psychologist
San Francisco Unified
School District
San Francisco, California

Jean Nakasato, M.S.
Speech-Language Coordinator
State of Hawaii
Department of Education
Honolulu, Hawaii

Chandra Shekar, Ph.D.
Department of Linguistics
California State University
at Fresno
Fresno, California

Ward Shimizu, M.A.
San Jose State University
San Jose, California

Huynh Dinh Te, Ph.D.
Senior Equity Associate
Southwest Regional Lab (SWRL)
Los Alamitos, California

Gloria Jean Wallace, Ph.D.
Department of Audiology
and Speech Pathology
University of Tennessee
Knoxville, Tennessee

ACKNOWLEDGMENTS

First of all, I would like to express my appreciation for two giants in the field of Communication Disorders: Drs. Sadanand Singh and Orlando Leroy Taylor for having the faith in me to accomplish this monumental task. Their words of encouragement, support, and wisdom, and their sense of humor have guided me through the course of this writing. Their insistence on inquiries and excellence compelled me to go one step beyond. I owe my deepest gratitude to them. Second, I want to thank all the contributors for spending endless hours writing, correcting and rewriting their manuscripts. It is their will power, devotion, and persistence that have sustained me through many long hours of hard work. Like me, many of the contributors of this book are not native speakers of English, and our struggle to express what we want to say formed the basis of our stories. Through the process of writing, interviewing, dialoguing, and debating we have learned so much from each other and have become empowered and yet more humble by the process. I also want to thank the children, their teachers, and their families for giving us such rich and powerful stories. Furthermore, this book could not have become a reality without the comments and reviews of Frances Chow, Kathee Christensen, Henriette Langdon, and John Tse. Andy Koopmans, Joyce Huey, Kristen Ogwaro, and Natasha Petroff provided me with excellent editorial assistance. Additionally, Pam Rider, Marie Linvill, and Angie Singh have been instrumental in their support for this project.

While attending the 1994 ASHA annual convention in New Orleans, I was so touched by many students and colleagues who have found my writing useful that I want to thank them for their recognition. It was such a heartening experience for me. Their continued work and struggle to have a better tomorrow inspired me greatly. I thank you all. I dedicate this book to my husband, Koun-Ping and my son Philip Si-Wei, whose love, understanding and caring for me have made it all worthwhile. Finally, for all of us who are life-long learners, this book marks the beginning of an everlasting relationship between you and the pursuit of truth, knowledge, caring, love, and empathy for all humankind. Thank you.

PART I

The first part of the book presents selected topics surrounding the social, linguistic, and educational dimensions of Asian-Pacific Islander populations from a special-needs perspective. It lays a theoretical foundation for discussing language, literacy, and the acquisition of knowledge. Furthermore, it discusses in-depth description and analysis of missed learning opportunities of students with special needs and provides suggestions for school intervention.

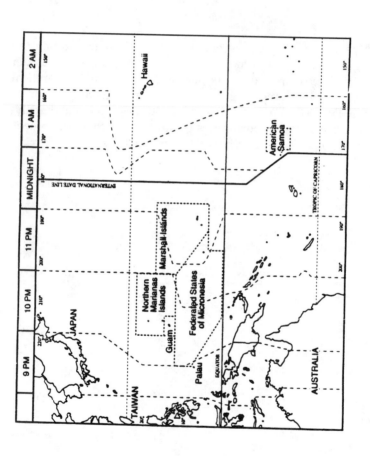

MAP OF THE PACIFIC

CHAPTER 1

ASIAN/PACIFIC ISLANDER STUDENTS IN NEED OF EFFECTIVE SERVICES

LI-RONG LILLY CHENG, PH.D.
JI-MEI CHANG, PH.D.

It has been two decades since Lau vs Nichols (1974), yet a close examination of our service delivery to language minority populations leaves a great deal to be desired. Twenty-five years ago, the Bilingual Education Act of 1968 was passed and then reauthorized in 1974 with full support from the federal government. Despite the passage of these laws, numerous reports have documented the inadequacies of U.S. schools in meeting the needs of Asian students and other groups with cultural and language differences (Olsen, 1988). Although the number of Asian/Pacific Islander students has increased over the past twenty years, support for bilingual education, including Asian programs, has dropped for limited English proficient (LEP) students with special needs. Currently, less emphasis is placed on a student's primary language than on English and questions are being raised about the feasibility of implementing new programs to upgrade educational services for Asian/Pacific language minority students (Ima, 1990).

⊔

DEMOGRAPHIC INFORMATION

In recent years there has been a significant influx of Asian/Pacific populations to the United States. They represented less than 1% of the total U.S. population in 1970, growing to 1.5% by 1980. Estimates predict a rise to 4% by the year 2000: a projected growth of 400% within 30 years and an additional 10% by the year 2050 (Gardner, Robey, & Smith, 1985; Rueda, 1993). The U.S. population currently stands at approximately 245 million. According to the 1990 Census, the official count of Asian-Americans and Pacific Islanders (API) was 7.3 million (U.S. Bureau of Census, 1991). Increasing numbers of Pacific Islanders have emigrated in recent years; data from the 1990 census shows an increase of 145% from 1980 to 1990 (U.S. Bureau of Census, 1991), indicating that APIs are the fastest growing ethnic minority in America, followed by Hispanics (Yu, 1993). In 1982, just under 12% of the U.S. population was African-American, 6.4% Hispanic, and 1.6% Asian, setting the White population at about 80%. By the year 2050, the estimated U.S. population will reach 3 billion. Whites will account for only 60% of the total, with Blacks at 16% and the population percentage of Hispanics will more than double to 15%. Estimates further predict that Asian populations will jump from 1.6% to as much as 10%. If these predictions are accurate, by 2050 more than 1 in 3 Americans will be non-White (Rueda, 1993).

Two historic events prompted an increase in the API populations in the United States: the Immigration Law of 1965, and the U.S. involvement in the Vietnam War, resulting in the flow of more than one million Southeast Asian refugees into this country (Ima & Cheng, 1989). Other political developments, such as Tienaman Square in 1989, led to the emigration of political refugees from the People's Republic of China. Also, in 1992, there were reports of Chinese "boat people" entering the United States illegally. Future events, such as the transfer of power in Hong Kong from Great Britain to the mainland government in 1997, and the political unrest in the Philippines, are likely to generate additional numbers of Asian immigrants.

Seventy-nine percent of APIs reside in California, New York, Hawaii, Texas, Illinois, New Jersey, Washington, Virginia, Florida and Massachusetts. The API population grew by at least 40% in all states except for Hawaii. In California, the API population rose 127% between 1980 and 1990, surpassing the national API growth rate of

108% (Yu, 1993). There are large pockets of Chamorro and Samoan populations in large cities on Hawaii and the West Coast of the U.S. mainland, specifically in California. Other Pacific Islander populations are scattered throughout the western states.

Prior to 1965, the Asians residing in the U.S. mainland were mostly Chinese, Filipino, Japanese, and Korean. In this chapter, we refer to these groups as traditional Asians. Many Chinese came to the United States to build railroads and to work in gold mines. Very few Japanese came to the U.S. mainland; however, many went to the Hawaiian islands to work in pineapple and sugar cane farms. The Filipinos also went to the Pacific and Hawaiian islands. Their numbers were few and they were relatively invisible. When the 1965 U.S. immigration law opened up the possibility of significant Asian migration, the resulting influx led to proportionally more Asian than European immigrants for the first time in U.S. history. From 1960 to 1970, the origins of U.S. immigrants were 34% Asian, 34% Latin American, and 16% European, with 16% from other countries. However, in 1979, 42% were from Latin America, 41% from Asia, and 14% from Europe. This trend of shrinking proportions from Europe and increasing proportions from Asia and Latin America has continued. The figures from 1985 also indicated that more than 80% of all immigrants came from Latin America and Asia. It is projected that more immigrants will come from Pacific Asia (U.S. Bureau of Census, 1994).

Reasons for the immigration trend stem not only from the openness of U.S. policy, but also from factors within the native countries that have caused Asians to leave their native lands. These factors include civil wars, political oppression, internal unrest, economic depression, opportunities for trade, and educational opportunity. The top 10 countries of origin for immigrants in the fiscal year 1992 were Mexico with 22%; Vietnam, 8.0%; Philippines, 6.3%; Soviet Union, 4.5%; Dominican Republic, 4.3%; China, 4.0%; India, 3.8%; El Salvador, 2.7%; Poland, 2.6%; and United Kingdom, 2.1% (U.S. Bureau of Census). (See Table 1–1.)

On the whole, Southeast Asian immigrants are far younger than the U.S. population. Their school-age population will continue to grow because they are young and have higher-than-average reproductive rates, compared with settled American rates. Consequently, Southeast Asian family size in this group is likely to grow faster than the average American and traditional Asian families. An estimate of the relative number of youths of different ethnic groups is presented in Table 1–2. Another indication of the continued high rate of growth

TABLE 1–1

Top ten countries of origin for immigrants in fiscal year 1992.

Countries	Percent
1. Mexico	22.0
2. Vietnam	8.0
3. Philippines	6.3
4. Soviet Union	4.5
5. Dominican Republic	4.3
6. China	4.0
7. India	3.8
8. El Salvador	2.7
9. Poland	2.6
10. United Kingdom	2.1

Source: Adapted from U.S. Bureau of Census. Statistical Abstract of the United States: 1994 (114th ed.). Washington, DC.

TABLE 1–2

Projections of Asian/Pacific Islanders in the United States by age (× 1000).

Asian Pacific Americans	1990	2020
<15	1,749	3,706
15–24	1,224	2,509
25–44	2,659	5,309
45–64	1,187	4,333
65+	454	2,057
Total	**7,274**	**17,914**

Source: Adapted from "Growth of the Asian Pacific American Population" in *The State of Asian Pacific America: A Policy Report* by X. Ong and X. Hee (1993). Los Angeles: UCLA Asian American Studies Center.

of the Southeast Asian populations is the fertility rate. Fertility rates of various ethnic groups are provided in Table 1–3.

The overall birthrate for traditional Asian groups is proportionately low compared to Latinos, African-Americans and Whites. A more accurate or appropriate statement should include the high birthrates among Southeast Asians. Among the more recent arrivals from Southeast Asia are the very young, who tend to be more fertile. Thus, the newer Asian groups will probably grow more rapidly than both previous Asian arrivals and the general U.S. population—posing a more critical problem for schools. At the K–12 level, their numbers exceeded California's African-American enrollment in 1985. Currently, Asians constitute 10.2% of the California K–12 population, whereas African-American students constitute 8.9% of that population (Ima, 1990; Trueba, Cheng, & Ima, 1993; Yu, 1993).

Over half of all Asian youth come from homes where a primary language other than English is spoken (Chan, 1983). According to a 1992 report by the Office of Bilingual Education and Minority Language Affairs (OBEMLA), the following states have the largest LEP populations: California with 42%; Texas, 15%; New York, 8%; Illinois, 4%; Puerto Rico, 3%, New Mexico, 3%; Arizona, 3%; and Florida, 3%. In 1994, a report prepared by the United States General Accounting Office indicated that "[al]though 72 percent of LEP students are concentrated in six states (California, Florida, Illinois, New Jersey, New York, and Texas), about one-sixth of the counties (533 out of 3,140) located in 47 states have substantial numbers of LEP students" (U.S. GAO, 1994, p. 5). In California, one-fourth of LEP students are Asians (University of California Linguistic Minority Research Institute, 1994). In 1970, the California school-age population was 27% minority, and

TABLE 1–3
Fertility rate of Asians.

1983 San Diego	Chinese	Hmong	Khmer	Lao	Vietnamese
Total fertility rate	4.7	11.9	7.4	6.6	3.4
Household sizes	5.8	8.7	8.3	6.3	5.5
Percent urban	95.4	8.3	46.3	79.1	94.0

Source: Ngoan Le. (1993). *The Case of Southeast Asian Refugees: The State of Asian Pacific America*. Los Angeles: UCLA Asian American Studies Center.

by the year 2000, it will be 57%. By the year 2000, 35% of students in California will be Hispanic, 11% Asian, and 9% African-American. And by 2010, California will become the first mainland state with no single ethnic group as a majority (Rueda, 1993).

⊔

DIVERSITY WITHIN API POPULATIONS

More than 100 languages are spoken in the school systems of New York City, Chicago, Los Angeles, and Fairfax County, Virginia. The top 10 languages are listed in Table 1–4. According to the 1992 California Department of Education Annual Language Census, from the population of 1,078,705 LEP students, 76% spoke Spanish, 4% Vietnamese, 2% Hmong, 2% Korean, 2% Cantonese, 2% Khmer, 2% Filipino, 1% Armenian, 1% Mandarin and 6% all other languages. In California public schools, 1 out of 6 children was born outside the United States and 1 out of 3 children speaks a language other than English at home. The Los Angeles school system absorbs 30,000 new immigrant children each year.

TABLE 1–4

The top 10 languages spoken in the school systems of New York, Chicago, Los Angeles, and Fairfax County, Virginia.

Top Languages	Number of Speakers in Millions
1. English only	198.6
2. Spanish	17.3
3. French	1.7
4. German	1.5
5. Italian	1.3
6. Chinese	1.2
7. Tagalog	.8
8. Polish	.7
9. Korean	.6
10. Vietnamese	.5

Source: Adapted from U.S. Bureau of the Census. *Statistical Abstract of the United States: 1994* (114th ed.). Washington, DC.

Within the API groups, there are subpopulations; within each subpopulation there is an array of variables such as language, home environment, and socioeconomic status (SES). The range of ethnic groups includes students from wide geographic areas in Asia, including the East Asian countries of China, Japan, Korea, and Taiwan, the countries of Indochina (Vietnam, Thailand, Laos, Cambodia, and Burma), the Indian subcontinent, the Philippines, and the thousands of islands in the Pacific Ocean (Chan & Kitano, 1986; Cheng, 1987; McKay & Wong, 1988).

The hundreds of different languages and dialects spoken in East and Southeast Asia and the Pacific Islands can be categorized into five major families. These are (1) Malayo-Polynesian (Austronesian) family: Chamorro, Ilocano, and Tagalog; (2) Sino-Tibetan family: Thai, Yao, Mandarin, and Cantonese; (3) Austro-Asiatic family: Khmer, Vietnamese, and Hmong; (4) Papuan family: New Guinean; and (5) Altaic family: Japanese and Korean (Ma, 1985). (For more information about the Asian/Pacific languages, see Cheng 1991, 1993.)

The challenges of providing meaningful instruction to these diverse groups of students are tremendous. Most teachers are not bilingual and have not received training in bilingual education. They face cultural dissonance and linguistic incompatibility. Even trained bilingual educators are reluctant to provide a full bilingual program for Asians; there are logistical problems associated with the development of such programs in schools. The diversity of primary languages among API groups challenges schools that attempt to provide bilingual or native language services to these groups.

To illustrate the impact of diversity on educational programs for Asians, a few selected issues regarding diversity in Chinese languages are presented in this section. Aside from Mandarin, the designated national language in both the Republic of China and the People's Republic of China, are various dialects spoken by Chinese speakers from various regions (Cheng, 1991; Wong, 1988). Furthermore, the Chinese spoken and written language systems are two distinctively different entities. In the Chinese logographic writing system, the script-speech mapping is on the morphosyllabic level, although in an alphabetic system, such as English, writing is mapped onto a deeper morphophonemic level (Tzeng & Hung, 1988). Chinese written language consists of morphemes, which are represented by characters or logographs. These Chinese logographs then represent the units of meaning rather than phonemes as in an alphabetic writing system. However, more than 80% of Chinese characters are formed on the basis of phonetic compounds, which consist of two components: phonetic for sound clue and radical for meaning (Chang, Hung, & Tzeng, 1992; Tzeng & Hung, 1988). The character is like a monosyllable, or morpheme, and it in itself can also be a word. However, many of the spoken words are composed of more than one character. Given the unique nature of Chinese languages, the one-to-one correspondence between spoken and graphically represented words may not occur in various dialects; Cantonese is one such dialect. Cantonese-speaking or other Chinese dialect-speaking children may face increased information-processing challenges while acquiring Chinese characters in print (e.g., Chu-Chang, 1982).

The diversity within Chinese language groups noted here does not mean that non-Mandarin speakers will face difficulties in attaining their native language and literacy proficiencies. We merely point out the basic needs for conducting research and developing effective native language literacy programs and support networks for diverse API groups.

⊔

EDUCATIONAL REALITY

The necessity of examining the education of Asian/Pacific Islander students is apparent to API educators who feel that Asian students are not being adequately served by schools throughout the United States. A large number of those with LEP and special needs are placed in all English-speaking classrooms without ESL services. In this section we present a few selected issues that are relevant to the educational experiences, treatment, and challenges faced by the diverse groups of API students both inside and outside of school contexts.

GAPS BETWEEN THEORIES AND PRACTICES

Given the longer history of Spanish bilingual programs and the larger number of native Spanish speakers, the Spanish language bilingual programs have received the most attention, both in theoretical studies and program development (e.g., Guthrie, 1985). But in the face of the greater maturity and sophistication of Spanish-language-based programs, questions are raised by Asian bilingual professionals on the propriety of those programs and approaches for use among various

Asian language minority students. In part, there is a feeling among Asian educators that special attention should be paid to API students, as approaches that may be successful with Hispanic LEP students may not be appropriate for use in designing school programs for Asian students since there are major cultural differences among the groups.

The California State Bilingual Education Office (BEO) sponsored a series of API handbooks which have, over time, progressively incorporated the 1981 theoretical framework. The Handbook for Teaching Lao-Speaking Students (Lewis & Luangpraseut, 1989) attempts to incorporate Cummins' (1981) and Krashen's (1981) (see Chapter 7) theoretical framework into a format appropriate for Lao students. The Khmer booklet even suggests that teachers seriously consider using the Khmer language for teaching Cambodian LEP students. The Vietnamese book (Te, 1987) provides substantive information about the historical, linguistic, and cultural background of Vietnamese students and their families. These Asian handbooks reflect an attempt by the BEO to address the specific needs of a variety of Asian groups. Nevertheless, the books are largely based on anecdotal information and, for the most part, are not complete and are not helpful in developing full-service programs.

In addition, academic success entails not only a need for cognitive academic linguistic proficiency (CALP) (Cummins, 1981), but also for "comprehensible input" in classroom interactions (Krashen, 1981). API LEP students who find classroom discourse and its oral, written, and nonverbal rules incomprehensible or difficult are at a constant disadvantage. These rules exist tacitly both in and out of the classroom, in what might be called the "hidden curriculum." This curriculum exists in all schools and social encounters, and many Asians may not be aware of it. In *Life in Classrooms,* Jackson (1968) defined the hidden curriculum as the praise and the power that combine to give a distinctive flavor to classroom life. Each student and teacher must master the hidden curriculum to make his or her way through academic life.

For a student, mastering the hidden curriculum requires an understanding and willingness to accept the teacher's educational values; the teacher must incorporate his or her values into each student's education in order to become cross-culturally competent (Cheng, 1990a). High dropout rates among certain groups may be attributed to a disengagement brought on by LEP students being ignored during classroom interactions, and the situation, on the whole, may be a result of LEP students' failing to master the hidden curriculum (Pang, 1988).

NOT ALL API STUDENTS ARE MODEL STUDENTS

Many teachers will likely assume that Asian students are higher achievers than their peers (Wong, 1980). Asian Americans are often perceived by many teachers and peers as smart, hard working, and more likely to value education. This stereotype involves significant fallacies since there is a wide range of intergroup and intragroup differences among the diverse Asian populations. Many individuals not only do not fit the stereotype but need special assistance. Additionally, some students are under such pressure to succeed that they drop out (Trueba et al., 1993). For example, traditionally, Asian students coming from middle or upper-middle class families have succeeded in schools in the United States (Hirschman & Wong, 1986; Hurh & Kim, 1986). However, some recent immigrants from Southeast Asian countries (e.g., Indochina) have suffered from years of war, relocation, and disrupted schooling. Furthermore, many have been subjected to emotional and physical trauma as a result of their histories. The debilitating effects on the school performance and emotional well-being of these students perhaps are not being adequately addressed in U.S. schools (Chinn & Plata, 1986). Hence, a large number of Asians do not fit the "model minority syndrome"(see Chang, Chapter 2, and Ima and Kheo, Chapter 6). As teachers, specialists, and educators, we need to go beyond stereotypes, to identify students who are at-risk and in need of special services, and we need to improve our delivery of such services.

There are many at-risk Asian students who carry a combination of special characteristics and circumstances and who need to be identified and given special assistance in order to survive, not only within school but outside of it as well. Those who fit into the "at-risk group" will most likely drop out of school because they are incapable of functioning within the difficult context of their situation. This group comprises the "LEP forever students" (see Ima and Kheo, Chapter 6). These individuals are not likely to find adequately paid jobs and usually end up receiving welfare or taking odd jobs for an indefinite time. The failure of the at-risk group is a clear indication of the lack of an educational policy oriented toward accommodating the diverse needs of these individuals. It also points to the absence of a curriculum aimed at dealing with issues related to basic functional and survival skills.

BARRIERS AND CHALLENGES IN SCHOOLS AND FUTURE EMPLOYMENT

Because the API population is so diverse, sectors of the population are likely to be at-risk and in need of educational assistance beyond what is currently provided. This is especially true among immigrants and refugees who entered the United States during adolescence and were immediately placed into various public schools without adequate emotional or special academic support. Factors related to API populations illustrated in this section extend beyond ethnic boundaries and may be applicable to other at-risk groups within the culturally and linguistically diverse communities.

Some of the common indexes identifying students who are in need of guidance, counseling, and educational intervention in our schools are: poor school attendance, lack of participation in class, lack of supervision at home (no parents or parental figures), disrupted schooling, past physical or emotional trauma, experience of long duration in refugee camps, poor health, lack of previous schooling, lack of progress in English, lack of participation in extracurricular activities, and lack of guidance and counseling for career or life goals.

Acculturation and identity crises are additional factors that are influential on school and social performance of language minority students. Acculturation deals not only with acquisition of a new language, giving up an old language, and retaining or changing one's own culture, but also includes the issue of identity. These issues are much more complex than any single indicator would suggest. The difficulty that "bicultural" individuals confront is whether to make decisions based on the mainstream cultural values or to strike a compromise between their own cultural background and the mainstream. This difficulty often results in ambivalence (Trueba et al., 1993). Such ambivalence may be observed particularly in Asian students whose families are bonded to traditional cultures. Such families often inad- vertently interfere with their children's acculturation into the mainstream culture. These immigrant families should be provided with support and guidelines to enable them to better adapt to their new environment, especially during the transitional or adjustment periods, allowing a smoother transition for students and families.

Students may see acculturation as fundamental to achieving acceptance by mainstream peers. This often entails learning to speak, dress, eat, and behave like other students. Consequently, traditional patterns and values established by a family are often abandoned in favor of those held by valued peers, causing an unpleasant and even tragic dissonance between parents and children. Educators and other school personnel are in a strategic position because they can demonstrate the feasibility and value of bilingual and bicultural interaction. If successful in doing so, educators can minimize conflict in the school and in the home.

Expectations of students at home and at school may often be in conflict. For example, an Asian parent may want a teacher to assign a particular book for reading, although the teacher prefers to have children go to the library to find books of their own choosing. Under such conditions, teachers may view parents as rigid and demanding, and, at the same time, the parents may view the teachers as being lazy and unresponsive. LEP students and families must reconcile their goals, plans, and outlook, not only to the parameters of American culture, but to the personal values held by teachers about education.

Self-image is an important factor in the process of acculturation. Children desire to fit in with others in school, and if a child behaves differently than his or her peers, a feeling of alienation can arise. This situation may cause difficulties for teachers, as well as the child, as alienation may hinder educational progress. Because immigrant children must deal with their parents looking, behaving, and speaking differently than the parents of their peers, all of these children will face conflicts. They will need to make complex decisions about how to balance family life, which for the Asian student is usually very strict and obedience-oriented, with the American school environment that emphasizes individuality and sociability. Compounding the effect of such conflict is that these concerns are not easily discussed. Some children may deal with these conflicts by rejecting the notion of belonging to an ethnic group because they feel they will not be accepted by their mainstream peers or, on the other hand, they may socialize exclusively with their ethnic peers. In some circumstances, the latter type of survival strategy may lead to the formation of gang groups, and case studies of delinquency situations as reported by the San Diego Police Department (Solis, 1995) suggest that gang development is a serious matter that should concern both educators and families (see Ima and Kheo Chapter 6).

Potentially detrimental elements inherent in our schools and in society toward students, language-minority students in particular, have been well documented. These elements may stem from school curriculum or instructional approaches (Bartoli, 1989; Campione, 1989; Cummins, 1989; Goodman, 1986). Teachers' use of language (Heath, 1983, 1986), interaction patterns between teachers and students, low expectations of language minority students, discrimination against minority students' cultural heritage and language (Cummins, 1986; 1989), and a persistent orientation of treating language and cultural differences as deficits rather than resources are among the problematic factors that especially affect language-minority students (Ruiz, 1988). These negative attitudes toward language and cultural diversity have a great impact on the sociopolitical and educational policies influencing the educational and future employment prospects of such students.

Presently, factors related to school practices are most crucial for this discussion. Many factors identified here should also be addressed for the educational welfare of monolingual and other non-Asian, language-minority students. Increasing dropout rates, poor achievement, and substandard literacy development in our schools reflect the failures of rigid, linear, disjointed, and reductionistic approaches in curriculum designs and instructional practices, as well as an over-reliance on competency-based standardized tests that equate educational achievement with information retention. The common practice of "ability grouping" not only interferes with social interaction among minority students and their mainstream peers but also fosters lowered expectations and self-fulfilling prophesies of mediocrity or failure. Additionally, the separation of special and bilingual education programs and personnel interferes with collaboration among educators and works against the pooling of shrinking economic resources.

Even though many Asians would like to assimilate into the American culture, they cannot ignore that after several generations of being in the United States they are still considered "strangers from a different shore" (Takaki, 1989). Although the degree of acculturation may be determined by an individual, the extent to which the structural assimilation is determined by those in power is so great that even the most acculturated individuals may never realize full structural assimilation (Gollnick & Chinn, 1990). Although many immigrants have penetrated the educational system, there still remains a "glass ceiling" (Takaki, 1989) in employment of Asians after leaving school. Stereotyping of Asians often results in APIs exclusion not only from employment, in general, but, even if they are able to find work, from being promoted to management or decision-making positions. Two explanations are frequently offered by theoreticians regarding the glass ceiling phenomenon: a lack of interpersonal skills and racism in the job market. Asians are often seen as lacking interactional and linguistic skills as well as aggressiveness. Many Asians are screened out in employment interviews because they are not assertive enough or because they lack the interpersonal skills characteristic of Americans (Trueba et al., 1993). The racism inherent in the U.S. employment structure denies Asians opportunities because of prejudice rather than any perceptible lack of personal or professional qualification.

⊔⊓

IMPLICATIONS FOR EDUCATION, SERVICE DELIVERY, AND RESEARCH

Critical information relevant to appropriate services for API students in American schools remains scattered and scarce, and relevant research regarding special education for API/LEP populations is extremely limited. The following issues need to be systematically examined to provide a comprehensive and holistic look at the macrocontext pertinent to the provision of sound educational programs for API language minority groups with special needs.

NEED FOR BILINGUAL SPECIAL EDUCATION AND RELATED SERVICES

Neither the bilingual nor the special education field seems to have carried out systematic research focused on programming issues with API LEP student populations who might have specific language and learning needs. An extreme paucity of research-based information exists on the social, language, learning, and literacy environment, as well as the use of specific learning and teaching strategies. Information about optimal instructional approaches suitable to these populations is equally lacking (Chan & Kitano, 1986; Chinn, 1989; Chu-Chang, 1983). Although this is true, referrals for special education placement are increasing among these linguistically diverse API students in our public schools (see Chang, Chapter 2; Chinn, 1989). Therefore, these students are being served in special education and related services without the much needed data required to help special educators design intervention programs to fit these learners' special educational needs.

BRIDGING THE GAPS BETWEEN LANGUAGE AND CULTURE

Learning American English requires an understanding of American culture and of the rules that the American culture dictates. To use the language properly, one must understand the cultural and social meaning of what is being communicated. For example, communicating by telephone often requires the use of certain ritualized phrases such as "How are you?" Each culture has a different set of conventions that determines what behavior is appropriate and inappropriate for each communication circumstance. Knowledge of these conventions is crucial to the success of communication. In acquiring a second language, exclusively focusing on the language form will not facilitate a true comprehension of what is required to properly employ the language; on the other hand, individuals who have the opportunity to interact within a diversity of social and cultural contexts will be more effective communicators because they will gain "hands-on" "real-life" experience, allowing them to pick up on the nuances of the language and its conventions.

For API LEP students, acquiring English requires the development of adaptive strategies of linguistic and cultural code-switching, and it is critical that teachers acknowledge and examine the intricate relationship between language and culture. This means enhancing cross-cultural sensitivities to enable students to retain their world view as they interact with the codes and structures of the American culture. Ultimately, for students to become successfully bilingual and bicultural and to achieve cross-cultural communication competence requires that both the student and the teacher recognize differences and similarities in their cultures, embrace diversity, and strive for mutual understanding and communication.

Showing respect for a student's primary language and culture fosters the positive self-image and higher self-esteem that is important for healthy academic and social development. Mutual respect needs to be an integral part of the overall educational planning for API students. Negative or hostile societal attitudes among peers, teachers, and communities toward diverse API groups instill a sense of insecurity early in these API children's lives and subsequently influence their performance in school (Trueba et al., 1993).

EMPOWERING TEACHERS AND SERVICE PROVIDERS

The diverse language and cultural populations place unprecedented demands on teachers, administrators, and service providers. In thousands of classrooms across the nation, teachers and students are confronted with the challenges of understanding each other. Teachers and specialists face the challenge of identifying the sources of a student's educational difficulties that may stem from either one or a combination of factors such as linguistic, cultural, trauma-, or neuro-physical-related components. If one observes heightened anxiety, confusion in the locus of control, withdrawal, or unresponsiveness of a linguistic minority student, can the assessment team determine whether the child is suffering from cultural shock, an emotional disability, or perhaps both? (See Ima and Kheo, Chapter 6.) This question points to the larger area of generally how poorly our schools have been prepared to deal with linguistically and culturally varied school-age populations.

Teachers and specialists need systematic support in their attempt to understand the diverse needs of API LEP students and to facilitate communication. For example, Philips (1983) emphasized the need for a deeper understanding of the processes of teaching and learning and an examination of the cultural dimensions of interaction between teachers and students. Trueba (1987) argued for an understanding of how the classroom is organized, as well as an understanding of the more abstract social levels of organization that channel students toward success or failure. Trueba further cautioned against excessive stereotyping that results from reliance on the creation of catalogues of cultural patterns, for example, learning styles. Teachers can provide effective guidance to Asian parents and children who have difficulties and/or ambivalence in the process of acculturation into mainstream culture.

EMPOWERING API PARENTS

Families of API language minority students need to be informed and encouraged to participate at all levels of their children's school experience. By involving families in the assessment process, clinicians are able to gain insights into the most appropriate assessment procedures for children. In this way, school personnel can also learn more about a child's use of home and school language as well as his or her literacy environment. In addition, by inviting families of language minority students to participate in classroom activities, teachers can gain access to the richness of community resources relevant to language minority students' particular needs (Moll, Velez-Ibanez, & Greenberg, 1988). Chang, Lai, and Shimizu (Chapter 9) regard parents as significant resources and discuss the LEP parents' role in their children's social, language, and literacy development.

EMPOWERING API STUDENTS

Factors contributing to API students' school and future life success have been presented earlier. To empower API students, teachers, administrators, and specialists can approach solutions in three different ways. First, they can collaborate across disciplines to provide meaningful learning experiences within comprehensible learning environments. The current disjointed instructional approaches provided for students with special needs result in these students' loss of learning opportunities (see Chang, Chapter 2). Collaboration between special education teachers and speech language clinicians are especially fruitful for API groups because many of their students are likely to be diagnosed as language delayed, particularly in the areas of expressive language (see Chang, Chapter 2) and will be served by both of these groups of professionals in schools. Second, as Cummins (1986, 1989) has indicated, is for schools to take on the role of reversing the general societal attitudes and values toward minority groups. The educational system plays an important role in shaping the public image of certain groups of students. Working together, we are likely to provide coherent curricula and meaningful activities to enhance opportunities for all groups of minority students to be academically successful. Third, it is essential that our schools not only recognize the specific educational needs of API students but that they also work to rectify the problems in employment equity. Foreign-born API students, in particular, need to be better prepared for the job market and should be helped to recognize nonacademic issues that will affect their future (for example, the influence of speech accent or an understanding of the importance of networking). These nonacademic areas should be included in any curriculum dealing with this population so that students may translate academic success into occupational success.

In addition, the educational needs of students in terms of social competencies must be stressed further. Students, in general, and language minority students, in particular, must be prepared for life outside of school. If an education is to properly prepare Asian students to "crack the glass ceiling," in the employment sector, that education must examine contexts beyond those of the school environment. Asian students need to be prepared to deal interpersonally not only with peers and teachers but with colleagues and decision makers in the work environment, even as that environment may be associated with the high stress factor of social interaction on grounds unfamiliar to Asians.

Although many students are socially competent within their own environment, they are unable to function well in mainstream social settings. It is paramount for students to develop biculturally appropriate social and interpersonal skills for personal and, eventually, professional well-being. Asians complain that despite their hard work and competency, they seldom advance beyond middle management positions. People in power in the dominant culture counter these complaints by citing deficiencies in Asians' verbal and social skills (Trueba et al., 1993). Teachers can influence and enhance the likelihood of API students enrolling in courses emphasizing development of communication skills. Teachers and administrators can then be trained to sensitize and provide a "safe" and nonthreatening environment in such classes for API students.

At-risk Asian students require a total support system that will make them more successful in acquiring the English language in school, and give them the skills required to become competent citizens outside the school domain. How do we get these children to participate fully in extracurricular activities? How do we prepare the parents to become members of the school community and provide opportunities for the nurturing and development of social skills? Social competency is a very important issue (Bauman, 1972). Ima and Kheo (Chapter 6) discusses the psychosocial dimensions of bilingual special education.

PROVIDING EFFECTIVE STAFF DEVELOPMENT/TRAINING

Excellence in education will require a culturally heterogeneous cadre of professionals who are knowledgeable about social, linguistic, cultural, educational, and economic factors. According to a report published by the National Center for Research to improve postsecondary teaching and learning (1989), if we want educators to be motivated to make their teaching more culturally sensitive, a system of rewards or appraisal may be necessary to help promote individual, personal, and professional growth. Multicultural and social literacy are necessary across the educational continuum. The following are some of the demands which need to be addressed for staff training (Banks, 1990; Banks, Cortes, Gay, Garcia, & Ochoa, 1976; Cheng, 1993, 1994).

- Provision of optimal language learning environment for our students.
- Matching teaching styles to the learning styles of diverse students.
- Infusing curriculum with information about the bilingual and
- multicultural population.
- Evaluation of our teaching effectiveness with diverse students.
- Giving students with special needs frequent, timely, performance-based feedback that supports improved performance.

RECRUITING API SCHOOL PERSONNEL AND RESEARCHERS

Although Asian minority students encompass a significant portion of many states' school enrollment, the number of API bilingual school personnel is neither proportionately represented in general, special and or bilingual programs nor in related service areas. For example, there are some Chinese, Tagalog and Thai speech-language-hearing specialists in the United States, but there is not a single certified specialist from the Southeast Asian groups (Cheng, 1991). The most advanced services have been extended only to Chinese speakers, but not to Khmer, Hmong, Lao, or Vietnamese language groups (Siegel & Halog, 1986).

There is a need for professional training programs and school districts to devise systematic mentoring, recruitment, and retention of
API bilingual personnel in all aspects of services. The recruitment and
retention of API diverse personnel and researchers will ensure that
much needed research will likely be done to gain a fuller understanding of the complex issues surrounding the education of API students
with special needs.

NEED FOR MULTIDISCIPLINARY COLLABORATIVE RESEARCH

There is a need to study the API population from sociological, linguistic, psychological, educational, and anthropological perspectives
(Cazden, John, & Hymes, 1972; Cheng, 1990a, 1994; Trueba, 1987).
Both qualitative and quantitative data will increase our understanding regarding a wide range of issues on how API students learn English, maintain home language and culture, socialize in diverse
contexts, survive in schools, fare in the job market, and, in general,
acculturate into American society. Many interrelated research questions need to be asked in order to understand the relationship
between sociocultural conditions and educational results (Cheng,
1987, 1990a; Trueba, Guthrie, & Au, 1981; Trueba, Jacobs, & Kirton,
1990, Trueba et al., 1993).

There is a need for the systematic study of the culture of the educational institution, plus self-perceptions and operations. Educators
and policy makers can benefit the API groups and all groups of language minority students by redefining themselves as culturally
plural, in keeping with the true fabric of the American tapestry and in
recognition of the many contributions of European, African, Asian,
and American Indian cultures and peoples.

As we approach an increasingly multiracial and multiethnic twenty-
first century, educators must continue to play an important role in
educating, studying, researching, and training our future generations
of diverse students—white and black, yellow and brown, immigrant
and nonimmigrant—if we are to continue to meet the human capital
needs that our technologically advanced society demands (Oliver &
Johnson, 1988). The collective wisdom of multidisciplinary researchers
can lay a foundation for understanding the interaction between language, thought, achievement, learning, teaching, and acculturation.

CONCLUSION

Demographic indicators show that by the year 2000, Asian/Pacific Islanders will have reached 10 million in number (U.S. Bureau of Census, 1988). In the state of California, the number of limited-English proficient students reached 1 million in 1993. More than 25% of the LEP population is API. Furthermore, although many API are fluent-English-proficient (FEP), they have difficulty with academic discourse. In the future, speech and hearing professionals will face heightened challenges, including shortages of personnel and resources as well as difficulty in recruitment and retention of API students in our schools. Additionally, there is insufficient information regarding language development of multilingual/multicultural API populations to use in planning for appropriate assessment and intervention. Some of our goals include an increase in the number of teachers, specialists, administrators, educators, and researchers who are competent to provide special services for API students with special needs, an increase in the health, medical, and educational support services for students and their families, an increased awareness of the special need for support services, and a continuation of research efforts to provide accurate and useful data relating to the clinical management of API and culturally and linguistically diverse (CLD) populations.

This chapter has presented selected concerns for the social, language, and educational issues of API populations from a special-needs perspective. Theories supporting the need to promote native language and literacy development for English acquisition and learning have been introduced. By valuing and supporting diverse API students' cultural and native languages, we are likely to facilitate the academic and life success of all individuals, particularly the nonmainstream API LEP groups. The success of our future generations depends not only on education, but also on how that education is provided. It is beyond the scope of this chapter to discuss program issues and their implications, but it is our hope that the challenges we face in meeting the needs of the API students are fully explored and that specific goals to enhance school performance and future employment of API students with special needs be attained.

⊓

REFERENCES

Accent on Improving College Teaching and Learning. (1989). National Center for Research to Improve Post Secondary Teaching and Learning. Ann Arbor: University of Michigan.

Banks, J. A. (1990, November). *Transforming the curriculum.* Oakland, CA. California Teacher Credentialing Commission Conference on Diversity.

Banks, J. A., Cortes, C. E., Gay, G., Garcia, R., & Ochoa, A. S. (1976). *Curriculum guidelines for multiethnic education.* Washington, DC: National Council for the Social Studies.

Bartoli, J. S. (1989). An ecological response to Coles's interactive alternative. *Journal of Learning Disabilities,* 22(5), 292–297.

Bauman, R. (1972). An ethnographic framework for the investigation of communicative behaviors. In R. D. Abrahams & R. C. Troike (Eds.), *Language and cultural diversity in American education* (pp. 154–166). Englewood Cliffs, NJ: Prentice Hall.

Bilingual Education Act, 20USC. (1968).

Campione, J. C. (1989). Assisted assessment: A taxonomy of approaches and an outline of strengths and weaknesses. *Journal of Learning Disabilities,* 22(3), 151–165.

Cazden, C. B., John, V., & Hymes D. (Eds.). (1972). *Functions of language in the classroom.* New York: Teachers College Press.

Chan, K. S. (1983). Limited English speaking, handicapped, and poor: Triple threat in childhood. In M. Chu-Chang (Ed.), *Asian- and Pacific-American perspectives in bilingual education: Comparative research* (pp. 153-171). New York: Teachers College Press.

Chan, K. S., & Kitano, M. K. (1986). Demographic characteristics of exceptional Asian students. In M. K. Kitano & P. C. Chinn (Eds.), *Exceptional Asian children and youth* (An ERIC Exceptional Child Education Report). Reston, VA: The Council for Exceptional Children.

Chang, J. M., Hung, D. L., & Tzeng, O. J. L. (1992). Miscue analysis of Chinese children's reading behaviors at the entry level. *Journal of Chinese Linguistics,* 20(1), 120–158.

Cheng, L. (1987). English communicative competence of language minority children: Assessment and treatment of language impaired preschoolers. In H. T. Trueba (Ed.), *Success or failure?* Cambridge, MA: Newbury House.

Cheng, L. (1989). Service delivery to Asian/Pacific LEP children: A cross-cultural framework. *Topics in Language Disorders,* 9(3), 1–14.

Cheng, L. (l990a). Facing diversity: A need for paradigm shift. *American Behavior Scientist,* 34(2), 263–278.

Cheng, L. (l990b). The identification of communicative disorders in Asian-Pacific students. *Journal of Childhood Language Disorders,* 13(2), 113–119.

Cheng, L. (1991). *Assessing Asian language performance: Guidelines for evaluating limited-English-proficient students*. Oceanside, CA: Academic Communications Associates.

Cheng, L. (1993). Asian-American cultures. In D. Battle (Ed.), *Communication disorders in multicultural populations* (pp. 38–77). Boston: Andover Medical Publishers.

Cheng, L. (1994). Difficult discourse: An untold Asian story. In D. N. Ripich & N. A. Creaghead (Eds.), *School discourse problems*, (2nd ed.) (pp. 155–170). San Diego: Singular Publishing Group, Inc.

Chinn, P. C. (1989). *Training specialists to serve Asian handicapped students* (Project # H-29E90011, Handicapped Personnel Preparation: Special Populations). Washington, DC: Office of Special Education Programs, U.S. Department of Education.

Chinn, P. C., & Plata, M. (1986). Perspectives and educational implications of southeast Asian students. In M. K. Kitano & P. C. Chinn (Eds.), *Exceptional Asian children and youth* (An ERIC Exceptional Child Education Report) (pp. 23–34). Reston, VA: The Council for Exceptional Children.

Chu-Chang, M. (1982). A study of speech recoding from the difficulty of learning to read Chinese among bilingual children. In H. Kao & C. M. Cheng (Eds.), *Psychological studies of Chinese language* (pp. 123–133). Taipei, Taiwan: Wen-Hur Publishing.

Chu-Chang, M.(Ed.). (1983). *Asian- and Pacific-American perspectives in bilingual education*. New York: Teachers College Press.

Cummins, J. (1981). The role of primary language development in promoting educational success for language minority students. In California State Department of Education, Office of Bilingual/Bicultural Education (Ed.), *Schooling and language minority students: A theoretical framework*. Los Angeles: Evaluation, Dissemination and Assesssment Center, California State University, Los Angeles.

Cummins, J. (1986). Empowering minority students: A framework for intervention. *Harvard Educational Review, 56*, 18–36.

Cummins, J. (1989). A theoretical framework for bilingual special education. *Exceptional Children, 56*(2), 111–119.

Evaluation, Dissemination and Assessment Center. (1986). *Beyond language: Social & cultural factors in schooling language minority students*. Los Angeles, CA: Author, California State University, Los Angeles.

Gardner, R. W., Robey, D., & Smith, P. C. (1985). Asian Americans: Growth, change, and diversity. *Population Bulletin, 40*, 1–44.

Gollnick, D. M., & Chinn, P.C. (1990). *Multicultural education in a pluralistic society*. Columbus, OH: Merrill Publishing Company.

Goodman, K. S. (1986). *Revaluing troubled readers* (Occasional Papers #15). Tucson: University of Arizona, Program in Language and Literacy.

Guthrie, G. P. (1985). *A school divided: An ethnography of bilingual education in a Chinese community*. Hillsdale, NJ: Lawrence Erlbaum Associates.

Heath, S. B. (1983). *Ways with words: Language, life, and work in communities and classrooms*. Cambridge, England: Cambridge University Press.

Heath, S. B. (1986). Sociocultural contexts of language development. In *Beyond language: Social and cultural factors in schooling minority students*. Bilingual Education Office, California State Department of Education. Los Angeles, CA: Evaluation, Dissemination and Assessment Center, California State University, Los Angeles.

Hirschman, C. Wong, M. G. (1986). The extraordinary educational attainment of Asian Americans: A search for historical evidence and explanations. *Social Forces, 65*, 1–27.

Hurh, W. M., & Kim, C. K. (November, 1986) *The "success" image of Asian Americans: Its validity, practical and theoretical implications*. Paper presented at the Annual Meeting of the American Sociological Association, New York, NY.

Ima, K., & Cheng, L. (1989). *Climbing new mountains: The Hmong*. San Diego, CA: Los Amigos Research Associates.

Ima, K. (1990). Asian newcomers in America. Unpublished manuscript..

Ima, K. (1993). Kenny Lau revisited. CAFABE Newsletter. November, 1993, p. 3.

Jackson, P. W. (1968). Life in classrooms. New York: Holt, Rinehart and Winston.

Krahsen, S. (1981). Bilingual education and second language acquisition theory. In California Department of Education, Office of Bilingual/Bicultural Education (Ed.), *Schooling and language minority students: A theoretical framework* (pp. 51–79). Los Angeles: Evaluation, Dissemination and Assessment Center, California State University, Los Angeles.

Lau v. Nichols, 411 U.S. 563(1974).

Lewis, J., & Luangpraseut, K. (1989). *Handbook for teaching Lao-speaking students*. Folsom, CA: Folsom Cordova Unified School District, Southeast Asia Community Resource Center.

Ma, L. J. (1985). Cultural diversity. In A. K. Dutt (Ed.), *Southeast Asia: Realm of contrast*. Boulder, CO: Westview Press.

McKay, S. L., & Wong, S. L. C. (Eds.). (1988). *Language diversity: Problem or resource?* New York: Newbury House Publishers.

Moll, L. C., Velez-Ibanez, C., & Greenberg, J. (1988). *Project implementation plan, community knowledge and classroom practices: Combining resources for literacy instruction* (Technical report, Development Associates Subcontract No. L-10). Tucson: University of Arizona, College of Education and Bureau of Applied Research in Anthropology.

Office of Bilingual and Minority Affairs (OBEMLA). (1992). Condition of bilingual education in the nation. *Report to Congress and the President*. Washington, DC: Author.

Oliver, M. L., & Johnson, J. H., Jr. (1988). The challenge of diversity in higher education. *The Urban Review, 20*(30), 139–145.

Olsen, L. (1988). *Crossing the schoolhouse border: Immigrant students and California public schools*. San Francisco: California Tomorrow.

Pang, V. O. (1988). Ethnic prejudice: Still alive and hurtful. *Harvard Educational Review, 58*(3), 375–379.

Philips, S. (1983). *The invisible culture*. New York: Longman.

Rueda, R. S. (1993, July). *Meeting the needs of diverse students*. Presentation at the Multicultural Education Summer Institute, San Diego State University, CA.

Ruiz, R. (1988). Orientations in language planning. In S. L. McKay & S. L. C. Wong (Eds.), *Language diversity: Problem or resource?* (pp. 3–25). New York: Newbury House Publishers.

Siegel, V., & Halog, L. (1986). Assessment of limited English proficient children with special needs. In N. Tsuchida (Ed.), *Issues in Asian and Pacific American education* (pp. 13–20). Minneapolis: Asian/Pacific American Learning Resource Center.

Solis, C. (1995). Presentation at Asian Affairs Board, City of San Diego, March 19, 1995.

Takaki, R. (1989). *Strangers from a different shore*. Boston: Little, Brown.

Te, H. D. (1987). *Introduction to Vietnamese culture*. San Diego State University, CA: Multicultural Resource Center.

Trueba, H. T. (Ed). (1987). *Success or failure?* Cambridge, MA: Newbury House.

Trueba, H. T. (1990). The role of culture in literacy acquisition. *International Journal of Qualitative Studies in Education, 3*(1),1–13.

Trueba, H., Cheng, L., & Ima, K. (1993). *Myth or reality: Adaptive strategies of Asian newcomers in California*. London: Falmer Press.

Trueba, H., Guthrie, G. P., & Au, K. H. (Eds.). (1981). *Culture and the bilingual classroom: Studies in classroom ethnography*. Rowley, MA: Newbury House Publishers.

Trueba, H. T., Jacobs, L., & Kirton, E. (1990). *Cultural conflict and adaptation: The case of Hmong children in American society*. Bristol, PA: Falmer Press.

Tzeng, O. J. L., & Hung, D. L. (1988). Orthography, reading, and cerebral functions. In D. de Kerckhove & C. J. Lumsden (Eds.), *The alphabet and the brain: The lateralization of writing* (pp. 273-290). Berlin: Springer-Verlag.

United States General Accounting Office. (1994). *Limited English proficiency: A growing and costly educational challenge facing many school districts*. Washington, DC: Author .

U.S. Bureau of Census. Statistical abstract of the United States: 1988 (108th ed.). Washington, DC: Author.

U.S. Bureau of Census. Statistical abstract of the United States: 1991 (111th Edition). Washington, DC: Author.

University of California Linguistic Minority Research Institute. (1994, October). More LEP students recieve no special services. *LMRI Newsletter, 4*(2), p. 1. UC, Santa Barbara: Author.

Wong, M. G. (1980). Model students? Teachers' perceptions and expectations of their Asian and White students. *Sociology of Education: A Journal of Research in Socialization and Social Structure, 53*(4), 236–246.

Wong, S. L. C. (1988). The language situation of Chinese Americans. In S. L. McKay & S. L. C. Wong (Eds.), *Language diversity: Problem or resource?* (pp. 193–228). New York: Newbury House Publishers.

Yu, E. (1993, December). *Issues in studying Asian/Pacific Islander Americans*. Presentation at the Biostatisics Conference, San Diego State University, CA.

LI-RONG LILLY CHENG, PH.D.

Dr. Cheng is Professor of Communicative Disorders and Assistant Dean of Student Affairs and International Development of the College of Health and Human Services at San Diego State University. She is also Director of the International Institute for Human Resources Development in Health and Human Services and a fellow of the American Speech-Language Hearing Association (ASHA). Dr. Cheng received a bachelor's degree in English and Spanish from National Taiwan University, a master's degree in Linguistics from Southern Illinois University, a master's degree in Speech-Language Pathology from Michigan State University, and a doctorate in Speech-Language Pathology and Multicultural Education from Claremont Graduate School and San Diego State University. Dr. Cheng has researched bilingual acquisition, language and culture, cross-cultural communication, and speech-language pathology of the bilin-gual/multicultural population and lectured on working with the ever-growing bilin-gual/multicultural populations in the United States. She has written several books and numerous journal articles and is on the editorial boards of several professional journals. Dr. Cheng has coordinated conferences and symposia on topics ranging from communicative disorders to curriculum development.

JI-MEI CHANG, PH.D.

Dr. Chang is an Associate Professor in the Division of Special Education and Rehabilitative Services at San Jose State University. She received her master's degree in 1978 and her doctorate in 1989, both from the University of Southern California. Dr. Chang has conducted a series of cross-language research on reading abilities and disabilities among Chinese children in Taiwan, Singapore, and Northern California. Her professional interests include promoting partnerships across home, school, and community for the benefit of students and supporting teacher-as-a-researcher activities to implement alternative assessment as well as monitor teaching effectiveness.

CHAPTER 2

LEP, LD, POOR, AND MISSED LEARNING OPPORTUNITIES: A CASE OF INNER-CITY CHINESE AMERICAN CHILDREN

JI-MEI CHANG, PH.D.

Tim and his family immigrated from Hong Kong to the United States when he was only 3 years old. He is 14 years old and in the eighth grade at a large urban middle school. He lives in an apartment with his parents and three older brothers and sisters in an inner-city Chinese community. Tim's parents speak only Cantonese-Chinese and are non-English proficient, but life in this inner-city Chinese community does not demand English proficiency. Both of his parents have low-paying jobs for which it is not necessary for them to speak English. His older brothers and sisters must act as translators when communication with English speakers is needed.

Tim attended an inner-city grammar school that had had a Cantonese-English bilingual program for 5 years. Although Tim was on the quiet side, his elementary school teachers frequently noted that he had good interpersonal skills. He was well liked and had a friendly smile for everyone. His classmates enjoyed having him in their group because he always worked hard and made a conscientious effort to complete his school work. While working in cooperative learning groups, he seemed enthusiastic, but was not doing grade-level work.

In general, Tim's after-school activities were limited. His parents often worried about his safety, so he did not venture out into the surrounding neighborhood very often. In fact, he would go right home after school, where his older siblings could supervise him while he did his homework. However, rather than watch Tim, the older siblings often teased Tim because he was experiencing difficulties in school. Tim neither attended any community-based tutorial programs, nor participated in after school activities. He did attend a weekend Chinese language school for 2 years, but he stopped going after he was identified as learning disabled in the third grade. His teachers suggested that learning two languages would create an undue burden on his learning abilities. By having his world reduced to school and his family's apartment, Tim's opportunities for social development and literacy learning activities were minimal at best.

After his first year in kindergarten, the teacher had recommended that Tim repeat kindergarten because of his language difficulties and lack of readiness for first grade work. In the first grade, Tim began working with a speech-language clinician to correct speech articulation problems and language delay. Tim's second grade teacher referred him for special education assessment because Tim was having difficulties following oral directions and reading comprehension in both Cantonese and English. He was found to have a specific learning disability (SLD). In the third grade, Tim was placed in a pull-out based resource specialist program (RSP) for reading and language arts.

During the next 3 years, Tim began spending time journeying between two or three different classrooms, anywhere from two to four times a week. While in his homeroom, Tim was very interested in participating in science and social science because it meant an opportunity to work with his peers in cooperative groups. However, he was often pulled out of one or both of these classes because of his RSP or speech therapy schedule. Tim, wanting to return to his regular class, learned to quickly negotiate the tasks presented to him in his learning disabilities (LD) resource room or speech-language therapy. In contrast to his homeroom learning environment, his special education classroom meant sitting alone, working independently on worksheets. The worksheets were identical to those of his other English-speaking peers, with little or no apparent modifications for his limited English proficiency. Once Tim completed his work, he would politely ask the RSP teacher, "Can I leave now?" However, he would not ask to leave unless he had completed all of his assigned seatwork. The special education teacher felt that Tim worked alone because, "He's LEP (limited English proficient) and he doesn't talk a whole lot."

In middle school (grades 6–8), Tim continued his RSP for reading and math. The remedial activities at this level consisted of doing daily independent worksheets, however he no longer received Cantonese support for any of the classes he was taking, as he had in elementary school. Instead, he was placed in an English as a second language (ESL) class taught by a teacher who had a heavy non-native English speaking accent. Tim was often confused and this resulted in receiving a failing grade in that class. He was placed back into an RSP for English by the seventh grade.

Tim's sixth grade math experience was particularly challenging. While in the sixth grade, he was promoted to work with a group of eighth graders, not because he was capable of handling the learning tasks, but because the sixth–seventh grade combination group had many students with severe behavioral problems, making it inappropriate for him. Tim's mother indicated that her son had once liked math, but not in the middle school because the math was too hard for him.

Presently, Tim is in the eighth grade and has continued his RSP for math and English. At age 14, he has been in special education for 7 years and will soon undergo his second 3-year reevaluation. With the types of assessment tools and criteria the school uses, Tim is likely to continue in special education. Even though there were no pull-out based special education programs for him in middle school, Tim was, nevertheless, placed in a disadvantaged track with limited access to learning opportunities when compared to his peers.

There was a strong resemblance between Tim's middle and elementary school assignments in the type of drill and practice worksheets used for reading and writing activities. For example, in an attempt to remediate his difficulty in detecting English sound and symbol relationships and his reading comprehension, special education teachers at both levels often provided Tim with worksheets that he was to complete each session. Yet, he had not read very many books since the fourth grade, because he was mostly separated from his homeroom reading groups.

However frustrating Tim's school experiences may have been, with support from his parents, he forged ahead and maintained a positive attitude toward school. Middle school played an important part in helping Tim maintain his positive attitude, because it provided him with guaranteed opportunities that he had never had in elementary school. In one of our interviews, Tim became excited when he talked about his best subject areas, social studies and science. Tim and his parents fought hard to get him enrolled in ESL classes for social studies and sciences, where he worked with many of his Cantonese-speaking peers. Tim did well in cooperative learning groups in these classes; he particularly enjoyed working on science projects. In an interview of his ESL social studies and science teachers, they both indicated that Tim functioned as well as peers, and they were surprised to learn that Tim was a special education student with SLD.

According to both of Tim's initial (1988) and triennial (1991) psychoeducational assessment reports, his learning disability (LD) was identified in the area of processing language. In addition, Tim had a significant discrepancy between his estimated ability and academic achievement in the areas of reading and written expression. Furthermore, a speech language evaluation conducted in 1986 indicated that he had a language delay. In short, according to school files and teachers' interviews, Tim's LD affected his school performance in the areas of reading and written expression. Tim's language delay and poor reading comprehension also affected his ability to perform math work beginning in the fifth grade and he continues to have difficulties with word problems to this day.

Tim's interpersonal communicative skills, in both Cantonese and English, appear equally strong. In the initial study conducted in the 1991–1992 school year, his fifth grade homeroom teacher and his special education teacher rated his pronunciation and intonation of English language as near-native. He occasionally made grammatical and/or word order errors in English, but, in general, these errors did not obscure his intended meaning. However, with respect to his cognitive/academic language proficiency (CALP), he had not mastered reading or writing in either language. His vocabulary in both languages appears very limited. If he doesn't know a word in English, he does not know it in Chinese, either. Furthermore, he continues to have more difficulties in using appropriate words or terms. In some instances, when he cannot make himself understood, he resorts to spelling out the word or rephrasing ideas.

Tim's parents have often been told by teachers that they could help strengthen Tim's English language proficiency if they spoke to him in English at home. Both of Tim's parents reported that their own limited English abilities have resulted in restricted communication between themselves and Tim since the fourth grade. In addition, Tim's homeroom and special education teachers asserted that Tim preferred to use English and he did not speak much Cantonese. However, in a series of interviews, Tim often said that he liked to speak in Chinese, because most of his friends speak Chinese, but he did use more English with his siblings at home.

Every professional who has worked with Tim has had a personal theory as to why Tim was unable to read or write; however, his ESL science and social studies teachers could not agree with any of the negative statements about Tim. According to their observations of Tim in their classes, he was no different than any other student in a group of 30 ESL students. They asserted that Tim, just like any other ESL student, needed time and English support to learn the concepts.

Based on Tim's educational history, since he was identified as learning disabled he has missed a series of learning opportunities that can be analyzed from a home, school, and community context. Within the home context, he was not exposed to a rich home language and literacy environment. Since withdrawing from his community-based Chinese language school, Tim has missed multiple opportunities by having extremely limited interaction with Cantonese-speaking peers. Furthermore, in a school context, he has missed learning opportunities in four major ways: (1) peer resources in social and learning interactions in cooperative learning groups in his homeroom, (2) use of Cantonese to clarify concepts or to communicate with his parents, (3) use of literacy skills, and (4) access to school core curriculum. In contrast, based on field observations and teachers' reports, Tim did well when he had the opportunity to use Cantonese to (a) clarify concepts as he had in elementary classes, (b) interact with his peers as he did in his ESL science and social science classes, (c) be involved in cooperative learning groups, (d) engage in hands-on tasks within thematically based units, and (e) receive support by his Cantonese-speaking peers.

⊔

INTRODUCTION

Theoretically, once students are referred, identified, and placed in a special education program, all special education students should have gained access to meaningful learning opportunities. This chapter reports research findings that may provide readers with insights into Chinese American LEP + LD children's educational experiences and their actual learning opportunities in the school environment. Information presented in this chapter is organized in three parts. Part I presents Chinese American children with reading and learning disabilities. Part II describes research data obtained from a group of 16 Chinese American LEP + LD children and the characteristics of their language, cognitive, and social-emotional profiles. Part III provides synthesized information regarding these children's missed learning opportunities in schools and presents four major needs pertinent to school interventions for these children.

The typical special education interventions that Tim experienced often had little or no connection to his homeroom activities or core curriculum. Instead, the special education intervention focused on the perceived deficits in academic areas, such as basic sound and symbol correspondence and mechanics of writing, provided through worksheets or workbooks. The majority of Tim's time in the pull-out special education program provided inconsistent interactive opportunities with his teacher for mediation of either his learning disabilities or limited English proficiency. In addition, he had little or no interaction with peers. Moreover, he was treated as if he were a proficient English speaker. There were no specific linguistic goals stated in his individualized education program (IEP) and little indication of any systematic involvement of bilingual educators or language development specialists to address Tim's need for English or native language development. The author acknowledges that Tim's case may not be generalizable across a wide range of elementary school settings across every school district. However, compared to the 16 cases looked at in this chapter of LEP + LD Chinese American children, Tim's school experiences are not unique.

As the title of this chapter indicates, this discussion focuses on a specific group of inner-city, ethnic Chinese American children who were identified by the school as limited English proficient (LEP) and learning disabled (LD). Although the author acknowledges that the term LEP is not an appropriate generic term for all students acquiring and learning the English language, it has nonetheless been so defined by the school system. As the 16 students were recognized by their schools as LEP and LD, the acronym LEP + LD is used to represent the specific characteristics of this group of children.

These Chinese American LEP + LD students' educational standing warranted a thorough examination for four important reasons: (1)

most of them were unlikely to have articulate parents or powerful professional groups advocating for their rights or needs; (2) their lack of progress was likely to perplex their school teachers, psychologists, parents, and related personnel; (3) their parents and surrounding community were unlikely to understand the nature of their specific learning disabilities; and, (4) they faced the triple threat of being poor, LEP, and LD (Chan, 1983; Chang, 1993b). This specific group of students facing triple challenges were ethnic Chinese and recent refugees from Southeast Asia or immigrants from Hong Kong or rural China.

Despite being LEP and closely associated with an inner-city community, a majority of ethnic Chinese students tend to succeed in their formal schooling. The high degree of sociocultural value placed on education by Chinese or Asian families and communities, in general, is manifested by their high expectations for their children to excel in school (e.g., Caplan, Choy, & Whitmore, 1992; Chang, 1993b; Mau, 1994; Peng & Wright, 1994; Schneider & Lee, 1990; Scott-Jones, 1984; Trueba, Cheng, & Ima, 1993).

Although we celebrate the high achievement shared by many Chinese children and their families, we cannot overlook those who require special assistance, understanding, and empathy from their own community to realize their full learning potential. Some Chinese American LEP children have been referred for special education and related services, such as speech-language therapy, by their classroom teachers because they have demonstrated slow English acquisition, poor oral expression, or poor understanding of verbal concepts in addition to their poor performance in language arts areas.

EXISTENCE OF LEARNING DISABILITIES IN CHINESE LANGUAGE GROUPS

Before reporting findings presented in this chapter, it is important to situate the current discussion within the general context of present knowledge of LD and within the general as well as Chinese communities. LD is an umbrella term that covers a heterogeneous group of individuals with various types of mild to severe learning or language disabilities across an individual's life span (e.g., Lyon, Gray, Kavanagh, & Krasnegor, 1993; National Joint Committee on Learning Disabilities, 1994; Smith, 1994). The phenomenon of learning disabilities is complex and its causes remain controversial. Detailed information regarding the definitions of LD can be found in Smith (1994).

Hypotheses related to LD range from within-child deficits of neurological origins (e.g., Kavanagh & Truss, 1988) to an interactive effect of multiple factors inherited in the learners and their environment (e.g., Bartoli & Botel, 1988; Coles, 1987; Lipson & Wixson, 1986). Briefly stated, LD can be associated with any individual who has low to average or above average intelligence and has specific discrepancies between the estimated intellectual ability and achievement in one or more of the following areas: oral expression, listening comprehension, written expression, basic reading skills, reading comprehension, mathematics calculation, or mathematics reasoning (*Federal Register*, 1977). Furthermore, the condition of LD is likely to persist into adulthood (e.g., Gerber & Reiff, 1994), but it does not prevent an individual from pursuing higher education and advanced studies (Chang, Kilbourne, & Shimizu, 1994; Vogel & Adelman, 1993).

Reporting the prevalence of LD has been as difficult a task as defining LD. Reports of individuals with LD across the United States have varied from 2% to 20% or more of the general student population. Vagueness of definition, lack of standardized criteria for subject selection in various prominent studies, and poor diagnosis of LD conditions have all contributed to this variance (Interagency Committee on Learning Disabilities, 1987; Silver, 1988). Nevertheless, in the absence of a good database, the percentage of people affected by LD in the United States has been estimated to be between 5% and 10% of the population (Silver, 1988). In California, students with LD represent the largest single group of special education students. An estimated 56% (293,902) of the total special education population in California (521,615) were identified as learning disabled in 1992 (Wright, 1992).

Even through LD may not a familiar term in many Asian countries, LD student populations prevail across the Asian/Pacific region. Within the heterogeneous grouping of LD, children with reading disabilities, a subtype of learning disabilities, have been the subject of investigations since late the 1970s in Taiwan (Chang, Hung, & Tzeng, 1992; Guo, 1982; Hsu, Soong, Shen, Su, & Wei, 1985; Stevenson, 1984; Stevenson et al., 1982). Based on the Western criteria for intellectual ability and achievement discrepancy, the findings obtained from cross-language research on reading disabilities across Chinese, Japanese, and English language groups (Stevenson et al., 1982) showed that a similar proportion of fifth graders who participated in the studies could be identified as reading disabled.

The prevalence of monolingual Chinese children with reading disabilities in Taiwan has led to the development of special education programs for disabled readers in primary grades in major cities (Lee, 1983, 1985). A series of studies of Chinese children with reading disabilities suggested that when measured by standardized cognitive tasks, these children shared similar cognitive profiles as disabled readers found in English language groups (Chang, 1990; Chang & Tzeng, 1992). They tended to perform poorly on tasks that required verbatim recall of language-related elements such as digits or unrelated words, but they performed equally well as their peers on tasks involved in recalling nonlanguage-related elements or visual symbols.

Through in-depth analysis of reading processes, Chang et al. (1992) also found that Chinese readers typically used language cues such as syntactic, semantic, and graphophonic in their attempts to construct meaning from print. However, specific orthographic effects, particularly the morphological factors, such as the formation of Chinese spoken words, which are often formed by more than one character (i.e., morpheme), will have specific influence on beginning readers. The disabled readers performed poorly on all measures of reading comprehension when compared with their peers. They were particularly troubled by the demand to detect Chinese word boundaries in print—that is, to parse among seemingly equally spaced Chinese characters. Hence, when they were asked to retell stories, the retold stories often bore little or no relationship to the intended meanings. The reading research conducted among Chinese monolingual children in Taiwan informed educators and researchers that reading disabilities exist among Chinese children.

In many of the inner-city schools in the district where the author conducted the home-school-community-based study of Chinese American LEP + LD students, Chinese American students constituted the largest language minority student population. A small group of these students were identified in schools as having reading or learning disabilities. However, within Chinese communities, the terms learning and language or learning disabilities have often been misunderstood. For example, the parents of the studied group of 16 Chinese American LEP + LD children were unfamiliar with these terms because they were not educational or administrative labels in many Asian countries where they attended schools. Because learning or language disability is often an invisible condition, parents participating in a study of Chinese American LEP + LD children (Chang, 1993b) often assumed that learning disabilities meant educational retardation, slowness, inability to concentrate, or laziness. They generally felt uncomfortable discussing their child's disability with relatives or friends.

Furthermore, they felt that learning disability was a condition that could be "cured" after a year or two of special education and academic intervention. These parents accepted their children being labeled as LEP + LD and consented to having their children placed in a pull-out special education resource program where they were served by a monolingual English-speaking LD resource specialist, or RSP as they are known in California. Although their children were in special education, these parents, nevertheless, had high expectations, believing that LD resource specialists would bring their child to grade level within a certain period of time. However, such expectations frequently met with disappointment and often resulted in parents requesting that their child be dismissed from special education services, particularly when these children entered middle school (Chang, 1994b).

In sum, the phenomenon of LD continues to puzzle educational and medical professionals, and it prevails across various Asian populations as well as American populations. Moreover, interventions for Chinese American LEP + LD students are likely to be even more complex.

卐

CHINESE AMERICAN LEP + LD CHILDREN IN SCHOOLS

Information presented in this chapter is a portion of a home-school-community based study of a group of inner-city Chinese American LEP + LD students. These children were enrolled in largely urban schools on the West Coast, where there were high enrollments of Chinese students. The study of this particular group of Chinese American LEP + LD children may provide unique baseline information for the discussion of language, cognitive, and literacy development among Asian LEP students with special needs and their learning opportunities in a multilingual and multicultural school context. Readers interested in the research design, data collections, analysis, and other findings related to home and community may refer to Chang (1993b), Chang and Maldonado-Colon (1994), and Chang and Fung (1994).

In broadening the conceptualization of LEP + LD, this study of Chinese American LEP + LD children was expanded to include investigations into the total language learning and literacy environment of the home, school, and community. To do this, an in-depth study of 16 Cantonese-speaking Chinese American children was launched to examine their total social, language, learning, and literacy environment.

SUBJECT DESCRIPTIONS

During the school year of 1991–1992 when this project was first launched, the 16 Chinese American LEP + LD children, plus 6 other LEP + LD students who participated in the pilot study, represented over 65% of the entire available subject pool of individuals who shared similar learner characteristics as presented in this chapter. The general learner characteristics of the 16 children participants is presented in Table 2–1.

DESIGNATED CRITERIA FOR LEP

The participating school district has a specific set of criteria for designating students as LEP. Students were considered LEP if English was not their first language, and they (a) scored below the 36th percentile on the California Test of Basic Skills Achievement test (CTBS), (b) obtained grades lower than "C" in major subject areas, (c) were rated by classroom teacher below level 4 on the Student Oral Language

TABLE 2–1
Learner characteristics of the 16 research subjects.

1. Ethnic Chinese born in the United States, China, Hong Kong, or Southeast Asia
2. Cantonese-speaking Chinese children
3. Primarily from inner-city working family environments
4. Seven 5th graders (four female and three male), four 4th graders (all male), and five 3rd graders (one female and four male)
5. Eleven received speech-language therapy prior to the referral
6. Three received community-based mental health services
7. Referred and identified as learning disabled by school
8. Placed in a pull-out-based LD resource program (or RSP) and served by a monolingual English-speaking LD resource specialists
9. Designated as LEP because they were unable to meet a set of criteria as fluent English proficient

Observation Matrix (SOLOM) (California Department of California, n.d.; Peregoy & Boyle,1993), (d) scored below expected level on formal tests of English Oral Language, or (e) scored lower than level 3 in their writing samples.

DATA SOURCE

A series of descriptive studies were conducted to collect various types of baseline information related to the Chinese American LEP + LD children. Profiles of the reasons for these children's referral and placement in a pull-out LD resource program were obtained from reviews of their cumulative school files, psychoeducational reports, and individualized educational programs (IEPs). Their educational and learning opportunities, as well as language and literacy environment were constructed from field observations and interviews of parents, child, teachers, and principals. These interviews suggested that observations be extended into a few community-based after-school literacy learning sites, such as an inner-city YMCA and a public library.

SUMMARY OF FINDINGS

The following sections present a summary of findings relevant to the discussion of educational treatment of Chinese American LEP + LD students. Each section provides baseline information addressing reasons, factors, and current level of cognitive, language, and literacy performance that jointly contributed to the composite of learner characteristics among the 16 inner-city Chinese American LEP + LD children who need special attention.

FACTORS CONTRIBUTING TO STUDENTS' LEP + LD STATUS

In this section, information is presented to address reasons for special education referrals, placement, and identification as having learning disabilities.

REASONS FOR REFERRAL.   The LEP students who participated in the study had been referred primarily by their 2nd and 3rd grade teachers for comprehensive assessment and special education services. As required by the school district, all of these children were first referred to a child study team involving parents, teachers, and various other professionals as needed for pre-referral consultation on classroom-based modifications. After receiving 6 months to 1 year of prereferral intervention, these LEP children continued to lag behind their peers; hence, as a last resort, their teachers felt that special education was the best place for them to receive appropriate educational services. The reasons for their special education referrals are summarized and presented in Table 2–2.

The first category of reasons for special education referral was for academic delays in the areas of reading, writing, and math. All 16 cases received referrals for delays in reading. Reading difficulties, not reading to class expectations, reading below grade level, and inability to understand English sound/symbol relationship were commonly cited reasons for the below-par level of reading performance. With respect to writing abilities, 8 cases demonstrated difficulties in expressing thoughts with writing and 2 in spelling. Interestingly, only 1 case was referred because of math difficulties.

The second category of reasons for special education referral dealt with students' cognitive function abilities. Poor memory for vocabulary was cited in 8 cases, in 7 due to poor attention span, and 8 were indicated as having poor listening skills. The third category related to

TABLE 2–2

Common reasons for special education referrals.

Referral Rationales	Third $N = 5$	Fourth $N = 4$	Fifth $N = 7$
Academic Delay			
Reading	5	4	7
Writing	4	2	4
Math	0	1	0
Cognitive Function Abilities			
Poor memory for vocabulary	0	4	3
Poor attention span	3	1	3
Poor listening skills	2	4	2
Oral Language Abilities			
Difficulties in oral language fluency	3	3	1
Limited expressive vocabulary	5	3	2

oral language ability. Seven cases were referred for difficulties in oral language fluency and 10 cases for limited expressive vocabulary.

REASONS FOR PLACEMENT IN SPECIAL EDUCATION. In general, there were two major criteria for identifying a LEP student as learning disabled: (1) a discrepancy was found between students' estimated potential and actual achievement level in one or more academic areas and (2) measured deficit(s) in basic psychological processes (Smith, 1994). These processes involve either auditory or visual processing ability, which is thought to be involved in understanding or in using either spoken or written language. The common reasons for placement cited in the subject students' files are summarized and presented in Table 2–3.

Language delay included the following characteristics: limited receptive and/or productive vocabulary, poor sentence structure, and difficulties in the areas of either comprehending complex sentence structure or in formulating sentences. Language delay qualified a large number of the studied youngsters for speech-language therapy. Memory problems can involve difficulties with encoding, retrieving, or verbatim recall of digits and unrelated words. Weak auditory processing and integration of stimuli (visual and auditory) were considered important problems in preventing academic progress among these students.

REASONS FOR REMAINING AS LEP. The CTBS was one of the criteria used for designating students' LEP status. At the time of the study,

TABLE 2–3
Common reasons for placement in speech-language therapy and RSP.

Reasons for Placement	Third N = 5	Fourth N = 4	Fifth N = 7
Speech-Language Therapy			
Language delay	5	4	4
LD Resource Program			
Memory problems	2	3	5
Basic psychological processes problems			
Auditory processing	4	3	5
Visual processing	1	0	2

these Chinese American LEP + LD students had all scored below the 36th percentile measured by the CTBS, particularly in the area of reading achievement. They also tended to score below expected levels on other formal tests of English oral language. Many of these children's continued status as LEP was determined by these two specific factors, even after they entered middle school (Chang, 1994b).

SELECTED PROFILES OF CHINESE AMERICAN LEP + LD CHILDREN

Profiles are presented in this section to help the reader identify the characteristics of these children's intellectual abilities, Chinese and English language proficiency, and social-emotional patterns. Selected learner characteristics also highlight these children's differential academic performance in schools.

ENGLISH ORAL LANGUAGE PROFILES RATED BY TEACHERS. Most of these Chinese American LEP + LD children have been rated at or above level 4 in SOLOM by their homeroom teachers; however, their LD resource specialist rated them much lower on the same items (see Figure 2–1). A level 4 observed across comprehension, fluency, vocabulary, pronunciation, and grammar measured by SOLOM indicated that the LEP + LD child, in general, (1) understood nearly everything spoken at a normal speed, although occasionally repetition might have been necessary; (2) could carry on everyday conversation and classroom discussion, but occasionally might lapse in their attempt to search for the correct manner of expression; (3) occasionally used inappropriate terms and rephrased ideas because of lexical inadequacies; (4) spoke intelligibly, although with a definite accent and occasional inappropriate intonation patterns; and (5) occasionally made grammatical and/or word-order errors that did not obscure meaning.

The difference observed between the rating of homeroom teachers and LD resource specialists is an interesting one. One discrepancy might have resulted from the differences in background knowledge of second language acquisition between the two professionals.

With respect to their oral language proficiency as observed in the classroom, these Chinese American LEP + LD students were perceived, in general, by teachers to have developed sufficient basic interpersonal communicative skills (BICS) in English. Based on their inability to score above the 36th percentile in CTBS and other formal measures, it might be plausible to suggest that the students had not developed

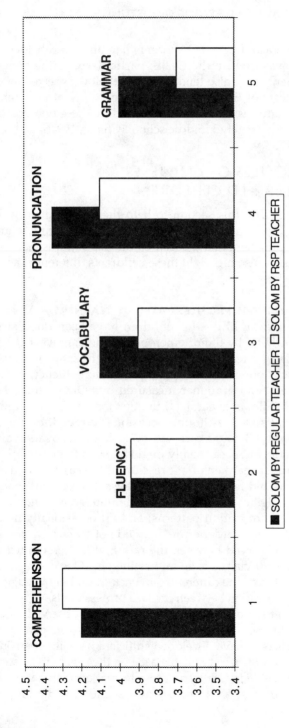

FIGURE 2–1
Level of Chinese American LEP + LD students' oral language proficiency as measured by SOLOM.

cognitive/academic language proficiency (CALP) in English (cf. Cummins, 1981, 1984). Based on teachers' observations and psychoeducational reports, the commonly observed difficulties of the youngsters' English language are summarized and presented in Table 2–4.

CHARACTERISTICS OF CANTONESE PROFICIENCY. Very few of these children could read or write in Chinese. Most of them had no formal instruction in Chinese written language. Many of them had few problems in expressing ideas when speaking in Cantonese, hence they had BICS in Cantonese (i.e., functional use of Cantonese in social contexts). However, these students did not have CALP in Cantonese (i.e., func-

TABLE 2–4
Some commonly observed difficulties in the target students' English oral language development.

Area of Difficulties	Descriptions
Semantics ■ Word meaning ■ Expressive and receptive vocabularies ■ Word choice	Generally 2–3 years behind their English speaking peers measured by clinicians and psychologists.
Syntax ■ Verb-tense agreement ■ Word endings and inflections ■ Word order ■ Sentence structure ■ Prepositions	Making grammatical errors, such as: Boy play ball. He go. Revealed Chinese word order. Used incomplete sentences. Inability to differentiate between the uses of "on" and "at" or "on" "in" revealed in test results.
Graphophonics	Difficulty in sound-symbol correspondence
Metalinguistics ■ Slang ■ Idioms	Generally 2–3 years behind their English-speaking peers.
CALP	Difficulty in answering "why" and "how" questions.

tional use of Cantonese in academic contexts). The level of sophistication in their use of language, vocabulary, length of sentences, and the like was usually below age level. Generally, they were unable to perform verbal or cognitive tasks in Cantonese. In short, their native language literacy skills were very limited and often not cultivated within or outside of school; hence, testing them solely in Cantonese was difficult. Furthermore, many parents reported that they did not read or discuss school-related subjects with their child in Cantonese, and many of these students had been withdrawn from a community-based Chinese language program when they were placed in special education. Thus, the limited access to CALP in Chinese may have also contributed to their inability to comprehend test items in Cantonese.

COMPARISON OF THE CANTONESE-CHINESE AND ENGLISH LANGUAGE PERFORMANCE.   In general, these students had BICS in both languages. However, it must be stressed that this level of interpersonal language proficiency in Cantonese and English cannot be generalized across a wide range of academic learning situations. Field observations and interviews showed that these students did not initiate much conversation with adults in schools, nor did they participate in class discussions in their regular education classrooms very often. In comparison, with respect to the BICS, these children all exhibited much lower levels of comprehension, fluency, vocabulary, and syntax in Cantonese than in English. Such an estimation of their Cantonese language proficiency was judged by LEP children themselves, their parents, and bilingual school psychologists.

Among the 16 cases, there were 11 who received speech-language therapy either before the referral or were concurrently referred for both special education and related services. Based on field observations, placing Asian LEP children in speech-language programs seemed to be a common practice in many schools with high enrollment of Asian students.

There are three possible reasons that may account for an Asian LEP students' placement in speech-language therapy. First, that they exhibited ESL types of speech patterns (e.g., many of them could not accurately produce the /r/, /s/, /th/, or /l/ sounds). Second, placing them in speech-language therapy programs was the alternative in schools with no ESL or language development support. Third, many inner-city Chinese American LEP students tend to have limited general information and basic concepts essential for scoring high in verbal tasks on standardized assessment tools. They were likely to show gaps in their language development.

COGNITIVE PROFILES. A review of the Chinese American LEP + LD students' psychoeducational assessment reports revealed profiles with discrepancies between their performance on nonverbal tasks versus verbal tasks. They performed age appropriately on nonverbal cognitive tasks. However, on verbal performance subtests such as general information and vocabulary, their performance was consistently low, regardless of the language in which the test items were given (English or Cantonese).

In addition, the reports revealed discrepancies between tasks demanding visual processing skills versus auditory processing skills. On tests assessing their visual motor integration and visual processing skills, the Chinese American LEP + LD students tended to have average or above average age-appropriate skills. However, their scores were lower on tasks demanding auditory processing ability. Moreover, the Chinese American LEP + LD students' profiles were consistent with the patterns observed among White American students with reading disabilities (Stevenson et al., 1982) and monolingual Chinese students with reading disabilities in Taiwan (Chang, 1990).

The Chinese American LEP + LD students' general cognitive profiles reflected average to low average abilities as measured by specific cognitive task performance. Nonverbal problem-solving tasks were used to objectively determine the cognitive functioning level of these LEP students. The student's verbal skills were measured in both English and Cantonese to validate their overall performance.

GENERAL PROFILES OF SOCIAL EMOTIONAL ASPECTS. The LEP + LD children's general social-emotional profiles shared some common characteristics. In general, the Chinese American LEP + LD children were characterized as cooperative, well-behaved, quiet, shy, insecure, anxious, eager to please teachers and examiners, and diligent workers in class. Only one fifth grader had been referred because of acting out behaviors as a third grader. Some may have had difficulties making friends, but, on the whole, they tended to work well in groups and got along with peers, teachers, and adults. As reported by parents at home, these children also got along well with siblings. Although they usually had friends in class, they seldom played outside, visited friends, or had friends over to their homes. Their hobbies included watching television, playing video games, doing homework, and going grocery shopping with parents or siblings. They tended to be fairly happy contented children.

BRIEF DISCUSSION

The learner characteristics of this group of Chinese American LEP + LD children are presented to highlight the need for systematic language support in both regular and special education classrooms and meaningful special education intervention. Based on these findings, the school education provided for a majority of the participating Chinese American LEP + LD students was ineffective. When these inner-city poor Chinese American LEP + LD students did not match the stereotype of Asians as model minority students (e.g., Trueba et al. 1993; Wong, 1980), many teachers, regular or special education, did not seem to have adequate training to provide intervention to meet their special needs. Typically, the pull-out-based special education intervention focused on traditional remedial activities without considering the frequency of these students' exposure to print outside of classrooms, prior experiences or schema, and CALP that are often required to make these traditional remedial instruction methods effective.

The prevalence of this type of service and the apparent neglect in addressing such students' continuing need for English development are likely to contribute to a series of missed learning opportunities for the these children. A detailed analysis is presented in the following section.

🗗

THE MISSED LEARNING OPPORTUNITIES AND MULTIPLE CHALLENGES

Early in the chapter, it was suggested that the Chinese American LEP + LD students faced three challenges: being poor, learning disabled, and limited English proficient. To have their special needs addressed or remediated, the Chinese American LEP + LD students met with an RSP largely on a pull-out basis for approximately 50 minutes a day, four or five times a week. The RSP focused on either compensation for remediation of students' specific learning disabilities. However, within the context of current practices, synthesized data from field observations, interviews of students, parents, teachers, principals, and community informants, as well as file reviews suggest that Chinese American LEP + LD students may face three additional challenges. These are: (1) a lack of connected instructional program, (2) a lack of CALP in first language (L1) and second language (L2), and (3) a lack of social capital for school learning (see Figure 2–2).

LACK OF CONNECTED INSTRUCTIONAL PROGRAMS

The first additional challenge refers to a lack of coordination between Chinese American LEP + LD students' special education intervention and homeroom activities. When the Chinese American LEP + LD students were pulled out for their special education services, they were often provided with instructional material which may or may not have resembled the core curriculum. Five out of eight RSP teachers indicated that they provided their own instructional program and materials for their students. The emphasis was on remediating these students' perceived learning disabilities in the areas of reading or writing. Furthermore, these Chinese American LEP + LD students received the same material as their English-speaking peers. In short, this lack of coordination has led to a discontinuous and incoherent school education for these Chinese American LEP + LD students. Futhermore, some of these same Chinese American LEP + LD children were also pulled out for speech-language therapy which often had little or no connection to classroom instructional activities, thus compounding the disruption of their typical school day.

Under these conditions, it is plausible to suggest that the educational treatment that these students received in school likely affected their language development in general and academic progress. Not only was the flow of their school day disrupted, but, more importantly, their learning experiences were incoherent and disconnected as well. For example, many of them traveled between two or three classrooms during precious school learning hours. There was frequent exiting and re-entry of their cooperative learning groups in the homeroom learning environment, often in the midst of a meaningful learning activity. The contrasting learning environments and new sets of classroom rules and instructional materials of the two or three disjointed programs created an unnecessary burden for these Chinese American LEP + LD students.

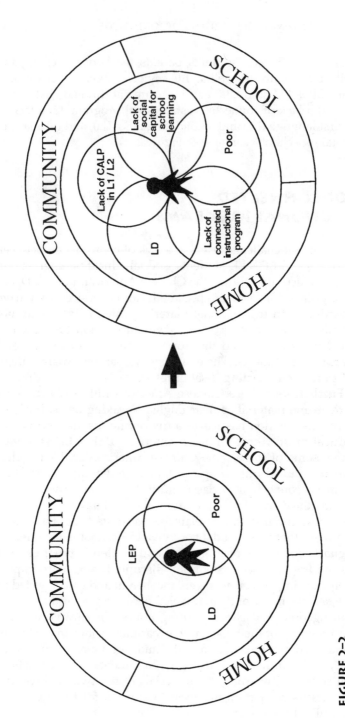

FIGURE 2–2
From triple to multiple challenges.

LACK OF CALP IN L1 AND L2

The second added challenge resulted from the lack of systematic support for students' home or first language and English language or second language. The aforementioned disjointed instructional programs left them with fragmented learning experiences; hence, they were likely to have reduced opportunities to develop CALP in either language. For Chinese American LEP + LD students to succeed in schools and later in life, they need to acquire and develop two levels of English language proficiency. In addition to most of them having acquired BICS, many of them struggled to acquire a more abstract level of cognitive and linguistic levels of English language proficiency (i.e., CALP). Acquiring knowledge and understanding of English instruction at this abstract level requires providing students with greater and systematic language support in the areas of semantics, syntax and graphophonic systems, and pragmatic competency in sociocultural contexts. Without built-in learning opportunities and systematic support from school and teachers, many Chinese American LEP + LD students coming from an impoverished family background will not achieve language and literacy competency as readily as their peers.

Another documented occasion of the students' missed learning opportunities has been the lack of support for the use of home language to facilitate their learning and acquisition of basic concepts, as well as opportunities for being bilingual and biliterate. It can be expected that peer-generated social mediation will contribute to their language and literacy development (e.g., Vygotsky, 1978). Many of the Chinese American LEP + LD students used Cantonese with their peers, siblings, and parents outside of the school context (see Chapter 9). In school, their homeroom learning often was mediated by their Cantonese-speaking peers (e.g., providing examples, further explanations, or filling in the missed directions for task completion when they were absent). However, in contrast, because many special education classrooms focused on individual work, these children were provided with few opportunities to interact with their peers in Cantonese, often not even in English, thus their learning opportunities were reduced.

LACK OF SOCIAL CAPITAL FOR SCHOOL LEARNING

Finally, the third added challenge relates to a limited access of social capital (e.g., Coleman, 1987) for school success as observed in some cases. In the context of inner-city Chinese American children's educational needs, social capital is broadly defined as the means by which LEP children's social, language and literacy development is generated through a network of peers, immediate and/or extended family members, adults, librarians, community informants, specialists, and teachers in an LEP child's home, school, and community-based multiple sites of learning (see Chang, 1993b; Chang & Fung, 1994).

A small group of Chinese American LEP + LD students were lagging behind because they had no access to either meaningful school instruction or community-based multiple learning sites, such as weekend or after school literacy learning programs, access to libraries or museums, and so on. These students' learning opportunities were limited because they received little or no support from their home, school, or community, or they received support from only one of these sources. Three parents indicated that their children did not have access to either school or community-based after-school programs for various reasons, such as time constraints, financial reasons, a need to be baby sitters at home, or the demands of other children. However, all Chinese parents reported their commitment to supervision of homework either by themselves or by older siblings. The students who have less access to multiple learning sites than other LEP + LD peers showed much less progress in school (Chang, 1993b).

⊥⊤

WHAT IS NEXT?

The information gathered from these 16 cases of Chinese American LEP + LD students provides us with a comprehensive set of data allowing the researchers to synthesize four major needs pertinent to those Chinese/Asian American LEP + LD students whose parents have a lower than high school education before coming to this country.

Before presenting the four sets of needs, we want to address a limitation of this chapter. Data obtained from a home-school-community based descriptive study are holistic, therefore a limitation of this chapter is that it can provide only part of the whole picture. For example, by focusing exclusively on the missed learning opportunities experienced by most of these Chinese American LEP + LD children, the few cases of effective special education practices and teacher characteristics (Chang, 1994a) are not reported here. In particular, there were three teachers (out of eleven) who, to one degree or another, met one or more of the following four major needs.

A NEED FOR SYSTEMATIC SUPPORT FOR DEVELOPMENT OF L1 AND L2

Chinese/Asian American LEP + LD students need systematic support for both their home language (L1) and English language to enhance their English language and literacy development. Inner-city Chinese American LEP + LD students were able to sustain school learning when they received social, language, and literacy support from the two of the following three sources: home, school, and/or community. Partnerships established between either home-school, school-community, or community-home can generate social capital for their academic advancement.

A NEED TO ACCESS MULTIPLE LEARNING SITES TO ACQUIRE KNOWLEDGE OF THEIR WORLD

A limited knowledge base tends to be associated with this group of children. Their inability to process language as efficiently as their peers and their limited access to community-based learning sites, such as public libraries, museums, and/or other social recreation sites, often contributes to their lack of prior knowledge to readily receive information presented in most of the school curriculum. Teachers and other service providers need to inform Chinese/Asian American LEP + LD students' parents about the value of prior experience and provide access to these children for field trips and hands-on activities. Through an integrated curriculum approach, curriculum content and experiences from the home environment can be connected.

A NEED FOR RESPECTING LEP PARENTS AS RESOURCES

Parents and caregivers who use the students' home language, can enhance basic concepts in the daily home environment. However, schools need to provide and train these parents with sets of workable strategies that will enhance their child's cognitive as well as home language development. Research conducted in teaching English as a second language indicates that the best context for concept development is providing children opportunities to discuss concepts in their native language with other children or adults (Saville-Troike, 1984).

A NEED FOR REMEDIATING THE MISSED LEARNING OPPORTUNITIES BUT NOT LEP + LD CHILDREN

Chinese/Asian American LEP + LD students need to have guaranteed access to various learning opportunities. This can be accomplished through a collaborative effort between regular and special education teachers as well as speech-language clinicians. Interrelated instructional activities within one holistic learning environment, in which they have access to peer resources for interactions and work on meaningful instructional materials can best mediate their learning in school.

⊐

ACKNOWLEDGMENT

This research was supported in part by Grant Number H02310050 from the Division of Innovation and Development, U. S. Department of Education, Office of Special Education Programs and by San Jose State University Foundation. The content and opinions expressed are of the views of the author.

⊐

REFERENCES

Bartoli, J., & Botel, M. (1988). *Reading/learning disability: An ecological approach.* New York: Teachers College Press.

Caplan, N., Choy, M. H., & Whitmore, J. K. (1992). Indochinese refugee families and academic achievement. *Scientific American, 266*(2), 36–42.

Chan, K. S. (1983). Limited English speaking, handicapped, and poor: Triple threat in childhood. In M. Chu-Chang with V. Rodriguez (Eds.), *Asian and Pacific-American perspectives in bilingual education: Comparative research* (pp. 153–171). New York: Teachers College Press.

Chang, J. M. (1990). Psycholinguistic analysis of reading processes by normal and disabled Chinese elementary readers. In S. C. Loo (Ed.), *Proceedings of the International Seminar on Chinese Language and Its Teaching in the World* (pp. 410–430). Singapore: Chinese Language Society.

Chang, J. M. (1993a, November). *Recruitment and retention of ethnic Chinese special education teacher-trainees: A Northern California experience.* Paper presented at the Conference on Asian Pacific Americans: Debunking the Model Minority-Myth and Reality, Sponsored by Teachers College, Columbia University, New York.

Chang, J. M. (1993b). A school-home-community based conceptualization of LEP with learning disabilities: Implications from a Chinese-American study. *Proceedings of the Third National Research Symposium on Limited English Proficient Student Issues: Focus On Middle and High School Issues* (Vol. 2, pp. 713–736). Washington, DC: U. S. Department of Education, Office of Bilingual Education & Minority Language Affairs,

Chang, J. M. (1994a, February). *Effective strategies of enhancing literacy development of Chinese/Asian LEP + LD children in RSP settings.* Paper presented at the 13th Annual California Association of Resource Specialists (CARS) convention, Burlingame, CA.

Chang, J. M. (1994b). *A follow-up study of Chinese children entering middle school.* (Research Report). San Jose, CA: San Jose State University, Graduate Studies and Research.

Chang, J. M., & Fung, G. (1994, April). *Literacy support across multiple sites: Experiences of Chinese American LEP children in inner cities.* Paper presented at the Annual Meeting of Educational Research Association (AERA), New Orleans.

Chang, J. M., Hung, D. L., & Tzeng, O. J. L. (1992). Miscue analysis of Chinese children's reading behavior at the entry level. *Journal of Chinese Linguistics, 20*(1), 120–158.

Chang, J. M., Kilbourne, J., & Shimizu, W. (1994, November). *Profiles of university students with learning disabilities: A multiple intelligences perspective.* Paper presented at the 45th annual conference sponsored by The Orton Dyslexia Society, Los Angeles.

Chang, J. M., & Maldonado-Colon, E. (1994). *A comparative study of learning and language disabilities across Chinese and Hispanic language minority groups.* Final Report (Grant #H023A10050). Washington, DC: United States Department of Education, Office of Special Education Programs.

Chang, J. M., & Tzeng, O. J. L. (1992). Reading ability and disability among Chinese beginning readers: Implications for educators. *Proceedings of Chinese Education for the 21th Century: An International Conference* (pp. 23–31). Charlottesville, VA: Curry School of Education, University of Virginia.

Coles, G. (1987). *The learning mystique: A critical look at "learning disabilities."* New York: Pantheon.

Coleman, J. S. (1987). Families and schools. *Educational Researcher, 16*(6), 32–38.

Cummins, J. (1981). The role of primary language development in promoting educational success for language minority students. In California State Department of Education, *Schooling and language minority students: A theoretical framework.* Los Angeles: Evaluation, Dissemination and Assessment Center.

Cummins, J. (1984). *Bilingualism and special education: Issues in assessment and pedagogy.* San Diego: College-Hill Press.

Federal Register. (1977, Thursday, December 29). (65082–65085) Washington, DC.

Gerber, P. J., & Reiff, H. B. (Eds.). (1994). *Learning disabilities in adulthood: Persisting problems and evolving issues.* Boston: Andover Medical.

Guo, Y. C. (1982). *A study of reading disability among the fifth graders in Tainan City.* (Collected papers.) Taipei: Taiwan Provincial Health Administration.

Hsu, C. C., Soong, W. T., Shen, S., Su, S. J., & Wei, F. W. (1985). Brain dysfunction as a cause of reading disabilities. *Psychiatry, 5*, 127–132.

Kavanaugh, J. F., & Truss, T. J. (Eds.). (1988). *Learning disabilities: Proceedings of the national conference.* Parkton, MD: York,

Lee, Y. C. (Ed.). (1983). *Annual report of the resource room program.* Taipei, Taiwan: Municipal Tun-Mang Elementary School.

Lee, Y. C. (Ed.). (1985). *The study of children's reading disabilities.* Taipei, Taiwan: Municipal Tun-Mang Elementary School.

Lipson, M. Y., & Wixson, K. K. (1986). Reading disability research: An interactionist perspective. *Review of Educational Research, 56*(1), 111–136.

Lyon, G. R., Gray, D. B., Kavanaugh, K. F., & Krasnegor, N. A. (Eds.). (1993). *Better understanding learning disabilities: New views from research and their implications for education and public policy.* Baltimore: Paul H. Brookes.

Mau, W. C. (1994, September). *Predictors of academic achievement: A comparison of bilingual Chinese, American-born Chinese, and White American high school students.* Paper presented at the annual conference of the Chinese American Educational Research and Development Association, New York.

National Joint Committee on Learning Disabilities. (1994). *Collective perspectives on issues affecting learning disabilities: Position papers and statements.* Austin, TX: Pro-Ed.

Peng, S. S., & Wright, D. (1994). Explanation of academic achievement of Asian American students. *Journal of Educational Research, 87*(6), 346–352.

Peregoy, S. F., & Boyle, O. F. (1993). *Reading, writing, and learning in ESL: A resource book for K-8 teachers.* New York: Longman Publishing Group.

Saville-Troike, M. (1984). What really matters in second language learning for academic achievement? *TESOL Quarterly, 18*(2), 199–217.

Schneider, B., & Lee, Y. (1990). A model for academic success: The school and home environment of East Asian students. *Anthropology & Education Quarterly, 21*, 358–377.

Scott-Jones, D. (1984). Family influences on cognitive development and school achievement. In E. W. Gordon (Ed.), *Review of research in education* (Vol. 11, pp. 259–304). Washington, DC: American Education Research Association.

Silver, L. B. (1988). A review of the federal government's Interagency Committee on Learning Disabilities report to the U.S. Congress. *Learning Disabilities Focus, 3*, 73–80.

Smith, C. R. (1994). *Learning disabilities: The interaction of learner, task, and setting.* Needham Heights, MA: Allyn & Bacon.

Southgate, V. (Ed.) (1972). *Literacy at all levels: Proceedings of the eighth annual study conference of the United Kingdon Reading Association.* Manchester, England: Ward Lock.

Stevenson, H. W. (1992). Learning from Asian schools. *Scientific American, 267*(6), 70–76.

Stevenson, H. W. (1984). Orthography and reading disabilities. *Journal of Learning Disabilities, 17*(5), 296–301.

Stevenson, H. W., Stigler, J. W., Lucker, G. W. , Lee, S. Y., Hsu, C. C., & Kitamura, S. (1982). Reading disabilities: The case of Chinese, Japanese, and English. *Child Development, 53*, 1164–1181.

Trueba, H. T., Cheng, L. L., & Ima, K. (1993). *Myth or reality: Adaptive strategies of Asian Americans in California.* Washington, DC: Falmer Press,

Vogel, S. A., & Adelman, P. B. (1993). *Success for college students with learning disabilities.* New York: Springer-Verlag.

Vygotsky, L. S. (1978). *Mind in society: The development of higher psychological processes.* Cambridge, MA: Harvard University Press.

Wong, M. G. (1980). Model students? Teachers' perceptions and expectations of their Asian and White students. *Sociology of Education, 53*, 236–246.

Wright, P. (1992). Sunset review finds funding, increased enrollment impacts special education programs. *Special Edge, 7*(1) 1, 6. Sacramento CA: Resources in Special Education.

PART II

The process of socialization begins at birth. Various experiences influence how we think, act, speak and interact. Our culture shapes our own values and lifestyles. Some cultures, such as Tibetan and Iranian, are dominated by religion. Other cultures, such as Haiti, Saipan, and Sarawak, are a blend of folk practices and religions. The various interactions and communications among people of different cultures often lead to adaptation and adjustment. The stories from Asia Pacific are a source of fascination because, for centuries, these diverse cultures have interacted with each other, and the results of these contacts have led these people to more enriched lifestyles. The dominant religions which influence Asian cultures are Buddhism, Hinduism, Islam, and Shintoism.

Southeast Asia is at the crossroads of Chinese and Indian cultures. The Southeast Asian cultures have been mainly influenced by Buddhism and Confucianism. The Conquistadors have had a great influence on Pacific Islanders, and many of them were Catholics or Christians. One religion, Islam, traveled to Asia from the Middle-East and has left a significant mark in Asia Pacific. As described in Part I, people from the Asia Pacific communicate with many languages and follow different religious and folk practices. They share similar, yet very different, pasts.

The second part of this book attempts to explore some of the lesser known histories, cultures, languages, and peoples of Asia Pacific. In Chapter 3, Cheng, Nakasato, and Wallace examine the cultures of Pacific Islanders and the Philippines; in Chapter 4, Te describes the Vietnamese culture; Shekar and Hegde, in Chapter 5, provide a comprehensive view of Indian languages, cultures, and religions; Ima and Kheo, in Chapter 6, discuss the intricate relationships between cultural adaptation, conflicts, and adolescent development among Southeast Asian youth and their family.

The main purpose of this section is to link background information about the Asia Pacific cultures and peoples with what educators, as service providers, are offering. The background information should guide educators' thinking and planning in regard to assessment and intervention and ultimately guide our overall policies of education and service delivery.

CHAPTER 3

THE PACIFIC ISLANDER POPULATION AND THE CHALLENGES THEY FACE

LI-RONG LILLY CHENG, Ph.D.
JEAN NAKASATO, M.S.
GLORIA JEAN WALLACE, Ph.D.

Within the United States in 1990, the total Pacific Island population was 365,051, a 53% increase since the 1980 census (U.S. Census, 1991). This population has immigrated to the United States from the many islands and atolls spread throughout the Pacific. The island-spattered Pacific Ocean covers 64 million square miles and is grouped into three main clusters—Polynesia, Melanesia, and Micronesia (also referred to as the Federated States of Micronesia). In addition to bordering the Pacific Ocean, the United States includes the Pacific islands of Hawaii.

Polynesian countries are located in the northeastern region of the Pacific Ocean and include populations of Hawaii, American Samoa, Western Samoa, Tonga, and Tahiti. Melanesian countries in the southwestern portion include Fiji, the Solomon Islands, New Caledonia,

Kiribati, Tuvalu, and Vanuatu. The Federated States of Micronesia, located in the northwestern section, includes Saipan, Ponape, Truk, the Marshall Islands, Yap, and Palau. Guam is culturally Micronesian. The listed entities are but a few of the homelands located throughout the Polynesian, Melanesian, and Micronesian areas.

Hawaii and Guam lie 5,000 miles apart; Fiji and Guam are 3,000 miles apart. Other smaller islands are very close together and are sparsely inhabited or uninhabited. Many atolls also have small populations (Cheng & Ima, 1989). Many western Pacific or Association of Southeast Asian Nations (ASEAN) countries—including Thailand, Singapore, Malaysia, Indonesia, Brunei, and the Philippines—share common interests with the Pacific Islands. ASEAN is the United States' seventh largest trading partner.

Limited technology makes communication between the Pacific islands quite difficult, and language variations hinder information sharing. A recent report indicates that English is the most frequently used language in inter-island broadcasts (Asian and Pacific Horizons, 1994). Colonization, including French, Spanish, Portuguese, German, British, Japanese, and American have left a considerable mark on Pacific Island cultures. American Samoa, for example, continues to follow the American educational system, with Western Samoa following the United Kingdom system. Spanish culture has heavily influenced the Chamorro people (of Saipan and Guam), as evidenced by names such as Martinez, Gutierrez, and Rodriguez.

The Pacific cultures have overlapping influences on one another and, as one might imagine, the Pacific Island populations are very diverse. Given the scope of these groups, it is not possible to provide a comprehensive review of all Pacific island cultures in this chapter. We do, however, describe the primary Pacific Islander groups represented in the United States, with emphasis on the needs of educators and clinicians working with these populations. Our discussion focuses on the Hawaiians, the Chamorro people of Guam, and the Samoans. We also present information about the Filipino people, who are often included within the Pacific Islander grouping and who are the fastest growing of all Asian/Pacific Islander groups.

Many cultures, including Chinese, Japanese, Korean, Filipino, and Portuguese, have heavily influenced the Hawaiian Islands. Japanese customs such as eating bento and wearing zori have been incorporated into everyday life and vocabulary. Kanahele (1980) has listed Hawaiian values that have been adopted throughout the Pacific and elsewhere, including aloha spirit, humility, spirituality, and generosity (Cheng & Ima, 1989).

The Chamorro people of the island of Guam are culturally part of Micronesia, although Guam is a U.S. territory politically, and not part of the Federated States of Micronesia. Family and festivities are the center of Chamorro social life. Fiestas in honor of the patron saints of the island's 19 villages include food such as fish, roast pork, taro, and breadfruit (Cheng & Ima, 1989).

The Samoan people are Polynesian. The extended families of Samoa are organized through a clan system. To Samoans, the social group is such an important factor that there is no word for "person" in the Samoan language; it is considered that an individual has no existence outside of his or her place in society.

The Philippines consists of many small groups of islands, the distance between which makes it difficult for people to live as a cohesive whole. Ninety-five percent of its population is of Malay origin, and other racial and cultural influences include Chinese, Spanish, Aboriginal, Amerasian, and Japanese.

⅃╗

PACIFIC ISLANDERS

The 1993 LEAP report indicates that the total Pacific Islander population in the United States amounts to 365,051 (see Table 3–1); this marks a 53% increase since the 1980 Census. The U.S. Census Bureau has officially identified nine groups of Pacific Islanders. Hawaiians account for 85% of the population, followed in number by Samoans, Guamanians, and Tongans (Akamatsu, 1993). Notice the population distributions of Asian and Pacific Americans as profiled in Table 3–1.

⅃╗

THE HAWAIIANS

HISTORY AND DEMOGRAPHICS

The Hawaiian islands, including Hawaii, O'ahu, Maui, Kauai, Molokai, Lanai, Niihau, and Kahoolawe, form a 1,500-mile archipelago. The first Hawaiians are thought to have settled on the islands

TABLE 3–1
Population statistics for Asian and Pacific Americans.

Total Asian Population	3,466,421
Asian Indian	387,223
Bangladeshi	1,314
Burmese	2,756
Cambodian	16,044
Sri Lankan	2,923
Chinese	812,178
Filipino	781,894
Hmong	5,204
Indonesian	9,618
Japanese	716,331
Korean	357,393
Laotian	47,683
Malayan	4,075
Okinawan	1,415
Pakistani	15,792
Thai	45,279
Vietnamese	245,025
Asian not specified	12,897
All other Asian	1,377

Source: From U.S. Bureau of the Census. Statistical abstract of the United States: 1980 (100th ed.). Washington, DC: Author.

about 400 AD and to have maintained contact with other Polynesian groups such as Tahitians for the next nine centuries. Since those early days, Hawaiians have developed distinct ways, different from those of other Polynesian peoples. Nevertheless, they share a racial background and strict system of laws set down by their ancestors (Cheng & Ima, 1990).

In 1778, the English explorer James Cook arrived in Hawaii and initiated European contact with the Hawaiians. During the next 40 years, an influx of Europeans and Americans changed the Hawaiian religion, language, and way of life. It is estimated that fewer than a quarter of native Hawaiians survived the onslaught of diseases brought by newcomers. Indigenous rulers lost political control to newcomers by the 19th century, and, in 1898, Hawaii was annexed by the U.S. Chinese, Filipino, Japanese, Korean, Portuguese, and numerous other peoples settled in the 19th century, working primarily on sugar cane and pineapple plantations. Cantonese, Mandarin, Hawaiian, Pilipino dialects (Ilocano and Tagalog),

Korean, Japanese, and Samoan are among the many languages spoken in Hawaii. Indigenous Hawaiians have intermarried with other ethnic groups and have all but lost their original languages.

Those still identifiable as native Hawaiians find themselves at the bottom of the social hierarchy, as reflected in lower education levels, higher rates of incarceration, lower income levels, and lower occupational status. These social conditions continue to influence the academic performance of students of Hawaiian ancestry. For more information about the Hawaiians, see Cheng and Ima (1990) and Kanahele (1980).

REVIVAL OF HAWAIIAN CULTURE

During the two centuries of rapid and diverse changes since the arrival of Captain Cook, native Hawaiians have felt a profound sense of cultural loss. Many feared that the Hawaiian people and their culture would simply disappear. Recently, however, there has been a resurgence of interest in the Hawaiian culture, indicating one of the most positive of all the educational trends. Indicators of this positive change include:

- In 1978, both Hawaiian and English were established as official languages of the state by the Constitutional Convention.
- Hawaiian history and culture are required courses in the state Department of Education for the fourth and seventh grades.
- Annually, thousands of people, Hawaiian and non-Hawaiian, participate in such events as the Merrie Monarch Hula Festival and the Molokai to O'ahu outrigger canoe race.
- A renewed pride in the navigational feats of the peoples of the Pacific has been generated by the voyages of the Hawaiian sailing canoe, Hokule'a.

Published in 1993, the Native Hawaiian Educational Assessment Project provides a good source of information on the problems facing native Hawaiians. A review and update of native Hawaiian needs include:

- Neonate health: Risk factors begin before infancy. It has been documented that some native Hawaiian women have only sought prenatal care late in their pregnancy or not all. In 1990, 45% of all teenage mothers in the state of Hawaii were native Hawaiian. The infant mortality rate for Hawaiians is 25% higher than for non-Hawaiians.

■ Health: National studies indicate that the mortality rate for Hawaiians is 34% higher than the national average. Heart disease, lung cancer, and diabetes continue to be prevalent among native Hawaiians. There is a high incidence of mild intermittent hearing loss among Hawaiian preschool children, and this is associated with long-term educational problems (Steward, Anae, & Gipe, 1989).

■ Language skills: On school achievement tests, Hawaiian students perform below national norms. Hawaiian youngsters entering kindergarten have lower vocabulary scores than other children in the nation. In the 1989–1990 school year, the average score for vocabulary achievement on the *Peabody Picture Vocabulary Test-Revised* for ethnic Hawaiian children was at the tenth percentile on the national norm. On the Total Reading subtest of the *Stanford Achievement Test* administered by the State of Hawaii Department of Education in 1991, Hawaiian sixth-grade students scored at the 37th percentile, the lowest among four major ethnic groups in the islands: Hawaiian, Filipino, Japanese, and Caucasian. On similar achievement tests, Hawaiian students scored lowest among major ethnic groups in science and social science and lowest in mathematics at grades 3, 6, 8, and 10.

■ Special education: Hawaiian students are over-represented in special education categories, particularly learning disabilities. In addition, there are a number of students of Hawaiian ancestry who were considered "at-risk," but who were not receiving special education services.

■ Educational aspirations: Only one-third of Hawaiian public school ninth graders aspire to complete four or more years of college, compared to 50% to 75% of their peers in other ethnic groups.

■ Higher education: Hawaiian students are under-represented in institutions of higher learning in Hawaii. In 1986, native Hawaiians were only 4.8% of the student body enrolled at the University of Hawaii Manoa campus. However, during the past four years, enrollment rates of Hawaiian students have been steadily increasing. At present, over 6% of the student body at the Manoa campus is made up of ethnic Hawaiians.

■ Alcohol and drug abuse: Hawaiian students rank the highest among major ethnic groups in the state of Hawaii for alcohol and drug abuse. However, during 1987 and 1989, drug and alcohol usage rates appeared to decline for Hawaiian students, suggesting that preventive education efforts had had a positive effect.

HAWAIIAN PUBLIC SCHOOL STUDENTS

A large proportion of Hawaii's public school population is Hawaiian or part-Hawaiian: 23.4%, or approximately 41,477 children (LEAP, 1993). Table 3–2 summarizes the ethnicity of students enrolled in the Hawaii Department of Education, 1992–1993.

Prevailing differences between Hawaiian-American and Caucasian-American values and learning styles, and differences in educational systems explain some of the difficulties encountered by Hawaiian students. Table 3–3 is a comparison chart (Kishi & Hanohano, 1992).

To improve special education services to students of Hawaiian ancestry, Pihana Na Mamo Native Hawaiian Special Education Project, a federally funded project, was implemented by the Hawaii State Department of Education in 1989. Departmental data revealed that 30.8% of the students in special education were of Hawaiian ancestry. In addition, there appeared to be a number of Hawaiian students who were considered "at-risk," but who were not receiving special educa-

TABLE 3–2

Ethnicity of students enrolled in the Hawaii Department of Education, 1992–1993.

Ethnicity	Number	Percentage
Hawaiian	41,477	23.4
Caucasian	38,025	21.5
Filipino	31,945	18.0
Japanese	23,313	13.2
Chinese	5,659	3.2
Samoan	5,288	3.0
Black	4,803	2.7
Hispanic	4,404	2.5
Korean	2,943	1.7
Other	19,252	10.9
Total Enrollment	**177,109**	**100.0**

Source: From LEAP (1993). *The State of Asian Pacific America: Policy issues to the year 2020.* Los Angeles: LEAP Asian Pacific American Public Policy Institute.

TABLE 3–3

Hawaiian-American compared with Caucasian-American values.

HAWAIIAN	CAUCASIAN
Overall Values	
Affiliation/maintenance of interpersonal harmony	Personal achievement
Group goals	Individual goals
Affirmation of relationships as status	Accumulation of material capital as status
Deference to rank and authority	Personal autonomy
Interdependency	Independency
Care and affection	Development of competencies
Learning Styles	
Na'au (sharing of personal information, establishing lineage, relationships)	Separation of public and private life
Ho'olehe (listen)	Questions encouraged
Ikepono (look)	Adult-child interchanges and feedback
Ho'opili (watch and mimic)	Originality encouraged
Peers as source of information	Adults as source of information
Risk minimization ("ain't no big thing")	Creativity and spontaneity rewarded
Educational Processes	
Hawaii Education Process	*Special Education Processes*
Group	Individual
Social-interpersonal skills	Individual achievement in math and reading
Ho'oponopono as conflict resolution	Due process
Verbal word important	Written paper trail
Deference to experts	Equal partnerships
Holistic view of child	Fragmented

Source: From Kishi, G., & Hanohano, M. (1992, November), *Hawaiian children.* Presentation at Council for Exceptional Children, Honolulu, HI, with permission.

tion services. Failing in school, having poor attendance, and lacking motivation and positive attitudes toward school and learning were all characteristics of these students.

The goals of the project addressed four components:

■ Preservice and inservice personnel preparation
■ Prereferral intervention and mainstreaming
■ School and community integration and transition, and
■ Parent and community liaison partnerships

Although the Pihana Na Mamo project is continuing and is being evaluated, it is evident that the integration of programs addressing special education, regular education, and at-risk students is enhancing students' learning. Significant in accomplishing this goal has been the use of cooperative learning, cross-age tutoring, hands-on activities, and cultural enrichment activities. Staff development and parent training have also made considerable contributions to the program's success. For further information and evaluation of individual school case studies refer to Nakamura, Cerveny, Kagehiro, Komo, and Saka, (1992).

INTERVENTION STRATEGIES

Another federally funded program aimed at early intervention (and particularly the improvement of language skills) was the Native Hawaiian Speech and Hearing Project at Kamehameha Schools Bishop Estate. Beginning in 1991, this 2-year model demonstration project confirmed the hypothesis that counteracting the negative educational effects of mild/moderate intermittent hearing loss would improve language competence of Hawaiian preschoolers (Stewart, 1993).

The six intervention strategies implemented in the experimental Kamehameha preschools were: (1) enhanced screening procedures for hearing loss, middle ear disorder, and speech; (2) a follow-up effort, ensuring every child who failed the screening received appropriate medical care; (3) the reduction of classroom ambient noise levels to educationally acceptable levels as specified by an acoustic engineer; (4) the amplification of instructional speech to an educationally effective signal-to-noise ratio; (5) special communication-enhancing classroom teaching techniques, a classroom speech center, and equipment designed to improve the language competence of children experiencing moderate speech and hearing difficulties; and (6) an individualized home and school communication therapy program for children identified as most needful.

Considered an integral component of success for the Kamehameha Project was the involvement of parents and caregivers, with inclusion of parent workshops and home speech and language stimulation activities.

EDUCATIONAL AND CLINICAL IMPLICATIONS

Given the historical, social, and health-oriented contexts, as well as the educational problems facing Hawaiian students and their families, enhancement of natives' scholastic achievement and advancement is challenging. The school environment provides numerous opportunities for social and cognitive growth, but life outside of the school provides an even greater arena for development because students spend less time in school than in their homes and communities.

To effect significant and life-long changes in the educational achievement of Native Hawaiian students, meaningful and effective parent training programs are essential. The children's learning skills can only be maximized with parental involvement.

The key to successful intervention programs lies with parent training programs. The essence of parent training lies in building partnerships, always being aware of the subtleties that trigger and maintain parent-child-professional relationships.

Professionals working with Native Hawaiian children and their families must not only be culturally sensitive to individual communities' needs, values, attitudes, and learning styles, but also highly attuned to unique variations from community to community. They need to understand that what works in one community will not necessarily work for the next.

Effective avenues for communicating and collaborating with parents are:

- Providing information to parents on a regular and consistent basis;
- Providing a balance between dissemination of information and hands-on-activities;
- Presenting information appropriate to the parents' interests and learning styles and using visual and concrete aids to emphasize critical information;

- Allowing parents to experience activities that are planned for their children;
- Making inservice training fun, motivating, and exciting;
- Informing parents of workshops and activities via the "talk story" approach: Hawaiians start any discourse by chatting about familiar topics and moving to the main topic of discussion after a relationship has been established (Au & Jordan, 1981; Cheng, 1993).

⅃

THE CHAMORROS (GUAM)

HISTORY AND DEMOGRAPHICS

The U.S. territory of Guam lies at the southern end of the Mariana Islands in the western Pacific; it is part of Micronesia, along with the Marshall, Caroline, and Gilbert Islands. Guam, at nearly 30 miles long and 4 to 9 miles wide, is the largest island in the Pacific Ocean between Hawaii and the Philippines. It is volcanic in origin and covers approximately 212 square miles. The official languages of Guam are English and Chamorro, both taught in public and private schools and used in official documents.

Guam's population was estimated at 116,000 in 1990. The Chamorros were the largest ethnic group, at approximately 42% of the total population, with Caucasians accounting for approximately 24% and Filipinos 21%. Other ethnic groups included Japanese, Koreans, Chinese, and those from other Pacific islands.

The Chamorros are believed to have migrated from Indonesia and the Philippines to Guam as early as 2000 BC. In 1521, Magellan sailed into Umatac Bay, Guam, and was followed in the 1600s by Spanish missionaries, soldiers, and government officials. Guam consequently became a colony of Spain. The Spaniards left an enduring legacy in Chamorro religion, culture, architecture, family names, and language. In 1898, when the United States defeated Spain in the Spanish-American war, Guam was placed under the administration of the U.S. Department of Navy. The Japanese occupied Guam for 2½ years during World War II, but the United States soon regained control.

LIFESTYLE

Although some islands are located thousands of miles apart and their inhabitants differ in terms of politics and language, Micronesians, including Guamanians, share many customs, beliefs, superstitions, and proverbs. Most Micronesian societies are matriarchal. Legends are part of the rich heritage of the oral literature, and islanders generally believe in the magic that prevails in the stories. The narratives, often with an integral sea theme, focus on important aspects of Micronesian culture, such as values, and include proverbs that serve as lessons for both adults and children.

EDUCATIONAL IMPLICATIONS

The scarcity of Chamorro people in higher level occupations relates directly to their attitude toward life which is vastly different from the typical mainland outlook. Timelines for getting things done are considered less important than making people comfortable among Chamorro. Consequently, they seem, by typical American attitudes, to lack the motivation needed to achieve challenging goals, such as doctoral degrees. Their approach to life entails enjoying it and being good to people. At the same time, they place little emphasis on schoolwork or discipline. For example, absenteeism rates among Chamorro teachers in primary and secondary schools are occasionally so high that schools have to close for shortage of teachers. Poor attendance by students further reinforces the notion that Chomorros give low priority to academic pursuits.

In general, a lack of role models and low self-esteem prevent the Chamorro from raising academic goals and standards, increasing attendance, and realizing the benefits of academic motivation.

THE SAMOANS

HISTORY AND DEMOGRAPHICS

The Samoan people are Polynesian. The islands on which they reside are located 2,200 miles southwest of Honolulu in the South Pacific. The islands are divided into two parts—Western Samoa and American Samoa. Western Samoa, officially known as Samoa i Sisifo, is the more traditional of the two. Western Samoa, which is located in the western part of the Samoa island group, has an area of 1,100 square miles and a population of approximately 168,000. In 1980, residents of Western Samoa were 86% of the total Samoan population (Markoff & Bond, 1974).

The eastern Samoan islands form a territory of the United States, known as American Samoa. American Samoa has a land mass of 76 square miles and a population of 46,800 (American Samoa Statistical Digest, 1990). The projected population for 1995 is 54,000, and the population of American Samoa is expected to increase to 62,000 by the year 2000 (American Samoa Statistical Digest, 1990). This increase is mainly from the influx of residents from Western Samoa. The status of American Samoa as a trust territory has led to the adoption of American values among the residents of that country. Because the residents of American Samoa are American nationals, they are free to move to the United States. Their government and educational systems are patterned after those of the continental United States.

Many American Samoans emigrate to the United States in search of a better life, access to comprehensive health care, better education, and an opportunity to escape from Samoa's traditional authoritarian system (Cheng & Ima, 1989). The majority of Samoans migrate directly to the United States from American Samoa (Markoff & Bond, 1974). It is not uncommon for citizens of Western Samoa to move to American Samoa, establish residency there (gaining American citizenship), and then emigrate to the United States. Because of the pattern of migration, the population of Samoans in the United States is steadily increasing, especially in Hawaii and California.

WESTERN SAMOA OVERVIEW

Western Samoa comprises two large islands, Savai'i and Upolu, and several islets. The two large islands, which are rugged and mountainous, were formed by volcanoes. Two-thirds of the land is covered with tropical rain forests. Numerous streams and waterfalls can also be found throughout the islands. Apia, the capital of Western Samoa, is the largest city and chief port of the country. Apia also houses an observatory where scientists from Samoa and other countries conduct research; a teacher training college; an agricultural hospital (located near Apia); and a hospital.

The Samoans inhabited the western islands more than 2,000 years ago. Jacob Roggeveen, a Dutch explorer, was the first European to sight the Western Samoan islands in 1722. The first Christian mission was established there in 1830 by John Williams of the London Missionary Society, which is still the most popular church in the country. The missionaries were responsible for developing a written Samoan language system in the 1800s.

In the late 1800s Britain, Germany, and the United States all sought control over the Samoan Islands. In 1899, Britain and the United States gave up their claims to Western Samoa. Germany held claim over Western Samoa from that time until 1914. At the onset of World War I, New Zealand occupied Western Samoa. New Zealand continued to administer the islands after the war was over—first under a League of Nations mandate and then under a United Nations trusteeship. Western Samoa gained independence in 1962. New Zealand and the United Kingdom, however, continue to assist and to have a great influence on Western Samoa today. The school system adopted in Western Samoa, for instance, is very similar to the system used in the United Kingdom.

As in the United Kingdom, the head of the Western Samoa government is a prime minister, appointed by the head of state. Until 1963, two hereditary chiefs served simultaneous offices as heads of state. After one chief died, the other became the Head of State for life. When the current chief dies, heads of state will be elected for 5-year terms by the legislature. Members of the legislature are chosen by the residents, through the village chiefs, called matai.

In Western Samoa, most of the people live as their ancestors did hundreds of years ago in small family villages. Their homes, called fales, have thatched roofs made of palm leaves. The walls, which can be rolled open to let in air and light, are made of woven leaves. Mats made of coconut leaves cover stone floors.

The traditional ways are also preserved in colorful dances, songs, and traditional feasts and celebrations. The people still grow or catch most of their own food and make many of the things they need, rather than import them. The Samoans grow tropical fruits (banana, pineapple, papaya) and vegetables (breadfruit and taro), catch fish, and raise pigs and chicken for food. Copra (dried coconut meat) is the main export. Herds of cattle grazing in the coconut plantations control weeds and provide beef. There is little industry. Tourism is expanding; however, the Samoans are careful about not encouraging too rapid development of the tourist industry for fear that their traditional way of life may be affected.

AMERICAN SAMOA OVERVIEW

The country of American Samoa comprises six islands: Tutuila, Aunu'u, Ta'u, Ofu, Olosega, and two islets named Sand and Rose Islands. The majority of the residents of American Samoa live on the island of Tutuila, which houses governmental offices, a junior college, and the country's only major medical facility, LBJ Tropical Medical Center. A major tuna cannery is also located on the island of Tutuila. The cannery provides a large source of income for the country's residents. Traditional occupations in this country include fishing and farming. For the most part, traditional values still prevail in America Samoa, although not to the same extent as in Western Samoa.

In 1888, when Western Samoa was first acquired as a colony by Germany, the United States acquired American Samoa as a trust territory. American Samoa was desired because its geographical location and harbors made it a desirable location for a naval station. When in 1962 Western Samoa became an independent nation, American Samoa remained (and still remains) a trust territory of the United States. During World War II, many men from American Samoa were drafted into the U.S. military, and many individuals were hired as civilian employees of the United States. This resulted in a thriving economy for the country, and residents of Samoa became accustomed to imported luxuries and a lifestyle influenced by American values. However, when the war ended, so did the war economy. Because of the change in economy in American Samoa, many Samoans began to emigrate to the United States.

During the past several decades, American Samoa has been administered by the United States Department of the Interior under a governor appointed by the U.S. president. In November 1977, after years of declining to do so, the American Samoans elected their own governor for the first time.

LIFESTYLE

Culturally, the two Samoas are similar. At one time, they were united politically. Although the union has always been relatively loose, there are important cultural and family ties between the two Samoas.

Social classes, as such, are nonexistent for the people of Samoa. And although, from an outsider's perspective, the countries may appear to be economically depressed, the problems of poverty and homelessness as observed in the United States do not exist in Samoa. Everyone is linked within a closely knit family or extended family network, with food, shelter, and material wealth shared freely. In fact, in the Samoan language there is no word for "person," because in the Samoan culture a person is considered to be part of the whole group. Because family units tend to be large, older siblings are typically assigned the responsibility of caring for and raising the younger siblings. The social system is patrilineal (descends through the male side of the family).

For residents of Western and American Samoa, the basic unit of society is the extended family headed by a chief called a matai. All who are related by birth, adoption, religious, or other close affiliation are recognized as belonging to one aiga, a network comprising large closely knit family clans that may contain several hundred people. Each aiga is governed by a council, or fono, which is composed of matais.

There are about 10,000 matais in Western Samoa alone. Not all matais share equal rank in the fono and there usually is one senior member. Chiefly titles are of two types, ali'i or "high chief," and tulafale or "talking chief." The ali'i, who is the more prestigious of the two, has great responsibilities for decision making, with the tulafale serving as orator and speaking for the ali'i. Both are referred to by the generic name of matai. The chiefs speak a formal "high Samoan" language and others speak a more common form of the Samoan language. Succession to the title of chief is by election within a family and, though inheritance is a factor, general ability and popularity are the most important qualifications. The matais are responsible for representing village members before the government; helping to see that the laws are carried out in the villages; locating resources such as food, land, and housing; and having authority over bestowing titles (although titles can be inherited).

RELIGION

Religion is very important in Samoa and nearly every village has one or more large churches. About half of the people belong to the Congregational Christian Church of Western Samoa (formerly known as the London Missionary Society) or other Protestant churches. Other residents of Samoa are Roman Catholics. The Church of Jesus Christ of Latter Day Saints (Mormon) also has a particularly large membership among residents of the Samoa islands.

CHILD REARING

Although Samoan caregivers attend to infants often, they do not interact with them as communication partners in the way seen in European American middle-class mother/child dyads. Samoan caregivers cuddle, soothe, and play with their infants, but do not treat the child's early gestures and vocalizations as intentional or social (Ochs, 1988; Ochs & Schieffelin, 1984), resulting in the lack of emphasis on early onset of language development.

One of the most important features of the socialization of Samoan children is the constant physical presence of many individuals of varying social status. This provides young children with an opportunity to participate in interactions with multiple partners more often than in dyadic interactions. In the multipartite interactions, each participant may assume varying social identities, based on the social identities of others present. For example, a young untitled man may have a higher status than a younger sibling, but a lower status than a titled family member who may also be present. This requires conversational participants to continually calculate their social rank with respect to those they are interacting with. Interactions contain a great deal of social information, some relating to rights and responsibilities associated with rank; some relating to an ingrained understanding of who can say what to whom (Shore, 1977, 1982). In this way Samoan children come to understand their roles and identities in society based on social context.

Samoan children, from a very early age, are socialized to attend to and to serve others, especially those holding a higher rank. They are also socialized to listen carefully and give great respect to those of higher status. By the time children are 3 years old or so they begin serving higher status family members by running messages from one family member to another (Ochs, 1988). In the Samoan schools, this feature of respect carries over into the classroom context, where great reverence is given to teachers.

A final point of interest is the expectation that Samoan children will assume child-care responsibilities for younger siblings early in life. This aspect of socialization results in a mature repertoire of communication skills at an early age. By 4 years of age, Samoan children are able to interact with younger siblings, peers, older siblings, and a range of adult relatives, guests, and strangers of varying status (Ochs, 1988).

DISCIPLINE

Regardless of social position, Samoan caregivers use a range of verbal and nonverbal strategies to curb misbehavior in children. Caregivers prefer verbal control techniques, such as the use of negative imperatives, affective terms of address, warnings, threats, and public shaming. These techniques are more common than withdrawal of affection or physical punishment in the form of striking a child. Verbal control techniques, however, are usually followed by the latter techniques when deemed necessary. The order of sequence is almost formulaic, in which the caregiver first says "Aua" (don't), then "Soia" (I said stop it), then "Sasa" (I'm going to spank you). If the caregiver deems it necessary to follow through with a spanking, this action is taken because of a double, or paramount offense. From the perspective of the caregiver, the child would warrant a physical reprimand in such an instance because the original offense is compounded by the lack of respect for the caregiver's directive to stop the behavior (Ochs, 1988).

Typically, lower-ranking caregivers are responsible for the discipline of the children. However, if the lower-ranking caregiver cannot manage a behavior, a higher-ranking caregiver will take over. As household members higher up the social hierarchy become involved in the discipline, there is an increase in the punishment and shame experienced by the child. Samoan discipline is often criticized by Europeans, who view it as harsh. However this type of discipline is widely practiced and accepted in the Samoan culture, and is considered by Samoan children to be supportive and protective rather than abusive (Ochs, 1988).

AGGRESSION

There is a high incidence of violent aggression among the young male population in American Samoa (Baker, Hanna, & Baker, 1986; Gerber, 1975; Freeman, 1983; Keene 1978; Maxwell, 1969; Shore, 1982). This aggression has been most often attributed to stringent discipline practices in American Samoa, which generate high levels of anger with no outlet for expression. Although social constraints in the culture help to keep internal feelings of anger and hostility in check, display of anger is acceptable when one is presented with a challenge to status or a challenge to self-esteem, either of which is considered to be a severe affront.

LANGUAGE

The Samoan language belongs to the Western Polynesian or Samoic-Outlier subgroup of the Polynesian language group, along with languages such as East Futunan, Ellicean, Pukupukan, Tikopian, and Nukuoro (Chung, 1978; Pawley, 1966, 1967). The rules of language use in Samoa are situationally variable. Phonological, morpho-syntactic, and lexical constructions are associated with particular activities, affects and social roles and relationships (Gumperz, 1982).

There are two primary registers for the Samoan language (Duranti, 1981). One style of communication is used when conversing with those of high status, when conversing with Europeans, and when conversing in formal or Western-dominated settings, such as with pastors or high chiefs or when conversing during church services and conferences (Shore, 1977, 1982). It is also the language of radio and television programs, the Bible, and reading materials. The other style of communication is used between Samoan speakers in informal settings.

The Samoan alphabet consists of 14 letters: 9 consonants and 5 vowels. The consonants are "f, g, l, m, n, p, s, t, and v." The vowels are a, e, i, o u" (Ochs, 1988). In the Samoan language, there are a number of phonological rules that differ from those in English. These include:

1. Vowels are always long.
   a is pronounced ah
   e   eh
   i   ee
   o   oh
   u   oo
2. In cases of multiple vowel combinations, every vowel is pronounced.
3. Primary stress is typically placed on the second-to-last syllable.
4. the consonant "g" occurring after a vowel is pronounced "ng."
5. There are no consonants in the final position of words.
6. There are no consonant clusters (as in "st" in the English language).

Samoan words always end in a vowel and multiple vowel combinations are very common (Shearer, 1975). Based on these rules, the repertoire of phonemes and the vowel-oriented nature of the Samoan language, it might be expected that a native Samoan speaker can encounter challenges when attempting to use English. And as mentioned earlier, all aspects of Samoan language phonology, lexicon, and syntax are subject to context—two registers—further compounding difficulties for conversing in English.

Samoan is a well-described language. There are at least four dictionaries (Milner, 1966, 1993; Pratt, 1911; Violette, 1879), several grammars (Churchward, 1951; Marsack 1962; Neffgen 1918; Pawley 1966; Pratt, 1911; Tuitele, Sapolu, & Kneubuhl, 1978) and many grammatical descriptions (including Chapin, 1970; Chung, 1978; Duranti, 1981; Milner, 1962, 1973). The reader should refer to Ochs (1988) for a detailed discussion of Samoan language registers, and adult-child language features.

EDUCATIONAL IMPLICATIONS

The Samoan language and the English language are both spoken in Samoa; however, Samoan is typically the first language learned by children. During the preschool years, children are taught in the Samoan language. In American Samoa, formal English instruction begins in second grade. However, in most classrooms, both English and Samoan are used prior to this. Exposure to and use of English outside of the school setting depends largely on the language used by each child's immediate and extended family.

American Samoan children go to preschool in a fale, which is the name of the building. The children sit on the floor, which is usually covered with hand-woven mats. The older children go to schools that are composed of many separate fales, one for each class. These are constructed with relatively modern materials and are basically the same except that each fale has screened-in walls.

Despite the effort to incorporate both English and Samoan into the Samoan school system, many students from American Samoa encounter academic problems when entering American schools in Hawaii and the continental United States (Cheng & Ima, 1989; Rumbaut & Ima, 1988). Cheng and Ima reported that Samoan students in San Diego County have the lowest grade point averages of all ethnic groups. A similar profile of low academic performance has been reported in Hawaii (Cheng & Ima, 1989). Samoan children are, in fact, considered to be limited English proficient (LEP). It is presumed that the lack of proficiency in English hurts their academic performance.

ᛉ

THE FILIPINOS

HISTORY AND DEMOGRAPHICS

The Philippine archipelago consists of more than 7,200 islands situated south of China and southeast of Indochina. With 116,000 square miles of land area in the islands, the country is slightly larger than the state of Arizona (Cheng, 1991); however the islands are widely scattered. The nation's weather is tropical, with two seasons, dry and wet, plus many typhoons (hurricanes) during the summer.

Repeated colonization has forced the Filipinos to adapt and survive. They work extremely hard and thrive in a social mosaic that includes Spanish, American, Chinese, Malay, Indian, and other cultural influences. Their language is influenced by Sanskrit, Spanish, and English. Their culture is heavily influenced by the Spaniards who colonized their land, resulting in such Spanish holdovers as music, food, Christian names, and Catholicism. An emphasis on courtship and romance and appreciation for flowery oral recitation also reflect cultural traits introduced by Spanish colonizers.

Because of geographic proximity, the Chinese began traveling to the Philippines in the 16th century and contributed to cultural practices, particularly concerning food and hospitality. When one visits a friend, the first question asked is "How are you?" The second question asked is "Have you eaten?"—and food is promptly provided (Cheng & Ima, 1989). Recently, American influence has included the adaptation of American school curricula and teaching methodologies. Multicultural influences have made the Filipino lifestyle intriguing.

It is difficult to identify a single, comprehensive Filipino culture as Kitano and Daniels (1988) suggest there is a persistent tendency for groups to divide along lines of regional origins, language, ideology, and subgroup cultures. Also, the far-flung Filipino communities can be at odds with each other for varying reasons. Special attention should therefore be paid to diversity among peoples from the Philippines.

FAMILY SYSTEM AND OBLIGATIONS

Filipino people practice a bilateral family system, in which one obligates oneself to both sides of the family. Extended families live in the same house or in neighboring houses (Galang, Noble, & Halog, 1985). Age is revered in the Philippines, and asking someone's age is considered appropriate. Age denotes a particular status and place in the social hierarchy. Filipinos pay special heed to status and view education as a key measure for achieving it.

Filipinos place high value on the following roles and responsibilities:

- Grandparents: Family members accorded the most respect and authority. In traditional families, they live with the son's family. The daughter-in-law is expected to respect her mother-in-law's wishes in household and child-rearing matters.
- Father: Principal money earner and nominal head of the family. He is the dispenser of discipline and the decision maker, who nonetheless shares authority with the mother.
- Mother: Shares in husband's authority, duties, and responsibilities. She manages the household, the rearing of children, and family religious obligations. She augments family income by undertaking professional employment or household industry.
- Children: Center of family life. They must respect and obey and not question. They must also fulfill specific duties at home.
- Older sons: Share in authority over and care of younger children, set examples, sacrifice for younger children. The eldest assumes his father's role when the father is absent.
- Older daughters: Also share in authority over younger siblings: dressing, feeding, and protecting them. The eldest assumes her mother's role when the mother is absent.
- Younger daughters/sons: Must listen, obey, and follow examples set by older siblings.

These roles continue to serve as binding forces long after children have reached adulthood.

LANGUAGE

The people of the Philippines speak 87 mutually unintelligible languages, all stemming from the Malayo-Polynesian group. The major ones are Pilipino (central Luzon), Ilocano (northern Luzon), and Visayan (central Philippines) (Cheng, 1991). Pilipino (also known as Tagalog) is a polysyllabic language with dialectal variations and 27 phonemes: 5 vowels, 6 diphthongs, and 16 consonants. Sounds that are different from those in English are the glottal stop, tap/trill, and consonant clusters /nj/ and /lj/. There are some vowel and diphthong sounds and nine consonant sounds in English that do not exist in the Filipino sound system.

Speakers of Pilipino (the national language) must learn sounds that do not occur in Pilipino when they learn English. In most English nominals, the "s" ending indicates plurality, but in Pilipino, the plural is indicated by the word "onga" placed before the nominal or by another word, such as a number. Some sounds are similar in the two languages, so that speakers have no difficulty learning to pronounce them. Others are dissimilar, and when pronounced incorrectly lead to serious distortions in meaning. Allophonic vowel deviations that occur do not usually affect intelligibility (Elgo, 1989). For more information, see Cheng, 1991.

Pilipino borrows heavily from Spanish and English. For example, the Spanish *destinar* (to destine, appoint, designate, or assign) may be equated with the English *destine* (to determine beforehand; to assign for a specific purpose; to direct toward a given destination). A Pilipino speaker may say, "My father was destined in the province for a year" instead of "My father was assigned to the province for a year" (Cheng, 1991). Most words consist of substantive, verbal, and adjectival roots and affixes to show respect, focus, and mode. Root and affix combinations determine word meaning.

The Pilipino alphabet has 20 letters, consisting of 15 consonants: b, k, d, g, h, l, m, n, ng, p, r, s, t, w, y and 5 vowels: a, e, i, o, u. The orthographic rules were modified by the Department of Education and Culture of the Philippines in 1976 to accommodate the rapidly changing Pilipino language due to linguistic additions from different languages.

This is the system in which Filipino children learn to read and write. Word order for simple sentences in English is reversed in Pilipino, so that the predicate precedes the subject, except in formal language, which takes on an alternate word order similar to English. Phonetic and syntactic differences between the two languages cause many frustrations for native Filipinos, as expressed by a 10th grade student who immigrated to the United States at age 14: "There is lots of teasing me when I don't pronounce right. Whenever I open my mouth I wonder, I shake, and worry—will they laugh? They think if we speak Tagalog that we are saying something bad about them, and sometimes they fight us for speaking our language. I am afraid to speak English, I am afraid to try. And I find myself with fear about speaking Tagalog" (Olsen, 1988).

Filipinos from various parts of the Philippines have different traditions, customs, languages, and religious beliefs. The main religions are Catholicism, Protestantism, and Islam. Their diversity is reflected in regional loyalties often associated with language—Visayan (44% of Filipinos), Tagalog (25%), and Ilocano (16%). Ilocanos were most numerous among immigrants to the United States from about 1910 and 1940, and Tagalogs dominated the immigrants post World War II. Most Filipinos speak Tagalog as a second language, because it is the national language. Filipino American communities contain numerous organizations reflecting occupational interests, politics, and cultural activities. Filipinos in the United States tend to live in communities with inviduals from their native regions who speak the same language.

IMMIGRATION TO THE UNITED STATES

The U.S. Filipino population is often grouped with Pacific Islanders. It will have reached 2 million by the year 2000 (Kitano & Daniels, 1988). According to the 1990 Census, at least 800,000 Tagalog speakers and more than 1 million Filipinos live in the United States. They are among the fastest growing and most numerous Asian/Pacific Islander American communities.

The United States maintains Naval and Air Force bases in the Philippines. This close connection has had extensive ramifications from the U.S. Navy's long-standing practice of recruiting personnel from the Philippines. Many Filipino men who joined the U.S. Navy and became naturalized citizens sponsored their families to emigrate to the United States. Today, these families concentrate in Hawaii, California, New York City, Illinois, Guam, and Micronesia.

Many Filipino Americans were born in the Philippines or are children of first generation immigrants. It is estimated that 90% of Filipino-American students are fluent English proficient (FEP). They do not present the same linguistic challenges as other Asian communities, such as some Southeast Asian refugee students, among whom as few as 33% are FEP at the high school level.

The Filipino population varies from region to region in the country, making it difficult to generalize about the Filipino-American experience. Unstable political climates, poverty, the search for better economic and educational opportunities, and family reunification have all drawn immigrants to the United States in the past. Asia's explosive economic growth and political ferment have yielded dramatic changes as seen in the Philippines with intense social pressures shattering an authoritarian political system and initiating democratic reform (Solomon, 1989).

Three major waves of Filipino immigrants have come to the United States. The first wave, between 1910 and 1940, consisted of young men seeking college education (the pensionados) and intending to return to their own countries. Many stayed in the United States.

The second wave, which started at approximately the same time and continued until 1934, consisted of agricultural workers. The U.S.-legislated Tyding-McDuffie Act of 1934 granted the Philippines independence and placed a tight quota on Filipino immigration.

A third wave of Filipinos began in the period following World War II. A family reunification policy (the McCarren-Walter Act), permitted many to enter the United States outside of their national quota, which stood at 100 persons per year in 1953. For the 13 years following the act, 1,300 Filipinos entered the United States within quota numbers, and more than 32,000 under the family reunification clause. In 1965, the Immigrant Act was passed to revise the Filipino quota, and a dramatic jump occurred in the number of immigrants entering the United States, including many "brain drain" professionals, who were given preferential treatment.

The 1965 immigration law resulted in a shift from European to Asian immigrant prevalence in the United States, with people of Asian origin making up approximately 40% of all new immigrants. Prominent among new immigrants were Filipinos, the largest single group of Asian immigrants. This ongoing third wave included many educated families seeking more stable economic conditions and educational opportunities. This change in Filipino immigration has changed the demographic composition of many communities here. For example, Filipinos were more than 11% of Hawaii's overall population in 1983, and this percentage is still growing (Cheng, 1989).

EDUCATIONAL IMPLICATIONS

In classrooms in the Philippines, students are told to be quiet and remain in their seats. They look down when spoken to, giggle when embarrassed or reprimanded, and hand papers to teachers with both hands (Cheng, 1991). Such gestures of compliance are well suited to elementary school environments, but less appropriate at higher levels where students are encouraged to take the initiative, challenge convention, and seek innovative solutions. Students at higher levels engage their teachers' attention as co-equals in a mutual search for knowledge and wisdom. This underlying assumption exists more commonly in elite educational institutions. But public school teachers should consider it a part of education for all students.

FILIPINO STUDENTS

Most students from the Philippines have learned English in native or U.S. schools, and many were born here. In the San Diego Unified School District, in 1988, of approximately 2,000 Filipino sophomores, juniors, and seniors, just 11% were limited English proficient (Cheng & Ima, 1989). Approximately 39% speak only English and about half spoke both a Filipino language and English. As the Philippine economy has deteriorated, more recent Filipino immigrants have a history of disrupted or poor quality schooling. Data indicate that earlier Filipino migrants were more likely to have completed college than more recent arrivals, and increasing numbers have been coming to the United States without literacy or knowledge of English. An increased number of at-risk students have pre- or low-literacy skills.

Although elementary education is compulsory in the Philippines, it is not enforced. It is entirely possible to have a mix of students in a U.S. classroom that includes a teenage student from the Philippines with little previous schooling and significant problems both in learning English and in general literacy. Information on such a student's prior education and school experience is essential.

Filipinos bring prior experience and values—including politeness, courtesy, and reserved mannerisms—with them to school. They are generally bilingual because English is taught in Philippine schools. During their early school experience, they learn to be respectful towards teachers and elders. Teachers in the homeland stress rote memory and hard work, so that critical thinking, exploration, questioning, and problem solving will have to be taught from scratch. Because of their seemingly competent skills in communicating, teachers may overestimate the transferability of Filipino students' previously acquired skills and knowledge.

Assessment tools should be appropriately designed for new non- and limited-English speaking immigrants. Some currently implemented ideas include translating core text materials, developing tapes that present basic U.S. educational concepts in native languages, tutoring, using cooperative learning methods, reducing class loads, and providing sheltered English classes where English is reduced to the simplest units for comprehension (Olsen, 1988). Filipino students (except for those who may have become gang members) are unlikely to show a need for special attention.

High cumulative grade-point averages (GPAs) and low dropout and suspension rates had led to Filipino students in California high schools being identified as "immigrant success stories." However, problems show up in graduation GPAs and on verbal and quantitative SAT scores (King, 1988). Azores (1986–1987) studied a group of Filipino high school seniors who aspired for higher education but lacked the grades necessary for college admission. She suggested three possible reasons: (1) Filipino students have unrealistic expectations, (2) their aspirations lack personal commitment, and (3) they feel that characteristics other than grades define a good student (Cheng & Ima, 1989).

Filipinos often sacrifice financially for the sake of their children's schooling (Watkins & Astilla, 1981). Given this observation, what are their educational needs? The California cities of Daly City, San Diego, Los Angeles, and San Francisco all have large Filipino enclaves. The state of Hawaii (particularly Kauai and O'ahu) also has a large Filipino population. Monzon (1984) observed that large numbers of Filipino students entering local universities had achieved high grade point averages. The high value Filipinos place on education and their efforts to achieve success lead to their depiction as a "model minority."

Filipino sophomore, junior, and senior level high school students in the San Diego Unified School District have had lower test scores than other East Asian immigrants—in spite of the Filipinos' longer exposure to the English language (Monzon, 1984). In light of Monzon's observation of Filipinos' high college level performance, this finding causes one to wonder whether elementary and secondary teachers might need to improve their approach to the education of Filipino American students. Perhaps teachers are permitting students to advance in school without sufficient skills.

Monzon suggested an educational need for Filipinos beyond English language development: to deal with cultural conflicts between the traditional collective orientation of the Filipino family and the individualistic orientation encouraged by schools. The interdependency engendered by Filipino parents directly conflicts with the self-initiation and self-sufficiency valued by U.S. culture. This dichotomy should alert the guidance and counseling services of public schools, even in light of the seeming lack of problems among Filipino students. Surely the "model minority" characterization might be limiting educational services for Filipinos by creating overconfidence in current practices.

Filipinos have consistently entered the labor market with extensive educational backgrounds and have received the same income as others who are less educated. Why? Have we prepared these youth with sufficient English language, critical thinking, and social skills for communicative competence (Damico, 1991)? Teachers should consider these pragmatic questions in preparing Filipino American youth for the future.

⌐⌐

CONCLUSION: PACIFIC ISLANDERS AND U.S. CLASSROOMS

Pacific Islanders did not regard formal education as part of their tradition until the Europeans came. Before that time, much of their education was still based on oral tradition. Today, Polynesians and Micronesians teach sustenance skills and more traditional educational subjects in an authoritarian style. Educators discourage individualism and teach students by the rote method. They are taught to speak and think from an Eastern point of view that emphasizes conformity. These children are struck by cultural contrast when they enter U.S. schools that emphasize individual variation and creativity. The American system not only contradicts their own system, but it undermines their sense of well-being. Their view of self-interest is vested in group cooperation and not in individual achievement.

Pacific Islanders treasure and value collective behavior (i.e., group reliance) as opposed to individualism so highly valued in the United States. A student from the Pacific Islands in a U.S. classroom for the first time will be shocked and initially unaccepting toward the concept of reading in small groups rather than as a class. This certainly separates Pacific Islanders from U.S. mainstream educational traditions.

Earning higher degrees has never been a tradition for Pacific Islanders. Their traditions are largely premodern and preliterate; the cultural gap is coupled with a literacy gap. However, children with parental support can nonetheless succeed. Parents can help their children by creating community networks that gather information and resources through cumulative efforts. In this way, they can empower themselves as well as their children.

ATTITUDES TOWARD DISABILITY AND ILLNESS

Pacific Islander attitudes toward disabilities can be traced—at least in part—to folk beliefs and superstitions in all cultures. Through studying these beliefs, current family and societal perspectives on disability can be clarified and better understood. Asian cultural attitudes toward birth defects are little understood. A variety of mutually interactive folk beliefs exists. Views held in rural areas differ from those held in urban areas, depending on the accessibility of information. Variability of educational levels and personal experiences also contribute to differences in folk beliefs.

Views are also informed by major religions and philosophies among Pacific Islanders, which include Buddhism, Confucianism, Catholicism, and Islam. Catholicism and Christianity have influenced religious and philosophical beliefs in most of the Pacific Islands, so that people tend to operate with a mixture of native and imported beliefs. Cultural members must interpret each other's behavior along multiple paradigms. Buddhists believe that disability has been established by karma (fate) and that nothing can be done about it. Most Pacific Islanders view such a handicapping condition as the result of wrongdoings on the part of an individual's ancestors (e.g., talking about others behind their backs), resulting in guilt and shame. Some cultures, such as those in the Philippines, view disability as a curse and may ostracize individuals with disabilities. On the other hand, Chamorro culture views a birth defect or a disability as a gift from God; an individual with a disability belongs to everyone and is protected and sheltered.

Attitudes toward hospitalization also vary a great deal. Some view it as threatening and choose to rely on it only for fatal injuries, sicknesses, or permanently disabling diseases. When Chamorro children ask, "What does an ambulance do?" the common answer is "It takes sick people to the hospital to die," or "It takes dead people to the hospital" (Cheng & Ima, 1989). "Suruhana" and "suruhano" faith healers are respected among the Chamorro. Hawaiians also hold faith healing in high esteem. Persons with mental disorders may be viewed as healthy, as there may be no evidence of physical disability. On the other hand, persons with physical handicaps may be regarded as sick, even though they are otherwise in good health.

In some Pacific Island cultures, doctors of modern or Western medicine are appointed to cure people. Therapy and therapists are not involved in the healing process and may be viewed as unimportant. Parents of children with disabilities may not understand or appreciate therapy and resource teachers. This attitude might result in poor therapy attendance and participation. Educators should take it on themselves to explain the roles of speech pathologists, audiologists, psychologists and resource specialists to parents and/or respected community members.

KINSHIP

Traditional family values vary among families and are subject to such complications as individual needs, economic realities, and family hardships. Educators may be working with children of families separated from their broader family units (Galang et al., 1985). Pacific Islander households' traditional inclusion of non-nuclear family members indicates a greater reliance on extended kinship networks. This especially prevails among Filipino, Samoan, and Chamorro households. These extended family households will probably continue in the United States into the next decade for Asians as a whole, but will tend to move toward the American standard of the nuclear household.

How do extended households impact the academic achievement of children—especially those who are Limited English proficient (LEP)—who live in them? Extended households provide both effective support systems and added demands on family finances. Some large households have low social mobility because their collective financial support system encourages youngsters to leave school before having completed secondary or postsecondary schooling. There is a wide range of well-being and at-risk characteristics associated with school failure *and* with school success for Pacific Islanders in U.S. schools.

There is an apparent paradox limiting conditions existing along with overall statistics of well-being of Pacific Islanders in the United States as measured by income and educational achievement. This is a result of lumping statistics of well-educated and well-to-do immigrants with illiterate and poor newcomers and refugees from the same homelands.

Some 20 years ago, scholars began studying the relationships between language, culture, and learning in comparing African, Hispanic, Native Americans, and Pacific Islanders (Cazden, John & Hymes, 1972). They presented group differences but not relevant parameters within which to address students from various Pacific Island backgrounds. This is because measures are often culturally biased. We have made little progress in our empirical understanding of these populations.

IMPACT OF DEMOGRAPHIC CHANGES IN THE UNITED STATES

There is a paucity of information and statistics about Pacific Islander groups in the United States, which largely relies on census data of 1970 and 1980, along with estimates for 1990, taking into account changes which occurred between 1980 and 1990. Asian/Pacific Islander growth is now concentrated in a few areas of the United States. Nevertheless, populations will soon be seen in areas formerly sparse in Pacific Islanders. Rural areas will likely be the least equipped to provide appropriate instruction to Pacific Island LEP students. Education will have to accommodate both affirmative action goals and the need for a trained labor force. Newer minority groups have traditionally had little say in the political arena and need, in many ways, more attention as they develop a capacity to participate more fully in this society.

Some hidden at-risk populations include the English-only Pacific Island population, whose grasp of English just suffices. But many Pacific Islanders and Filipinos from so-called English-speaking homes manifest problems in English language development. Immigrants' children born in the United States have divergent needs, and poor English language proficiency is one of the principal barriers to full educational achievement.

Aside from those "misclassified" as proficient, many Pacific Islanders demonstrate nonstandard language development, such as Hawaiians who speak pidgin English. Although they are of lower priority than immigrants with no or limited English, immigrant students whose proficiency levels fall between limited and mainstream should be granted some consideration. "In-betweens" constitute a hidden, but significant component of the Pacific Island student population.

Standardized verbal tests have continually reflected below-average performance by Pacific Island students. Little information is available on the English-only Pacific Island population, whose language needs are, indeed, diverse. California State School Superintendent Honig's

Advisory Council of Asians and Pacific Islanders suggested and then launched a special California Academic Performance (CAP) study of Asian/Pacific Island 8th graders (Fong, Hom, Ima, & Yung, 1989).

CHALLENGES FACING ASIAN/PACIFIC ISLANDERS

The past decade has seen a plethora of reports documenting the inadequacies of U.S. schools in meeting the needs of their changing populations. The California Tomorrows report (Olsen, 1988) and the National Coalition of Advocates for Students report (First & Wilshire-Carrera, 1988) are among recent statements pointing out current schooling practices' failure to provide quality education to Pacific Islander language-minority students.

During the past decade, looser standards for requiring bilingual program services reflect diminished concern for LEP needs and a general relaxation of primary language emphasis. Bilingual educational programs have slackened not only for Spanish-language speakers, but also for Pacific Island students. Bilingual programs are facing reduced impetus, lowered emphasis on the primary language, and greater emphasis on English language methods. This does not really create a crisis, as the initial bilingual programs were actually not all that adequate.

If and when substantial bilingual legislation is passed, questions need to be raised about the feasibility of upgrading educational services to Pacific Islands language minority students to a level that approximates the quality of services rendered to native English-speaking students. Schools must deal with the cultural and social conditions and *special needs* of Pacific Islands newcomers.

One impetus for examining the education of Pacific Islanders is the uneasy feeling among educators that Pacific Islands language minority students' needs are inadequately served by bilingual programs throughout the country. Many schools appear to have a "sink or swim" language policy that contradicts the country's long-standing policy of bilingual education. Pacific Islands bilingual professionals have raised major questions concerning this.

EDUCATIONAL CONSEQUENCES OF GROWTH OF DIVERSE POPULATIONS

Educational institutions are taking in increasing numbers of students with different language and cultural backgrounds. Are they prepared? How can service providers live up to this challenge? The Lau v. Nichols decision requires schools to take a student's home language into account. But, because of the large numbers of Spanish-speaking students in U.S. schools, the public expects bilingual programs to primarily serve Hispanics. Although Pacific Island language minority students are a significant portion of student enrollment, most school districts have not yet fully incorporated them into special education, bilingual, and other programs commensurate with their numbers.

Teachers must ascertain possible sources of students' problems: Are difficulties linguistic, cultural, psychological, or neurological (possibly associated with trauma)——or perhaps a combination of the above? What resources do teachers have to distinguish between acculturation, handicapping, or combination problems when they observe heightened anxiety, confusion in the locus of control, withdrawal, or unresponsiveness among language minority students? This alludes to a larger question: How well have our schools prepared themselves to deal with linguistically and culturally varied school-age populations? Schools need to examine the student population they serve and be sensitive to their needs.

BILINGUAL EDUCATION FOR PACIFIC ISLANDERS

Where do Asians and Pacific Islanders fit into bilingual education? The California State Department of Education document *Schooling and Language Minority Students* (California State Department of Education, 1991) provides a theoretical framework. It is based on data from international sources on the phenomenon of second language acquisition, including famous Canadian studies of French language acquisition by children from English-speaking homes (Lambert and Tucker, 1972). Numerous theoretical developments regarding second language acquisition as well as effective methods and political considerations for developing bilingual services span the recent past (see Cummins, 1989; Krashen and Biber, 1988). Results have all pointed to the need for promotion of primary language development, the academic benefits of bilingualism, the importance of comprehensible input, and positive recognition of students' social standing. Krashen and Biber (1988) cited successful bilingual programs based principally on experiences with Spanish language programs. Their data supported the need for development of primary language literacy before successful transferral into English language-based classes.

Most proposed theoretical frameworks appear to be equally applicable to Asian/Pacific Islanders and other LEP student populations. But there is concern about the transition from ideas to action at school sites with Asian/Pacific Islander language minority students. Materials, curriculum, and staff have not been adequately developed to support primary language services to these populations. Initial efforts by the San Francisco Unified School District to develop Chinese language services have atrophied. Today, the district has just one fully bilingual elementary school, whose most-used transition program is English-based transition, despite large numbers of Chinese-speaking LEP students. Although the theoretical framework takes into account a full range of alternatives—from full primary language maintenance to English-only programs—an uneasy connection between theory and application persists, especially in programs serving Pacific Island language minorities.

WHAT IS NEEDED:
EDUCATION AND PACIFIC ISLANDERS

The following summarizes critical information concerning Pacific Islander student populations:

■ Home language(s): Language(s) spoken at home may impact students' quality of schoolwork. Degree of acculturation will also influence education and employment.

■ Birth history: Pregnancy, birth, and early developmental histories are important in detecting problems.

■ Religious beliefs: Religions lead to differing views on disabilities and their treatment. Culturally sensitive inquiries should be made.

■ Life history: Facts of immigration and secondary migration, including family, medical, psychosocial, educational, and language histories are vital in evaluating needs of Asian/Pacific Island students.

■ Social and family factors: Parents' home and employment status; older children's responsibilities; a given students' place in the family structure need to be explored.

■ Educational expectations and learning styles: Culturally based differences between expectations and styles of learning and communicating held by parents, students, and educators can lead to difficulty in detecting roadblocks to U.S. educational success.

EDUCATIONAL IMPLICATIONS

Collaborative inquiry is needed into the multifaceted bonuses and challenges of Asian/Pacific Islander students in U.S. classrooms and should be based on the Vygotskian paradigm (1962, 1978). This model asserts that robust knowledge and understanding are socially constructed through talk, activity, and interaction around meaningful problems and tools. The approach is particularly useful for language minority students, with students defining the problems to be explored. Questions asked by students are followed by a gap-bridging process that delineates school culture from the home culture (Heath, 1983). The approach is meant to challenge thoughts and beliefs, encourage negotiation of meanings, and resolve conflicts. Students must construct and reconstruct their knowledge to arrive at some common understanding of their best strategy for U.S. educational success.

The collaborative inquiry process validates and employs Asian/Pacific Islander sociocultural values such as collective stories (Cheng, 1989). Because it does not emphasize individual performance, students with collective values fare well. A number of studies have shown that students participate more actively if they can set their own agendas as to when and how they participate (Au, 1980; Cazden, John, & Hymes, 1972; Philips, 1982).

Teachers should involve API students in purposeful communicative interactions that promote the use of language. Heath (1986) presented six genres of teaching that encourage discourse and stress the multiple uses of language. These are:

- Label quests: These language activities involve naming items and their attributes or *asking* for their names and attributes. Labeling precedes higher order knowledge such as answers for "why," "how," and "when."
- Meaning quests: Adults infer the meanings of what young children say or imply through word or action; they interpret their own or others' behavior, and often ask for explanations of what is meant or intended. In school, students must learn to state their meanings, know their intentions, and anticipate results—such as how their statements will be interpreted or valued.
- Recounting: The speaker retells experiences or information known to both teller and listener. Teachers ask children to provide summaries, recount facts known to all class members, and display knowledge through oral and written accounts.

■ Accounting: A speaker provides information that is new to the listener or new interpretations of old information. Schools typically allow few occasions for such accounts.

■ Event-casting: An individual gives running narrative to a current event and/or forecasts an upcoming event.

■ Story-telling: Fictional story-telling can move through events with goal-directed narration.

API students can benefit greatly from exposure to language in productive contexts, such as during problem solving. Literacy activities, including purposeful talk, reading, and writing, mediate intellectual efforts (Warren, Rosebery, & Conant, 1989).

Teachers need to provide contextualized learning (Cheng & Ima, 1989; Cummins, 1981; Hakuta, 1986; Van Dongen & Westby, 1986), being careful not to use U.S. culturally loaded terms without explanation, such as U.S.-only words about foods, money, music, geography, eating and kitchen utensils, furniture, and animals. Furthermore, they need to take into consideration the students' prior knowledge by building on what the students know linguistically and experientially.

Many culturally diverse families view the U.S. educational system as complex, intimidating, and bureaucratic (Correa, 1989). Parents usually find it to be different from their own educational experience (Lynch & Stein, 1987). API children interacting in the school and home when such differences exist may be receiving conflicting messages.

API children are generally viewed as extensions of family generations rather than as individuals, and the family is seen as a *unit*. Members of traditional U.S. society may regard such interdependency as threatening to the American ideal of self-sufficiency and therefore excessive.

Social interaction between Asian/Pacific Island students and non-Asian students needs to be facilitated. Educators need to devise activities for classrooms, schools, and after-school programs to promote interaction (Sugarman & Brockel, 1989). The commonplace expectation of the "quiet" Asians needs to be confronted and all students must be encouraged to express themselves.

Pacific Islanders present an enormous educational challenge that requires teachers to go beyond their students' linguistic needs, to talk with them and their families about their current and past experiences. These students' special needs demand a restructuring of curricula to make it relevant, valid, and meaningful.

⅃⊤

REFERENCES

Akamatsu, C. T. (1993). Teaching deaf Asian and Pacific Island American children. In K. M. Christensen & G. L. Delgado (Eds.), *Multicultural issues in deafness* (pp. 127–142). New York: Longman.

American Samoa Statistical Digest. (1990). America Samoa: Economic Development Planning Office Research and Statistics Division, American Samoa Government.

Asian and Pacific Horizons (1994). Fall Newsletter, *1*(1). Asian Studies Institute, San Diego State University, San Diego, CA.

Au, K. (1980). Participation structures in a reading lesson with Hawaiian children: Analysis of a culturally appropriate instructional event. *Anthropology and Education Quarterly, 11*(2), 91–115.

Au, K., & Jordan, K. (1981). Teaching reading to Hawaiian children: Finding a culturally appropriate solution. In H. Trueba, G. P. Guthrie, & K. H. Au (Eds.), *Culture and the bilingual classroom.* Rowley, MA: Newberry House.

Azores, T. (1986–1987). Educational attainment and upward mobility: Prospects for Filipino Americans. *Amerasian Journal, 13*(1), 39–52.

Baker, P. T., Hanna, J. M., & Baker, T. S. (1986). *The changing Samoans: Behavior and health in transition.* New York: Oxford University Press.

California State Department of Education. (Ed.). (1991). *Schooling and language minority students: A theoretical framework.* Los Angeles: Evaluation, Dissemination and Assessment Center, California State University.

Cazden, C. B., John, V., & Hymes D. (Eds.). (1972). *Functions of language in the classroom.* New York: Teachers College Press.

Chapin, P.(1970). Samoan pronominalization. *Language, 46*(2), 366–378.

Cheng, L. (1989). Service delivery to Asian/Pacific children: A cross cultural framework. *Topics in Language Disorders, 9*(3), 1–14.

Cheng, L. (1991). *Assessing Asian language performance: Guidelines for evaluating limited English proficient students.* Oceanside, CA: Academic Communication Associates.

Cheng, L., & Ima, K. (1989). *Understanding the immigrant Pacific Islander.* San Diego: Los Amigos Research Associates.

Cheng, L., & Ima, K. (1990). *Understanding the Filipino immigrant.* San Diego: Los Amigos Research Associates.

Chung, S. (1978). *Case making and grammatical relations in Polynesian.* Austin: University of Texas Press.

Correa, V. (1989). Involving culturally diverse families in the educational process. In S. H. Fradd & M. J. Weismantel (Eds.), *Meeting the needs of culturally and linguistically different students: A handbook for educators.* Boston: Little Brown.

Churchward, S. (1951). *A new Samoan grammar* (2nd ed.). Melbourne: Spectator Press.

Cummins, J. (1981). The role of primary language development in promoting educational success for language minority students. In California Department of Education, Division of Instructional Support and Bilingual Education (Ed.), *Schooling and language minority students: A theoretical framework* (pp. 3–49). Los Angeles: Evaluation, Dissemination and Assessment Center, California State University.

Cummins, J. (1989). *The empowerment of minority students.* Los Angeles: California Association for Bilingual Education.

Damico, J. S. (1991). Clinical discourse analysis: A functional approach to language assessment. In C. S. Simon (Ed.), *Communication skills and classroom success: Assessment and therapy methodologies for language and learning disabled students.* Eau Claire, WI: Thinking Publications.

Duranti, A. (1981). The Samoan fono: A sociolinguistic study. *Pacific Linguistics, 8*(80).

Elgo, J. S. (1989). *Phonological analysis of 3- and 4-year old bilingual Tagalog-English speaking children's utterances.* Unpublished master's thesis, San Diego State University.

First, J., & Wilshire-Carrera, J. (1988). *New voices: Immigrant students in U.S. public schools.* Boston: National Coalition of Advocates for Students.

Fong, E., Hom, G., Ima, K., & Yung, K. (1989, April). *Academic achievement patterns of Asian/Pacific Islander students on the eighth grade CAP (California Assessment Program).* Paper presented at the annual conference of the American Educational Research Association, San Francisco.

Freeman, D. (1983). *Margaret Mead and Samoa: The making and unmaking of an anthropological myth.* Cambridge: Harvard University Press.

Galang, R., Noble, V., & Halog, L. (1985). *Assessment of Filipino speaking limited English speaking students with special needs.* Unpublished manuscript.

Gerber, E. R. (1975). *The cultural patterning of emotions in Samoa.* Unpublished doctoral dissertation, University of California, San Diego.

Gumperz, J. (1982). *Discourse strategies.* Cambridge, England: Cambridge University Press.

Hakuta, K. (1986). *Mirror of language: The debate on bilingualism.* New York: Basic Books.

Heath, S. B. (1983). *Ways with words: Language, life, and work in communities and classrooms.* New York: Cambridge University Press.

Heath, S. B. (1986). Sociocultural contexts of language development. In California State Department of Education, Bilingual Education Office (Ed.), *Beyond language: Social and cultural factors in schooling language minority students,* (pp. 143–186). Los Angeles: Evaluation, Dissemination and Assessment Center, California State University.

Kanahele, G. (1980). *Stand tall: A search for Hawaiian values.* Honolulu: University of Hawaii Press.

Keene, D. T. P. 1978. *Houses without walls: Samoan social control.* Unpublished doctoral dissertation, University of Hawaii, Honolulu.

King, B. (1988). *The educational experience of the Filipino student.* Unpublished manuscript.

Kitano, H. L., & Daniels, R. (1988). *Asian Americans: emerging minorities.* Englewood Cliffs, NJ: Prentice-Hall.

Kishi, G., & Hanohano, M., (1992, November). *Hawaiian children.* Presentation at Council for Exceptional Children, Honolulu, HI.

Krashen, S., & Biber, D. (1988). *On course: Bilingual education's success in California.* Sacramento: California Association for Bilingual Education.

Lambert, W. E., & Tucker, G. R. (1972). *Bilingual education of children: The St. Lambert experience.* Rowley, MA: Newbury House.

Lau v. Nichols, 411 U.S. 563 (1974).

LEAP. (1993). *The state of Asian Pacific America: Policy issues to the year 2020.* Los Angeles: LEAP Asian Pacific American Public Policy Institute.

Lynch, E. W., & Stein, R. C. (1987). Parent participation by ethnicity: A comparison of Hispanic, Black, and Anglo families. *Exceptional Children, 54,* 105–111.

Markoff, R., & Bond, J. (1974). The Samoans. In W. Tseng, J. F. McDermott, Jr., & T. W. Maretzki, (Eds.), *People and cultures in Hawaii: An introduction to mental health workers.* Honolulu: Transcultural Psychiatry Committee, Department of Psychiatry, University of Hawaii School of Medicine.

Marsack, C. (1962). *Samoan.* London: Hodder and Stoughton.

Maxwell, R. J. (1969). *Samoan temperament.* Unpublished doctoral dissertation, Cornell University, Ithaca, NY.

Milner G. B. (1962). Active, passive or perfective in Samoan: A fresh appraisal of the problem. *Journal of Polynesian Society, 71,* 151–161.

Milner, G. B. (1966). *Samoan dictionary.* London: Oxford University Press.

Milner, G. B. (1973). It is aspect (not voice) which is marked in Samoan. *Oceanic Linguistics, 12,* 1–2, 621–639.

Milner, G. B. (1993). *A Samoan dictionary: Samoan-English and English-Samoan.* Auckland, New Zealand: Polynesian Press.

Monzon, R. I. (1984). *The effects of the family environment on the academic performance of Filipino-American college students.* Unpublished master's thesis, San Diego State University.

Nakamura, R., Cerveny, L., Kagehiro, G., Komo, H., & Saka, S., (1992). *Pihana Na Mamo Native Hawaiian Special Education Project.* (Evaluation Report 1991–1992). Honolulu: College of Education, University of Hawaii.

Native Hawaiian Education Assessment: 1933 Summary Report. (1993). Honolulu: Department of Education Office.

Native Hawaiian Hearing and Speech Project. (1991). *Conteracting the negative educational effects of otitis media in Native Hawaiian preschoolers.* Honolulu: Kamehameha Schools Bishop Estate.

Neffgen, H. (1918). *Grammar and vocabulary of the Samoan language.* London: Kegan Paul, Trench, Tubner.

Ochs, E. (1988). *Culture and language development: Language acquisition and language socialization in a Samoan village.* Cambridge, England: Cambridge University Press.

Ochs, E., & Schieffelin, B. B. (1984). Language acquisition and socialization: Three developmental stories and their implications. In R. Shweder & R.

LeVine, (Eds.), *Culture theory: Essays on mind, self and emotion*. Cambridge, England: Cambridge University Press.

Olsen, L. (1988). *Crossing the schoolhouse border: Immigrant students and the California public schools*. San Francisco: California Tomorrow.

Olsen, L. (1989). *Bridges: Promising programs for the education of immigrant children*. San Francisco: California Tomorrow.

Pawley, A. (1966). Polynesian languages: A sub-grouping based on shared innovations in morphology. *Journal of Polynesian Society, 75*, 39–64.

Pawley, A. (1967). The relationships of Polynesian outlier language. *Journal of Polynesian Society, 76*, 259–296.

Philips, S. (1982). *The invisible culture: Communication in classroom and community on the Warm Spring Indian Reservation*. New York: Longman.

Pratt, G. (1911). Grammar and dictionary of the Samoan language (4th ed.) (rev. and enlarged by the Rev. J.E. Newell). Apia: Malua, Samoa.

Rumbaut, R. G., & Ima, K. (1988). *The adaptation of Southeast Asian Refugee youth: A comparative study*. Washington, DC: U.S. Office of Refugee Resettlement.

Shore, B. (1977). *A Samoan theory of action: Social control and social order in a Polynesian paradox*. Unpublished doctoral dissertation, University of Chicago.

Shore, B. (1982). *Sala'ilua: A Samoan mystery*. New York: Columbia University Press.

Shearer, A. (1975). *Understanding Samoans*. Wellington, New Zealand: Government Printer.

Solomon, R. H. (1989). *Cambodia and Vietnam: Trapped in an eddy of history?* (Current Policy No. 1206). Washington, DC: United States Department of State, Bureau of Public Affairs.

Stewart, J. L., Anae, A. P., & Gipe, P. N. (1989). Pacific Islander children: Prevalence of hearing loss and middle ear disease. *Topics in Language Disorders, 9*(3), 76–83.

Sugarman, A. W., & Brockel, R. J. (1989). *Facilitating social interaction between Asian and non-Asian students: A resource booklet*. Fort Lee, NJ: Fort Lee School District.

Tuitele, M. T., Sapolu, M., & Kneubuhl, J. 1978. *La Taatou Gagana: Tusi Muamua (Our language: first volume)*. Pago Pago: Bilingual/Bicultural Education Project of American Samoa, Department of Education, Government of American Samoa.

U.S. Bureau of Census. Statistical abstract of the United States: 1980 (100th ed.). Washington, DC: Author.

U.S. Bureau of Census. Statistical abstract of the United States: 1990 (110th ed.). Washington, DC: Author.

U.S. Bureau of Census. Statistical abstract of the United States: 1991 (111th ed.). Washington, DC: Author.

Vygotsky, L. S. (1962). *Thought and language*. Cambridge, MA: MIT Press.

Vygotsky, L. S. (1978). *Mind in society*. Cambridge: Harvard University Press.

Van Dongen, R., & Westby, C. (1986). Building the narrative mode of thought through children's literature. *Topics in Language Disorders, 7*(1), 70–83.

Violette, L. (1879). *Dictionnaire samoa-francais-anglais et francais-samoa-anglais, precede d'une grammaire de la langue samoa*. Paris: Maisonneuve et cie.

Warren, B., Rosebery, A. S., & Conant, F. R. (1989). *Chech Konnen: Learning science by doing science in language minority classrooms*. New York: Bolt, Beranek and Newman.

Watkins, D., & Astilla, E. (1981). Antecedents of personal adequacy of Filipino college students. *Psychological Reports, 49*, 727–732.

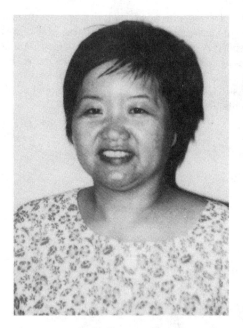

JEAN NAKASATO, M.S.

Jean Nakasato is the speech-language coordinator with the Hawaii Department of Education. She received her bachelor's degree in 1972 from the University of Hawaii and her master's degree in 1974 from the University of Washington. She is active in developing and implementing programs and materials for public school personnel. Among her special interests are preschool programming, transdisciplinary teaming, and working with families in rural areas.

GLORIA JEAN L. WALLACE, PH.D.

Dr. Wallace is an Associate Professor in the Department of Audiology and Speech Pathology at the University of Tennessee-Knoxville. She received her master's degree in 1977 from the University of Colorado and her doctorate in 1981 from Northwestern University. Her research, teaching and clinical interests are in the area of neurogenics. She is particularly interested in issues pertaining to stroke and traumatic brain injury rehabilitation for culturally and linguistically diverse underserved populations. Dr. Wallace has done extensive research and clinical work in the Pacific Island region.

CHAPTER 4

UNDERSTANDING SOUTHEAST ASIAN STUDENTS

HUYNH DINH TE, Ph.D.

Southeast Asia, as a geographical term, refers to Vietnam, Laos, Cambodia, Thailand, Mynanmar (formerly Burma), Malaysia, Indonesia, Brunei, and the Philippines. However, in the educational circle and the media, "Southeast Asians" includes only Vietnamese, Laotian, and Cambodian refugees and immigrants. In this article the term "Southeast Asian" is used with the restricted meaning because no other term refers to these three groups exclusively. The term "Indochinese," which is often used to refer to these groups, includes all people living on the Indochinese peninsula. On the other hand, this term carries a bad connotation for some people. For those who were born before 1945, this word reminds them of the French occupation era and the term "Indochinois" used by the French with some condescension.

Besides the Filipinos, few immigrants come from the larger Southeast Asia. Chinese residents in Southeast Asia who emigrate to the United States are often referred to as Southeast Asians, although geographically speaking, they belong to the East Asian group, which consists of Chinese, Japanese, Koreans, and Mongolians.

Most Cambodians, Laotians, and Vietnamese came to the United States as refugees, at the fall of "the smaller Southeast Asia" to the communists in April 1975. They differ from other Southeast Asian immigrants. They did not have the freedom to choose the country of asylum or the time to prepare for life in a new country by learning new language and job skills. When fleeing their native countries, the Southeast Asians did not even know which country would give them asylum. Sometimes, they had only a few days, even a few hours, to prepare for their escape. Many of these refugees went through traumatic experiences before, during, and after the escape from their countries because of war conditions, political repression, persecution, and physical and moral hardship while hiding and during escape, and the sordid living conditions in refugee camps.

ᛡ

HISTORY OF SOUTHEAST ASIAN IMMIGRATION

The first exodus of Southeast Asian refugees, about 130,000 people, started in April 1975. The bulk of this refugee population was Vietnamese who, for the most part, belonged to the bureaucracy and armed forces of the defeated government of South Vietnam. The second wave of Southeast Asian refugees started in 1978, following the intensified conflict between China and Vietnam. More refugees came from Laos and Cambodia because of the new political developments in those two countries such as Pol Pot's reign of terror in Cambodia and the intensified persecution of the Hmong in Laos. Southeast Asians continued their attempts to flee from their countries since the fall of their countries to the communists. Most of the Vietnamese refugees who escaped after 1975 did so by small boats, hence the term *boat people*. These refugees were generally less educated than the first wave, and many were rural people.

The third wave of Southeast Asian immigrants to the United States began in 1982. The Orderly Departure Program (ODP) was agreed upon by the U.S. government and the communist government of Vietnam to help reunite relatives in Vietnam with relatives residing in the United States. The Homecoming Act of 1988 allowed Amerasians to settle in America. These Amerasians are the children of American citizens, mostly members of the U.S. armed forces stationed in

Vietnam during the war years, and Vietnamese mothers who were left behind when the U.S. armed forces withdrew after the Paris Agreement in 1973. Recently, the Humanitarian Operation (H.O.) Program allowed former detainees in communist concentration camps to come to the United States to be reunited with family members. It is estimated that between 1975 and 1990 1,101,054 Southeast Asian refugees were admitted into the United States, approximately half of whom were under 18 years of age (Chuong & Van, 1994).

ㄐ

ASPECTS OF SOUTHEAST ASIAN CULTURE THAT ARE RELEVANT TO EDUCATORS, PSYCHOLOGISTS, AND SPEECH SPECIALISTS

Southeast Asians belong to three different nationality groups, speaking different national languages, which are not mutually intelligible, and use different writing systems. The significant differences among these people should be taken into consideration when curriculum and programs are devised and instructional materials and teaching approaches are selected for teaching these students.

Within each nationality group, there are ethnic differences. For example, the Laotians consist of the Lao majority and various ethnic minorities such as the Hmong, Iu-Mien, Khmu, Lahu, and so on. (Lewis, 1994). The Cambodians and Lao are predominantly influenced by Indian culture whereas the Laotian ethnic groups are predominantly influenced by Chinese culture. The Vietnamese are influenced by both Indian and Chinese cultures. Socio-economic and educational backgrounds are also diverse among the three nationality groups of Southeast Asians. Further differences are found within each group. For example, children of Vietnamese refugees who came to the United States in 1975 were better educated, more proficient in English and more exposed to American media than the children of the "boat people" and the "H.O." people who came more recently.

In spite of those differences, Southeast Asians share certain common experience and backgrounds. English is not their native or even second language, as is the case of some other Southeast Asian groups. Most of them did not learn English in their home countries. English is very different from Southeast Asian languages, phonologically, grammatically, and lexically. Lao and Cambodian students have to learn a new writing system, even if they are literate in their native language. It should be noted that a substantial number of Southeast Asian students are preliterate in their native language and may have had no schooling.

One of the common characteristics of Southeast Asians is the naming system. In Southeast Asia, people are referred to, or called by, their given name, with or without a title, and never by the family name. One of the reasons why they are not called by the family name is the limited number of Southeast Asian family names. For instance, the Vietnamese have about twenty common names for a population of 69 million people. Like Americans, Lao people write their given name first and their family names last. Vietnamese, Hmong, and Cambodians, on the other hand, write their family name first and their given name last. Therefore, when asking for a student's name, an educator should ask for the family and given names rather than for the first and last names. Lao family names are borrowed from Sanskrit, which is a polysyllabic language. Therefore, Lao names are longer than Vietnamese, Hmong, or Cambodian names. Among Southeast Asians, only the Vietnamese have a middle name .

Another cultural characteristic shared by Southeast Asians is the extended family. Contrary to the widespread belief of the Southeast Asian family consisting of several dozens of members living under the same roof, the Southeast Asian extended family is more of an organizational power structure than a physical entity. It is a network of immediate families which are somewhat comparable to, but still different from, the nuclear family of the West. The Southeast Asian immediate family usually includes the married couple and their children, often the parents of the husband, and sometimes, the unmarried brothers and sisters of the couple or some other unmarried close relatives. Members of the extended family are bound together by collective responsibility and mutual obligations. They are expected to give one another moral and material assistance, especially during stressful times. The same responsibilities and obligations are also held for members who live far apart.

Respect is the cornerstone of interpersonal relationships in Southeast Asian societies. Among people who are highly respected are elderly people, religious leaders, and teachers, even though the latter may be younger than the parents. Respect is expressed in everyday language and nonverbal behavior. In making an utterance, the Southeast Asian expresses, along with any concept or idea, an attitude of respect, or lack of it, toward the interlocutor. This expression is so natural—because it is inherent in the nature of the words used—that generally both the speaker and hearer are not aware of it. But if the speaker unintentionally or purposely uses a word which reflects an attitude of disrespect, the listener will immediately recognize it and respond accordingly. The Southeast Asian concern for expressing respect in language can be illustrated by comparing the English word "yes" and its Vietnamese equivalents. The English word "yes" expresses agreement and does not reflect any attitude of respect or disrespect. Vietnamese has three words for "yes," and a speaker of Vietnamese must choose between "Dạ," "Vang," and "ʊ." No Vietnamese would use "ʊ" when talking to parents, teachers, employers, or older people .

Respect is also expressed through nonverbal communication. Avoidance of eye contact from the student while talking or listening to the teacher is a demonstration of respect toward the teacher. Direct eye contact with an interlocutor who is senior in age or status or of the opposite sex is a sign of disrespect. Elderly people and teachers enjoy special respect in Southeast Asia. Teachers are not addressed by their names but by their respected title of "Teacher." Consequently, Southeast Asian students tend to address their American teacher as "Teacher."

⊔

LANGUAGE AND COMMUNICATION STYLES OF SOUTHEAST ASIAN STUDENTS

Southeast Asians speak different languages that are not mutually comprehensible. Lao is the national language of Laos. Its minority languages include Hmong, Iu-Mien, Khmu, Lahu, and so on. These languages belong to the Sino-Tibetan language family and are classified as tonal languages. In a tonal language, a change of pitch and contour brings about the change of meaning of an utterance. Unlike tones, intonation can change the grammatical or attitudinal value of a sentence but cannot change the lexical meaning of its constituent words. Although Lao is primarily monosyllabic, it borrows a substantial number of words from Sanskrit which are polysyllabic.

Cambodian, or Khmer, is the only language of the refugee groups which is nontonal. But, like other Southeast Asian languages, it is essentially monosyllabic and uninflected. Cambodian also borrows a great number of words from Sanskrit.

Vietnamese is a tonal, monosyllabic, and uninflected language of the Austro-Asiatic language family and consists of many words borrowed from Chinese (Handbook for Teaching Vietnamese-Speaking Students, 1994). Loan-words from French and English most often came into Vietnamese through Chinese. The following are common characteristics of Southeast Asian languages.

PHONOLOGY

All these languages are essentially monosyllabic but contain many polysyllabic words. In Lao and Khmer, a substantial number of polysyllabic words are loan-words from Sanskrit. Word stress is not phonemic. Generally, there are no consonant sound clusters in those languages, except for the initial clusters in Khmer. Only a limited number of single consonants occur in the final position. This raises the need for Southeast Asian students to learn to recognize and produce the contrastive features of English stress, intonation, final consonants, especially voiced consonants, and consonant clusters, especially final clusters.

MORPHOLOGY AND SYNTAX

All these languages are uninflected. This means that words are always invariable. Grammatical meaning is not expressed by suffixes or internal vowel changes, but by the context or individual words, called grammatical markers. There is no change of endings for gender, number, tense, case, or voice .

Word order is also a distinct characteristic of Southeast Asian languages. The syntax of affirmative statements is similar to that of English but word order in qualifying phrase structures is different: The modifier usually follows the noun, as in "house big" versus "big house." Interrogative sentences are distinguished by question markers and not by subject-verb inversion or auxiliary verbs as in English. An imperative sentence is formed by adding *imperative markers* to the affirmative statement. Usually, the imperative sentence does not contain a subject. Due to these differences in sentence and word structures, Southeast Asian students will encounter difficulties learning English inflections for the plural, tenses, and cases, subject-verb inversion, and the use of auxiliaries, articles, pronouns, and prepositions.

LEXICON

As with any language, words in Southeast Asian languages do not always cover the same area of meaning as their English "equivalents." In English, the word "hair" includes hair on the head and on any part of the human or animal body, but excludes feathers. In Vietnamese, specific terms for hair are used. The word for hair on the head, "tóc," is different from the word for hair on other parts of the body, "lông," which also refers to hair on animals and to the feathers of a bird. In some cases, English has only one generic term while Southeast Asian languages have several specific terms corresponding to the English generic term. For instance, the English term "carry" does not indicate how the carrying is done. Cambodian and Vietnamese have more than a dozen terms for "carry," depending on how the carrying is done, what or who is being carried, and the feeling of the person who does the carrying for the person or thing being carried. Southeast Asian languages, in other cases, have only one generic word while English has several specific words. For instance, the Vietnamese word "tủ" corresponds to "bookcase," "closet," "cupboard," "file cabinet," "safe," and so on. From these lexical differences, we can see that Southeast Asian students will experience difficulties in mastering English words which do not cover the same area of meaning as their Southeast Asian "equivalents" and words that are specific in one language and generic in the other.

English and Southeast Asian languages are unrelated languages, therefore, there are no cognates—as is the case in Spanish and English—which can help students to build up a common core vocabulary for immediate use and future expansion.

WRITING

Lao and Khmer writing systems are derived from Sanskrit and Pali, the old languages of India. Although they appear different from English, they are still an alphabetic writing system that comes from the Phoenician alphabet from which English and other Indoeuropean languages are derived. The relationship between Lao and Cambodian symbols and sounds is more consistent than symbols and sounds in English. Cambodian has 33 consonant letters and 24 vowel letters. Lao has 27 consonant letters and 24 vowel letters. The vowels can be written before, after, above, and below the consonant letters according to contexts. Because of the different alphabets used, Cambodian and Lao students who are literate in their own languages still experience difficulty in learning the English alphabet.

The Vietnamese writing system, "chū quố́c-ngū" is derived from the Roman alphabet. Diacritic marks are used to represent the tones. It was devised by European missionaries in the 16th century for the purpose of translating the Bible into the vernacular. However, it was not adopted as a national writing until the First World War. It is now the only writing system used by the Vietnamese. In appearance, the Vietnamese alphabet does not differ much from English. However the phonetic value of Vietnamese letters is not the same as that of the English alphabet. A written word which looks identical in English and Vietnamese may have different pronunciations. For instance, "loan" is pronounced /loʊn/ in English but /lwan/ in Vietnamese. Vietnamese spelling is more consistent than English spelling and adheres more closely to the principle of "one symbol per phoneme and one phoneme per symbol."

The alphabetic writing systems for Hmong and Iu-Mien people are of recent date. They were devised by American and European missionaries during the 1950s and 1960s. Very few Hmong or Mien could read and write in those alphabets which were not taught in Laotian schools prior to 1975. In fact, it was forbidden to disseminate those alphabets. For recording important events in their lives, the Mien used Chinese characters. There has been a continuous effort to disseminate the use of the Hmong alphabet among the Hmong living in the United States today.

COMMUNICATION

Because most Southeast Asian students are limited English or non-English proficient, they experience much difficulty in communicating with mainstream students, and with teachers and other school personnel. Difficulties arising from the lack of English proficiency are compounded by differences in communication style which often lead to misunderstanding, even for students who do speak English.

It is common for Southeast Asian students to use the nonverbal mode of communication when the teacher expects a verbal response. Teachers often complain that those students lack manners because they never use such words as "Thank you" in response to a gesture of kindness or a compliment. They never say "I'm sorry" when an expression of apology is expected of them. What the teacher receives instead is a simple smile. Some teachers even wonder whether there are any equivalents for "Thank you" and "I'm sorry" in Southeast Asian languages. These phrases do exist, but are used differently in the two cultures.

Even when both students and teachers speak English, they do not understand the same term in the same way. American teachers are often puzzled by the fact that most Southeast Asian students always say "yes" instead of "no" when asked whether they have understood what the teacher has said. In saying "yes," the Southeast Asian student wants to "save face" and avoid the disappointment or bad feelings that a "no" answer may generate.

When the teacher uses a question containing a negative word, for instance," Didn't you do your homework?" Southeast Asian students tend to reply with a "yes" which means "Yes, you are right, I did not do that."

Nonverbal communication is an area in which misunderstanding may occur. The use of silence by the student does not imply a lack of interest or a passive attitude. Southeast Asians are taught to listen and not to talk unless and until they are asked to do so by an older person. A smile may mean several things, the exact meaning of which will be determined by what precedes and what follows the smile. Avoidance of eye contact does not indicate guilt, mischievousness, disinterest, or lack of attention. Rather, it shows respect for the teacher. These are only a few examples of Southeast Asian nonverbal communication patterns that may be misunderstood by school personnel.

⊔

THE EDUCATIONAL NEEDS OF SOUTHEAST ASIAN STUDENTS

Southeast Asians have a very high percentage of limited English proficient (LEP) students. In the 1993–1994 school year, there were 11,926 Lao LEP students, 26,219 Hmong LEPs, 21,040 Cambodian LEPs, and 48,890 Vietnamese LEPs in California public schools (California Department of Education, Language Census, 1993) (see Table 4–1).

Although these students have different linguistic, cultural, and educational backgrounds, Southeast Asian LEP students share the same general educational needs. The most critical need is, no doubt,

TABLE 4–1
Southeast Asian Students in California Public Schools.

LANGUAGE	LEP	FEP	TOTAL
Cambodian	21,040	7,219	28,259
Lao	11,926	4,701	16,627
Hmong	26,219	4,516	30,735
Khmu	332	92	434
Lahu	440	30	470
Iu-Mien	4,691	661	5,352
Vietnamese	48,890	28,613	77,503

Source: Language Census Report R-30 LC, California Department of Education, Sacramento, Spring 1993.

acquisition of English proficiency, without which they would not be able to be successful in their school work or in the world of work later on. They need both the basic interpersonal communication skills (BICS) and the cognitive academic language skills (CALP). As mentioned earlier, English and the Southeast Asian languages are completely unrelated; the inflected structure of English poses several learning problems to native speakers of Southeast Asian languages. Cognates are nonexistent and loan-words are extremely rare.

The second critical need is to master the content areas that are taught in English. Because of their limited English proficiency, Southeast Asian students cannot fully understand what is taught in English. Language is not the only obstacle in their study. They also lack the life experiences that give meaning to many concepts in the content areas. The teaching style of American teachers, which is predominantly auditory, also contributes to their learning difficulties. Southeast Asian students are more visual-graphic oriented. Therefore, a multisensory teaching approach would help them learn better. This approach may be epitomized in the following sentence: "I see what I hear, I hear what I see, I understand what I hear and see, and make use of what I understand." The most crucial factor in the learning process is comprehension. Learning would not occur without it. For the limited English proficient student, comprehension is much easier through the medium of the primary language. However, it is not always possible to have a teacher who can communicate in a Southeast Asian language. In 1993, California had 87 certified bilingual teachers for 159,380 Southeast Asian LEP students, with 1 Lao-speaking teacher, 1 Cambodian-speaking teacher, 2 Hmong-speaking teachers, and 83 Vietnamese-speaking teachers. Primary language support was provided mostly by bilingual teacher aides. The number of Southeast Asian LEP students has increased from 80,370 in 1985 to 159,380 in 1993 while the number of certified teachers who speak a Southeast Asian language has increased by only 12 teachers (California Department of Education, Language Census Report, 1993) (see Table 4–2).

Twenty years after the Bilingual Education Act of 1974, bilingual education is still a matter of controversy, in light of the "English Only" movement. However, there is consensus among educators on one belief; that comprehension is crucial for learning. The use of the primary language helps LEP students to understand what is taught in English. Although the Supreme Court decision in the Lau versus Nichols case did not mandate instruction through the primary language, it did rule for school districts to provide instruction in a manner that is comprehensible to limited English proficient students (Supreme Court Decision, Lau versus Nichols, 1974).

If the primary language support is not available, comprehension can be achieved, to a certain extent, by the use of visual aids such as pictures, slides, films, videos, and realia and the use of "simplified" English. This approach is commonly known as "Sheltered English." A new term for this approach is "Specially Designed Academic Instruction in English" (SDAIE).

A third critical need for Southeast Asian students is social and cultural adjustment. These students bring with them certain social behaviors and communication styles that hamper their efforts to become proficient in English and culturally adjusted. Acculturation and English proficiency are equally important areas. However, the need for acculturation has often been left unfulfilled. The school usually emphasizes English and content areas, not social and cultural adjustments.

TABLE 4–2
Southeast Asian Bilingual Teachers in California Public Schools.

Language	Certified Bilingual	Bilingual Teacher Aides	LEP Students
Cambodian	1	287	21,040
Hmong	2	415	26,219
Lao	1	153	11,926
Vietnamese	83	778	48,890

Source: Language Census Report R-30 LC, California Department of Education, Sacramento, Spring 1993.

⌐

SERVICE TO SOUTHEAST ASIAN STUDENTS WITH MILD DISABILITIES

NEEDS ASSESSMENT

As we have seen in the previous section, Southeast Asian students are confronted with many learning barriers due to their cultural, linguistic, and educational backgrounds. Disabled Southeast Asian students face still greater problems in U.S. schools. Special education is a concept which is virtually nonexistent in Southeast Asian countries. The only special education school in Southeast Asia was a school for the blind in Saigon. No other educational opportunity existed for disabled Southeast Asian children. This condition resulted from the shortage of special education teachers and instructional materials in Southeast Asia and from the negative attitude of parents and school toward children with disabilities. Most Southeast Asian parents believe that disabled children cannot be educated. In addition, the parents believe in the theory of Karma, which explains that disabilities are God's way of punishing the parents for the sins committed in their previous lives. Therefore, parents tend to hide their disabled child to avoid the feeling of disgrace that the public might have toward a disabled child. Schools refuse to accept a disabled child because they do not know how to educate disabled students. The education of disabled Southeast Asian children, therefore, should begin with cooperation between the school and the family to impart the belief that a child with a disability can indeed be educated. Additionally, parents should not be ashamed about having a disabled child.

How many Southeast Asians are there who need special education? At present, there are no accurate figures available. There is a need for a state by state systematic survey of Southeast Asian students to approximate the number of special education students. These students would be classified according their disability; whether "socially and emotionally disturbed," "mentally retarded," "physically handicapped," or "learning disabled." The survey should also examine programs and agencies which deal with special education students whose primary language is Southeast Asian. With this information, educators could develop more appropriate programs to target the needs of this student population.

ASSESSMENT INSTRUMENTS

The instruments currently being used to assess Southeast Asian students with disabilities are intended for native English-speaking students. Even a Southeast Asian child without disability would experience difficulties in taking these assessments. Errors that occur during acquisition of a second language have often been attributed to language delay and language disorders. Consequently, a number of Southeast Asian students who are identified as having language disabilities may be nondisabled students who are limited English proficient. To the writer's knowledge, there are no commercially available assessment instruments in any Southeast Asian language. Appropriate assessment instruments for Southeast Asian students are urgently needed .

SPECIAL EDUCATION PERSONNEL AND INSTRUCTIONAL MATERIALS

Assessment instruments are mainly administered by monolingual specialists who may not have the necessary knowledge of the linguistic and cultural backgrounds of the students who take these tests. There is a small number of credentialed Southeast Asian teachers in special and bilingual education. San Jose State University is now the only institution of higher education in California that has a training program for bilingual special education elementary school teachers in Vietnamese and English. No information on any programs for other Southeast Asian languages in other states is available. Furthermore, school psychologists and specialists in testing and measurement who speak a Southeast Asian language are extremely rare.

Special education teachers who are monolingual English speakers should also learn how to communicate and work with Southeast Asian parents to gain their support and cooperation. These teachers often call upon interpreters to help them assess Southeast Asian students; but unless they are proficient in both English and Southeast Asian languages and are knowledgeable in special education test procedure and terminology, these interpreters would not be effective in the assessment process. With the present salary of educational paraprofessionals, it is not easy to recruit bilingual aides and interpreters who meet the above requirements.

Like other disabled students, Southeast Asian-speaking students identified as disabled are routinely placed in the same class with native English-speaking students. Because of their limited English proficiency, Southeast Asian students cannot fully benefit from the instruction of special education teachers. In addition, there are no instructional materials available for disabled Southeast Asian students.

Educators and education policy makers who are really concerned about the education of disabled Southeast Asian students could adopt the following actions to help improve special education for the Southeast Asian student with disabilities:

1. Training of bilingual special education teachers and specialists whose native language is a Southeast Asian language. There should be a cooperative effort between institutions of higher education and school districts to plan, recruit, train, and place teachers and specialists in bilingual special education programs for Southeast Asian students .

2. Training of bilingual interpreters in test procedure and special education terminology. These interpreters would assist monolingual special education school personnel.

3. Training of special education teacher aides to work with monolingual English teachers in programs for disabled Southeast Asian children. The salary should be commensurate with the high professional standards required of these paraprofessionals. There should be a career ladder program to help these aides become certified teachers.

4. In-service training for monolingual special education teachers and specialists to help them address problems caused by linguistic and cultural backgrounds of disabled Southeast Asian students.

5. Training parents of disabled students. If they are trained, parents can reinforce learning with instructional activities conducted at home. Southeast Asian parents are, in general, unfamiliar with the education system of the United States, including special education programs. The training should aim at raising parents' awareness of problems that their children may have to confront and at providing a formal practicum that includes clinical sessions on how to reinforce desirable behavior. It should also restore the faith of the parents in special education. Paraprofessionals and parents must be viewed as valuable resources for educating the disabled limited English proficient child.

6. Developing appropriate testing and instructional materials. The following three efforts should be made to improve these areas:

    a. revise current testing and instructional materials in English to adapt to the needs of Southeast Asian special education students, thereby removing cultural biases from these materials .

    b. develop supplementary bilingual materials for disabled Southeast Asian children; and

    c. develop handbooks for teachers, specialists, paraprofessionals, and parents working with Southeast Asian student with disabilities.

⊐

CONCLUSION

The influx of Southeast Asian refugees/immigrants to the United States has not subsided after the first wave in 1975, when Vietnam, Laos, and Cambodia fell to Communist rule. From 130,000 in 1975 to 1,101,054 in 1990, (Chuong & Van, 1994) the Southeast Asian population in the United States has steadily increased. In California, there were 159,370 Southeast Asian students in the 1993-1994 academic year. In this population, there were 113,538 limited English proficient students. Consequently school districts now face several problems in providing this student population with a quality education. The two most critical problems are (1) the shortage of teachers who can provide comprehensible input in the instruction of English and the subject areas and (2) the scarcity of instructional materials for limited English proficient Southeast Asian students. For a population of 113,538 LEP students, there are only 87 credentialed teachers throughout California's school districts who canx communicate in a Southeast Asian language. The demand for more bilingual teachers and more bilingual instructional materials in English and Southeast Asian languages is at a critical point. Without qualified teaching staff and appropriate instructional materials, schools cannot offer effective curricula. This message is conveyed when Justice Douglas stated in his Supreme Court decision, "We know that those who do not understand English are certain to find their classroom experience totally incomprehensible and in no way meaningful" (Lau versus Nichols, 1974).

⌐

REFERENCES

Chuong, C. H. & Van, L. (1994). *The Amerasians from Vietnam: A California study.* Sacramento: Southeast Asia Community Resource Center.

Handbook for Teaching Vietnamese-Speaking Students. (1994). Sacramento: California Department of Education.

Language Census Report. (1993). Sacramento: California Department of Education, Educational Demographics Unit, Research and Technology Division.

Lau versus Nichols. (1974), 94 S.Ct 786, 788.

Lewis, J. (Ed). (1994). *Minority cultures of Laos: Kammu, Lua, Lahu, Hmong and Iu-Mien.* Sacramento: Southeast Asia Community Resource Center.

HUYNH DINH TE, PH.D.

Dr. Te is currently senior equity associate at the Southwest Regional Laboratory (SWRL), Los Alamitos, California. He earned a D.E.S. degree from the University of Provence, France, and his doctorate from Columbia University. He was formerly Associate Professor in the Graduate School of Education, California State University, Long Beach. His areas of special interest are second language acquisition, crosscultural communication, teacher education, and Southeast Asian languages and cultures.

CHAPTER 5

INDIA: ITS PEOPLE, CULTURE, AND LANGUAGES

CHANDRA SHEKAR, Ph.D.
M. N. HEGDE, Ph.D.

One of the ironies of history is that the United States was discovered, and the natives were named Indians, because Columbus was looking for India and its surrounding countries ("Indies"), the mysterious lands of gold, spice, and fine fabrics. That he arrived in the Americas was sheer serendipity. If Columbus had not set sail looking for the Indies, the history of the Americas may not have been the same. Although the native Americans came to be known as Indians, the Indians of Asia and Asians of other countries only began to arrive in the United States in any significant numbers in recent years.

According to the 1990 census, there are nearly 7 million Asians in the United States (U. S. Department of Commerce, 1993a, 1993b). This represents a 99% increase over the 1980 census figure. Major Asian American groups included in the 1990 census are the Asian Indians, Cambodians, Chinese, Filipinos, Hmong, Japanese, Koreans, Laotians,

Pakistanis, and Thai. Other Asian Americans included are the Afghanis, Bangladeshi, Nepali, Sri Lankan (of former Ceylon), Burmese, Malayan, and Indonesian.

As Table 5–1 shows, people from India are the fourth largest Asian American population in the United States. Only the Chinese, Filipino, and Japanese are in the U.S. in larger numbers. There are numerous books and articles on India, its history, culture, and languages. However, books and articles on multicultural issues in communication sciences and disorders that have dealt with Asian Americans have focused mostly on the Chinese, Japanese, and the Southeast Asians. In the clinical literature in communicative disorders, there is very little written about the people of the Indian subcontinent, especially its largest group: the Asian Indians. Therefore, this chapter gives an overview of the people of India and their languages.

⌐

THE INDIAN SUBCONTINENT AND ITS PEOPLE

The Indian subcontinent, a region in South Asia, includes India, Pakistan, Bangladesh, Nepal, Sri Lanka, and Bhutan. Of these countries,

TABLE 5–1
The distribution of Asian populations in the United States.

NATIONALITY	PERCENTAGE OF THE TOTAL (6,908,638 PERSONS)
Chinese	23.8
Filipino	20.4
Japanese	12.3
Asian Indian	11.8
Korean	11.6
Vietnamese	8.9
Laotian	2.2
Cambodian	2.1
Thai	1.3
Hmong	1.3
Pakistani	1.2
Other Asian	3.2

India is the largest and the most populous. Therefore, among the countries of the subcontinent, India is the biggest contributor to the pool of Asians in the United States.

Before they gained their independence from Britain in 1947, India and Pakistan (as well as the current Bangladesh) were one country. The majority of people in India were (and still are) Hindus. However, there was a majority of Muslims in two regions of the country: the northwest and a small portion in the northeast on the Bay of Bengal. At the time of independence, India was divided into two countries: the predominantly Hindu India and the predominantly Muslim Pakistan, which had its Eastern and Western portions. East Pakistan was bordered on three sides by India (Spear, 1966). In 1971, during the course of a 9-month civil war between the two portions of Pakistan, East Pakistan proclaimed its independence from West Pakistan and became Bangladesh.

ANCIENT INDIA

India is the place of origin for three major and ancient religions: Hinduism, Buddhism, and Jainism (Basham, 1975). Hinduism is the oldest living religion of the world and its origins are traced to prehistoric times. Hindu philosophy, part of Hinduism, is the oldest philosophical thought in the world. Buddhism, which is believed to have been established around 500 B.C.E., was a dominant religion in India until around 800 C.E. As it spread to other parts of Asia, especially to Sri Lanka, China, Korea, and Japan, Buddhism declined in India. Jainism, another ancient Indian religion, also was developed around 500 B.C.E. In India, of the 900 million people, roughly 650 million are Hindu. Minority religions in order of decreasing size include Muslims (120 million), Christians (14 million), Sikhs (18 million), Buddhists (4 million), and Jains (3 million). A small number of Pharisees and Jewish people also live in India. Pharisees are the people who originally traveled to India from Persia (modern Iran).

The Indian culture and civilization can be traced back at least 3,500 years. Along with the Chinese and the Egyptian civilizations, Indian civilization is among the oldest of civilizations. Ancient historical records of India (Chatterji, 1965; Mahajan, 1970; Majumdar, 1968) indicate that Dravidians, who migrated from the Mediterranean region around 3,500 B.C.E. settled in the Indus valley in northwestern India, which is now a part of Pakistan. They spoke such Dravidian languages as Kannada, Tamil, Telugu, Malayalam, and Brahui. The Dravidians were a community of agriculturists, artisans, and herdsmen. They lived in highly developed and fortified cities. Their cities had multistoried houses, public baths, and masonry drainage systems. It is believed that the well-known Harappa and Mohenjo Daro civilizations were built by Dravidians.

The ancient Hindus had a highly developed system of measurement and writing. The Hindu-Arabic numeral system now widely used in the world was originally developed in India (Smith & Karpinski, 1911). The Arabs, who learned the numeral notation system you see on this page from the Hindus, introduced it to the west. Ancient India also had highly developed science, especially astronomy, in addition to art and architecture (Basham, 1967, 1975). Ancient Indian temples and the later Mogul buildings (including the famed Taj Mahal) still provide examples of a rich architectural heritage.

A second wave of immigrants who migrated to the Indian subcontinent around 1,500 B.C.E. were the Indo-Aryans or Indo-Europeans (Indic people). They settled mostly in northern India and are thought to be responsible for the Dravidians moving south. The Indic people developed the Hindu philosophical and religious classics. The third wave of immigrants and invaders who settled in India were the Muslims. They travelled to India from the Arabian peninsula in the early 700s and from Persia and Afghanistan in the 1000s. The Moguls, who were Muslims and whose ancestors were from Mongolia, had established the Mogul empire in the late 1400s. It lasted until the early 1700s (Spear, 1966).

Among the Europeans who established a presence in India, the Portuguese were the first (early 1500s). Their goal was mostly to establish and control trade routes with India. The Portuguese were soon followed by the Dutch, English, and French, who united to fight the Indians, yet also fought among themselves. Eventually, the British took the upper hand and stayed in India, ruling the country until it became independent in 1947 (Spear, 1966).

MODERN INDIA

India is the seventh largest country in the world. It has an area of 3,287,782 square kilometers. With more than 840 million people, the country ranks second in the world in population. Like Canada and Britain, India is a parliamentary democracy in which the president is the figurative head of the country. It is a member of the British Commonwealth. The prime minister, who is the leader of the majority party elected to the parliament, is the executive head of the state. The country's capital is New Delhi, which is in Northern India.

India is geographically, culturally, linguistically, and ethnically diverse. It has high Himalayan peaks to the north, desert to the northwest, vast plains in the central part, and, mountain ranges that roughly divide the north and south, along with ranges in the southeastern and southwestern parts of the country. With rain forests, jungles, snow-capped Himalayan mountains, and tropical lowlands, the country offers a wide variety of landscape.

Politically, India is divided into 25 states, each headed by an elected chief minister. Most of the states are linguistically based, as people in different states speak their own languages. Although 15 major languages are recognized in the Indian constitution, the country is home to about 180 languages and more than 700 dialects. One Indian language, Hindi, is recognized as the national language, though a majority of the people in the country do not speak it. English is the official language of the government and education. Table 5–2 lists the major languages of India.

Ethnically, all major racial groups are represented in India. The majority are classified as Caucasians, who include the Indo-Aryans who migrated to India from central Asia and the Dravidians, who were the original inhabitants of the subcontinent. Besides these two major groups, there are numerous tribal communities with different ethnic backgrounds. Mongoloid (Chinese) and Australoid (related to the original people of Australia) also are represented.

India is not only a land of ancient civilization, but also of age-old customs, juxtaposed to modern contrasts and contradictions. Vast urban areas and millions of small villages, high-rise buildings and lowly huts, people below the poverty levels as well as those who are very rich, a low literacy rate and a pool of highly educated persons, all add to India's traditional linguistic and ethnic diversity. Independent India has made progress in increased food production, education, and housing for the poor. It still has a rapidly growing population. India now has over 200 million in its expanding middle class, although rates of poverty are still high. Although the literacy rate is only 52% for the country as a whole, several states and regions have a rate that exceeds 75% (Maps and Publications Ltd., 1991). India is unique among developing countries in that it has a large pool of highly educated professional persons.

In recent years, more open economic policies of the government have pushed production and privatization of industries, contributing

TABLE 5–2
States of India and their languages.

STATES	LANGUAGES
Andhra Pradesh	Telugu
Arunachal Pradesh	Hindi
Assam	Assamese
Bihar	Hindi/Bhojpuri
Goa	Hindi/Konkani
Gujarat	Gujarati
Hariyana	Hindi/Haryani
Himachal Pradesh	Hindi
Jammu & Kashmir	Kashmiri
Karnataka	Kannada
Kerala	Malayalam
Madhyapradesh	Hindi
Maharastra	Marathi
Manipur	Manipuri
Meghalaya	Hindi
Mizoram	Mizo
Nagaland	Naga
Orissa	Oriya
Punjab	Punjabi
Rajastan	Rajasthani
Sikkim	Nepali
Tamil Nadi	Tamil
Tripura	Tripuri
Uttar Pradesh	Hindi
West Bengal	Bengali

to a faster economic growth. The country has recently attracted several major U.S. firms. With expanding trade between the two countries, India and the United States are becoming major trade partners.

ᚃ

LANGUAGES AND LINGUISTICS IN INDIA

Linguistics was an advanced discipline in ancient India. In fact, Panini (400 B.C.E.), an ancient grammarian of Sanskrit, is considered the first phonetician and descriptive grammarian in studies on the history of languages. His *Treatise in Eight Chapters,* was a book of grammar of spoken Sanskrit of his time (Whitney, 1967). Its purpose was to produce phonologically, morphologically, and syntactically correct spoken forms of classical Sanskrit. Panini has given detailed description not only of rules of grammar, but also of sound systems based on sound production. He also analyzed the prosodic features of Sanskrit including such linguistic features as juncture, length, quantity, and tone. Panini's grammar was a strictly synchronic, formal grammar. The details and acuteness of Panini's linguistic analyses were not matched in the West until the latter part of the 19th century.

Other early linguistic scholars of India were greatly influenced by Panini's writings. Most of the post-Panini scholars wrote extensive commentaries on his grammar. Most of the grammars of other Indic and Dravidian languages are based on Panini's seminal work.

The ancient Indians spoke Sanskrit, an Indo-European language and one of the most advanced of ancient languages. Comparative linguistic studies have clearly established the link between Sanskrit and other Indo-European languages including Greek, Latin, and Germanic languages. Working in India in 1786, Sir William Jones, a British judge, completed one of the earliest comparative studies to show that Sanskrit and most ancient European languages belonged to a single family. He made the following observation on Sanskrit (Jones, 1796):

> The Sanskrit language, whatever be its antiquity, is of a wonderful structure; more perfect than the Greek, more copious than the Latin, and more exquisitely refined than either, yet bearing to both of them a stronger affinity, both in the roots of verbs and in the forms of grammar, than could possibly have been produced by accident. (p. 15)

Sanskrit was the language of the Vedas, the classical philosophical and religious treatises of the Indic people. It also was the language of the Brahmins, the priestly class. The more commonly spoken language was Pali, which was the language of religious texts of Buddhists and Jains. Sanskrit had its simplified versions, which, it is believed, may have given rise to such modern Indian languages as Hindi, Marathi, and Bengali.

The countries of the Indian subcontinent present a staggering linguistic diversity. There are at least four major language families in the region: Indo-European (Indic), Dravidian, Austro-Asiatic, and Tibeto-Burman. Each major family has many subfamilies. All families and subfamilies contain numerous languages. Each language has hundreds of dialects. The Indian branch of the Indo-European family contains such languages as Hindi, Bengali, Marathi, Punjabi, Gujarati, Sindhi, Oriya, and Assamese. These languages are spoken mostly in northern India, Pakistan, and Bangladesh.

The Dravidian family of languages has four major languages: Kannada, Malayalam, Tamil, and Telugu (Chatterji, 1965). These languages are spoken mostly in the four southern states of Karnataka, Kerala, Tamil Nadu, and Andhra Pradesh. About 95% of the population in southern India speak these languages.

The Austro-Asiatic languages are represented mainly by two language groups: Munda, or Kol, and Mon-Khmer. These two languages are spoken mostly by various tribes living in the central and northeastern parts of India and in some parts of Sri Lanka. The only member of the Mon-Khmer language group in the Indian sub-continent is Khasi, spoken in Assam, a northeastern state of India. It is believed that the Austro-Asiatic people migrated from the Mediterranean area to the subcontinent before the Dravidians arrived there.

Tibeto-Burman group of languages, which are usually regarded as a part of Sino-Tibetan family, are spoken mainly in Tibet, Burma, and a few northeastern states of India, including Manipur, Tripura, and Assam.

A majority of immigrants from India now living in the United States speak a language of the Indic or Dravidian family. Therefore, we focus our attention only on these two language families. In particular, we shall discuss some of the unique phonetic, phonological, morphological, and syntactic characteristics of two representative languages: Hindi from the Indic family and Kannada from the Dravidian family. Hindi is spoken in parts of northern India and Kannada is spoken in the southwestern state of Karnataka.

Although we describe some general characteristics of these two representative languages, it should be noted that the languages of the subcontinent vary to a great extent depending on the geographic region, socioeconomic class, level of formal education, and occupation. The Dravidian languages are highly diglossic, having formal and informal speech varieties. Often, the literary and formal forms of languages are very different from informal and spoken forms. To simplify our discussion, we concentrate only on the standard forms of Hindi, spoken in and around Delhi, the nation's capital, and Kannada spoken in and around Mysore, a city in the southern state of Karnataka. Although these two representative languages belong to two different language families, they share many common traits. This is expected because of mutual interaction between the two groups of people over the centuries.

PHONETICS AND PHONOLOGY

VOWEL SYSTEM

The literary varieties of Hindi and Kannada share a similar vowel system. Each language has five short vowels /a/, /e/, /i/, /o/ and /u/ and their long counterparts. Table 5–3 lists the vowel segments in Hindi (H) and Kannada.

Vowel length is phonemic in both languages. For example, in Kannada, *aTTa* means "attic" and *a:ta* means "play." However, Hindi differs from Kannada in that it has nasalized vowels. The following examples represent the nasalized vowels in Hindi.

[sãp] "snake"   [ãsu] "tear"   [sãs] "breath"

In fact, nasal vowels in Hindi are distinctive. Minimal pairs given on the next page illustrate the distinctiveness of the oral/nasal vowel contrast in Hindi.

TABLE 5–3
Vowels of Hindi and Kannada.

		FRONT		CENTRAL	BACK
High	Short	i			u
	Long	i:			u:
Mid	Short	e			o/ɔ (H)
	Long	e:			o:
Low	Short			a/ə (H)	
		æ (H)			
	Long			a:	

[sas] "mother-in-law"   [sãs] "breath"
[bas] "bad smell"   [bãs] "bamboo"

Dravidian languages, on the other hand, lack these nasalized vowels.

The long and short vowels of Indic languages differ from the English tense and lax vowels. The short vowels in Indic languages are longer than the tense vowels in English. Also, the lax vowels of English are shorter than the long vowels of Indic languages. For example, the tense vowel in "fit" [f I t] is shorter than the short vowel in the Kannada word čiTTe [čI T T e] "butterfly". Similarly, the long vowel in "feet" [f i t] is shorter than the longer vowel in the Kannada word i:ga [i g a] "now."

CONSONANT SYSTEM

Consonants in Indic and Dravidian languages are grouped on the basis of place and manner of articulation. The consonant system in Hindi and the literary variety of Kannada are presented in Tables 5–4 and 5–5.

The Indic and Dravidian consonants that are not found in English are: (a) Voiced bilabial and velar aspirated stops (e.g., g^h, b^h); (b) Dental and Retroflex consonants (e.g., Retroflex: T (ṭ), T^h ($ṭ^h$), D (ḍ), D^h ($ḍ^h$) and N (ṇ); Dental: t, t^h, d, d^h, and n; and (c) voiceless and voiced palatal affricates (e.g., $č^h$, $ǰ^h$) and palatal nasal (e.g., ñ). The closest sounds in English that correspond to dental sounds in Hindi and Kannada are the inter-dental sounds /θ/ (as in "think") and /ð/ (as in "this"). Retroflex sounds of Hindi and Kannada sound more like

TABLE 5–4

Stops and Nasals of Hindi and literary Kannada.

	UNASPIRATED	ASPIRATED	UNASPIRATED	ASPIRATED	NASAL
Velar	k	k^h	g	g^h	ŋ
Palatal	č	$č^h$	ǰ	$ǰ^h$	ñ
Retroflex	T (ṭ)	T^h ($ṭ^h$)	D (ḍ)	D^h ($ḍ^h$)	N (ṇ)
Dental	t	t^h	d	d^h	n
Labial	p	p^h	b	b^h	m

TABLE 5–5
Glides, sibilants, and laterals.

		BILABIAL	RETROFLEX	ALVEOLA	PALATAL	GLOTTAL
Glides	Voiceless					
	Voiced				y	
Fricative	Voiceless	(f)	S (ṣ)	s	š	h
	Voiced	v		z		
Laterals	Voiceless					
	Voiced		L (ḷ)	l		
Continuants	Voiceless					
	Voiced		r (ṛ)			

"r" sound in the Standard American English as in "America." Retroflex consonants are produced with the tip of the tongue turned back to touch the hard palate behind the alveolar ridge.

Dravidian languages differ from Indic languages in a number of ways. For example, as noted before, Indic languages have nasal vowels, which are absent in Dravidian languages. Although both the language groups share most of the consonants, voiced and aspirated stops are not native to Dravidian languages. In fact, voiced stops are allophonic variants in Tamil, a Dravidian language spoken in the state of Tamil Nadu. Voiceless stops are voiced when they occur between two vowels. For example, the Tamil word *ka:tu* "forest" is pronounced as [ka:ḍu]. Similarly, retroflex consonants are not native to Indic languages. They are incorporated into the phonemic system of these languages due to the interaction between the Dravidian and Indic languages over many centuries.

In contrast to the labio-dental fricative /v/ in English, most of the Indic languages have a bilabial fricative /v/. However, when /v/ is followed by a back vowel (e.g., u, u:, o, o:) it is pronounced as bilabial glide /w/. Therefore, the phoneme /w/ in English is only an allophonic variation of the bilabial fricative /v/ in Indian languages.

MORPHOLOGY

Morphology of the Indic and Dravidian languages is very rich. Nouns decline for three genders: masculine, feminine, and neuter; two numbers: singular and plural; and three cases: nominative, accusative, and oblique (Steever, 1993).

Gender distinction in Indic languages differs from Dravidian languages. For instance, in Hindi, masculine, feminine, and neuter genders are not always based on the biological sex of the noun, but on its grammatical category. In this sense, Hindi is similar to German and other Latinate languages like French, Italian, and Spanish. In the case of nouns denoting animate beings, grammatical gender almost always agrees with natural gender. Thus, *a:dmi* "man," *darzi:* "tailor" are masculine and *o:rat:* "woman" and *be:ti* "daughter" are feminine. However, the gender of many other nouns is harder to predict. For example, *kamara* "room" and *din* "day" are masculine, whereas *bo:tal* "bottle" and *me:z* "table" are feminine. On the other hand, gender distinction in Dravidian languages depends on the biological sex of the noun concerned.

Nouns in both languages are marked for case endings. In a normal declarative sentence, the subject is marked for nominative case, which is indicated as ø in both Hindi and Kannada. Object is marked with accusative marker *-annu* in Kannada, but it is null in Hindi and an indirect object is marked with dative case marker, *-ge* in Kannada and *-ko* in Hindi. Hindi also marks its nominal system with ergative marker *-ne*. Of course, there are several variations in case marking on the nouns depending on the type of sentence construction. The following examples illustrate the case marking pattern in Hindi and Kannada. The examples include nominative (ø), accusative (acc), dative (dat), ergative (erg), and the third person singular masculine/feminine (3psm, 3psf) forms.

Hindi:

a. ra:m-ø   pustak-ø   paṛta: hai
   Ram-nom   book-acc   read-imperfective be
   "Ram reads a book"

b. a:p-ø   si:ta:-ko   pustak-ø di:jie:
   you-hon-nom Sita:-dat book-acc give-imperfective
   "You give a book to Sita"

c. ra:m-ne   pustak-ø   paṛa:
   Ram-erg   book-nom   read-perfective
   "Ram read a book"

Kannada:
a. ra:manu-ø pustakaw-annu o:didanu
   Ram-nom book-acc   read+past+3psm
   "Ram read a book"
b. ra:manu-ø si:te-ge ondu pustakaw-annu koTTanu
   Ram-nom Sita-dat one book-acc   give+past+3psm
   "Ram gave a book to Sita"
c. ra:mani-ge taleno:wu-ø bandide
   Ram-dat headache-nom come-has
   "Ram has a headache"

As the examples given indicate, the case markers represent the grammatical functions of subject and object. Such case markers suggesting grammatical relations are absent in English.

The verbal system is complex in both the language groups. Most of the verbal bases are in their root form. Tense, number and gender suffixes are attached to the right periphery of the verbal base. Examples from Hindi and Kannada illustrate this point:

Kannanda:
a. bandanu   (bar + d + anu) "came"
   come+past+3sm   (verb root + past tense + 3sm)
b. bandaLu   (bar + d + aLu) "came"
   come+past+3sf   (verb root + past tense + 3sf)

Hindi:
a. a:ya: "came"
   come+past+3sm
b. a:yi:
   come+past+3sf

Verbal auxiliaries follow rather than precede the main verbs with which they are used in both the language groups. (e.g., Hindi: a: raha: hai "He *is* coming"; Kannada: bar-utta: idd-a:ne "He *is* coming").

Many Indian languages have constructions in which two independent verbal stems are combined to form a compound verbal stem with semantic properties slightly differing from those of either of the components. Usually the meaning of the entire compound is some variation of the meaning of one of the components. Thus in Hindi: *ma:rna* "to strike, hit," *ma:r Da:lna:* "to kill", *hona:* "to be," *ho ja:na:* "to become." Kannada also has similar compound verbs.

SYNTAX

Word order in Indic and Dravidian languages is *Subject Object Verb (SOV)*. Unlike English, languages in both the groups permit a fairly free word order. Speakers can switch around the sentential elements freely, more so in the Indic languages than in Dravidian languages. Although we can switch the subject and object around freely in a Kannada sentence, we cannot move the verbal element. The verbal element has to be in the final position, except in constructions used in poetry. Poetic license allows the movement of a verb to the sentence initial or medial position for special effects. However, free movement of the verb is possible in Indic languages. In this respect, word order variation is more flexible in Hindi than in Kannada. Examples illustrate the relatively free word order acceptable in Indic and Dravidian languages:

Hindi:

a. ra:m-ne   kela: kha:ya: (SOV)
   Ram-erg. (SUB)   banana (DO)   ate (V)
   "Ram ate a banana"

b. ra:m-ne   kha:ya: kela: (SVO)
   Ram-erg. (SUB)   ate (V)   banana (DO)

c. kela: kha:ya: ra:m-ne   (OVS)
   banana (DO)   ate (V)   Ram-erg. (SUB)

d. kela: ra:m-ne   kha:ya: (OSV)
   banana (DO)   Ram-erg. (SUB)   ate (V)

e. kha:ya: ra:m-ne   kela: (VSO)
   Ram-erg. (SUB)   ate (V)   banana (DO)

f. kha:ya: kela: ra:m-ne   (VOS)
   ate (V)   banana (DO)   Ram-erg. (SUB)

Kannada:

a. ta:yiyu-Ø maguw-ige ha:l-annu   kuDisidaLu   (S IO DO V)
   mother-nom   child-dat   milk-acc   feed-pst-3sf.
   "Mother fed milk to the child"

b. ta:yiyu-Ø   ha:l-annu maguw-ige   kuDisidaLu   (S DO IO V)
   mother-nom   milk-acc   child-dat   feed-pst-3sf.

c. ha:l-annu ta:yiyu-Ø   maguw-ige   kuDisidaLu   (DO S IO V)
   milk-acc   mother-nom   child-dat   feed-pst-3sf

d. ha:l-annu maguw-ige ta:yiyu-Ø   kuDisidaLu   (DO IO S V)
   milk-acc   child-dat   mother-nom   feed-pst-3sf

e. maguw-ige ha:l-annu ta:yiyu-Ø   kuDisidaLu   (IO DO S V)
   child-dat   milk-acc   mother-nom feed-pst-3sf

f. maguw-ige ta:yiyu-Ø ha:l-annu kuDisidaLu   (IO S DO V)
   child-dat   mother-nom milk-acc   feed-pst-3sf

Another syntactic feature that is shared by Indic and Dravidian languages is the formation of relative clauses. Unlike English, relative clauses precede the nouns they modify in both Indic and Dravidian languages. Similarly, other modifiers such as post-positional phrases and adjectives precede the nouns they modify in both language groups. On the contrary, it is possible to have prepositional phrase modifiers in English in the post nominal position, which is not allowed in Indic and Dravidian languages. For example, we can say in English, "The student of physics" with the prepositional phrase "of physics" modifying the noun "student." This construction is not possible in the languages of the Indian subcontinent.

SUBJECT-VERB AGREEMENT

Subject-verb agreement is quite complicated in Indic and Dravidian languages. Some languages show subject-verb agreement in person, number, and gender although others do not. Within the same language, some constructions show agreement and some do not. In Hindi, for example, if the verb is imperfective, then the verb agrees with the subject. But, if the verb is perfective, the verb agrees with the object and subject is marked with an ergative marker -*ne*. These examples illustrate this:

a. ra:m   roTi: kha:ta: tha:
   Ram (m.)   bread (f.)   eat (imp.m.) be (past.m.)
   "Ram (habitually) ate bread"

b. si:ta: kela: kha:ti: thi:
   Sita (f.)   banana (m.) eat (imp.f.)   be (past. f.)
   "Sita (habitually) ate banana"

c. ra:m-ne   roTi: kha:yi:
   Ram (m.) erg. bread (f.)   eat (perfect. f.)
   "Ram ate bread"

d. si:ta:-ne   kela: kha:yi
   Sita (f.) erg.   banana (m.) eat (perfec. m.)
   "Sita ate banana"

Subject-Verb agreement varies in Dravidian languages, too. The subject agrees with the verb in person, number, and gender in a simple declarative Kannada sentence. However, this agreement disappears in negative constructions.

> a. ra:manu   haNN-annu   tindanu
>   Ram-3sm   fruit   eat+past+3sm
>   "Ram ate the fruit"
> b. ra:manu   haNN-annu   tin-al-illa
>   Ram-3sm   fruit   eat+inf+Neg
>   "Ram did not eat the fruit"

On the other hand, Malayalam, another major Dravidian language, does not have any agreement morpheme on the verb in any construction. In fact, Malayalam is similar to Japanese in its agreement pattern.

THE DETERMINER SYSTEM

There are no definite and indefinite articles in the languages of the subcontinent. Instead, these languages use cardinal and ordinal numbers to denote indefiniteness. In English *a book*, for example, is roughly translated into *ondu pustaka* "one book" in Kannada. Because these languages do not have a definite article, speakers of the Indic and Dravidian languages have problem in using the definite article "the" in English.

POSTPOSITIONS

Both Indic and Dravidian languages are postpositional languages, as opposed to prepositional language like English. Such English prepositions as *on, in, under, above* and so forth occur post nominally in Indic and Dravidian languages. For example, in such constructions as *on the table, in the box, behind the door, under the table,* the prepositions *on, in, behind,* and *under* precedes the noun phrase *the table, the box, the door,* and *the table* in English. Corresponding constructions in Kannada are, *me:jina me:le* "table on," *dabbada oLage* "in the box," *ba:gila hinde,* "behind the door," and *me:jina keLage* "under the table." Here, the prepositions *me:le, oLage, hinde, keLage* follow the nouns.

ᒧ

LANGUAGE AND CULTURE

Several aspects of language structure and use in India reflect the close relation between culture and communication. The use of such formal linguistic devices as the pronominal system and kinship terms reflect individual and family relationships that are different from those in the Western cultures. Most languages have both formal and informal versions of language that vary than similar versions in the American English. Informal spoken versions of language, perhaps more like the British English, have variations that reflect social class. Generally, dialectal variations in Indian languages reflect the caste distinctions, although such variations have become less pronounced as the caste system has declined and formal education has become more common. Differences in dialects of people with and without formal education also can be significant. Because of historical lack of transportation and communication, dialects based on geographic regions are strong and often bewildering.

SOCIAL USE OF LANGUAGE

The social use of language reflects closely the type of personal relationships that are fostered in the speech community. Generally speaking, the use of informal forms of language is limited to communication between friends and family members. Unless they are close, people tend to use formal language. Individual relationships are more closely reflected in the use of language than they are in Western societies. For instance, it is a characteristic feature of the languages of the subcontinent to have multiple pronominal forms to address an individual or individuals. Hindi has three second person pronouns. A speaker's selection of a particular pronominal form depends on how close a person is and the degree of respect one intends to show to the listener. In other words, the different pronouns have different degrees of honorific values. The pronoun *a:p* is used to address older and more respected individuals; whereas, the pronoun *tum* is used to address individuals who are closer and, hence, a formal, respectful form of address is unnecessary. Therefore, the pronoun *tum* is used in addressing relatives who are not older than the speaker, friends, and servants. In the case of great intimacy and informality, the pronoun *tu* is used. This informal pronoun also may, depending on the communicative situation, imply contempt for the listener.

As in most Asian societies, teachers and children maintain more formal relationships than is the case in the U. S. schools. Therefore, children may not look straight in the eye when the teacher is talking. Also, children tend to use formal language when speaking to teachers. Communication is usually brief and to the point. Typically, the communication is limited to answering the teacher's questions.

Generally, the same pattern of communication exists when individuals speak with persons who are authority figures. Also, as in other Asian communities, silence is valued in the Indian culture. It is not assumed that the one who does not say much does not have much to say. Younger people talk less in the company of older people, but children are not generally isolated from adult conversation. In most family, religious, and cultural celebrations, adults and children mix freely.

KINSHIP TERMS AND FAMILY COMMUNICATION

Kinship terms in the languages of India provide an excellent means of understanding the close family structures and relationships that exist. Unlike English, languages of India have more refined and specific kinship terms. For instance, in Kannada, there are general terms for a brother (*sodara*) and a sister (*sodari*), but there also are specific, single terms for an older brother (*anna*), younger brother (*thamma*), older sister (*akka*), and younger sister (*thangi*). It is more common to use the specific single terms rather than the generic terms. The English term *uncle* refers to father's (and mother's) older as well as younger brothers. Similarly, the term *aunt* refers to mother's (and father's) older as well as younger sisters. In the languages of India, the terms are more specific. In Kannada, for instance, father's older brother is called *doddappa* and younger brother is *chikkappa*. Mother's older sister is called *doddamma* and the younger sister is called *chikkamma*. The term *appa* means father and *amma* means mother. The prefixes *dodda* means big and *chikka* means small. These specific Kannada terms imply a closer relationship than the English *aunts* and *uncles*.

To the contrary, counterparts of English terms that suggest distance between blood relatives are either nonexistent or not used in family communication in India. For instance, in Kannada, there is no equivalent for the English term *cousin*. In some communities, and in most family communications, a cousin may be referred to as a brother or a sister, suggesting greater closeness. Similarly, there is no specific term for father-in-law or mother-in-law. The term for father-in-law in Kannada is the same as that for mother's brother (ma:wa). The term for mother-in-law is the same as that for father's sister (atte). Some of the languages in India make greater distinctions than others, but generally speaking, terms that suggest closer relationships substitute those that suggest more remote relationships.

ᛩ

ASIAN INDIANS IN THE UNITED STATES

A majority of people from the Indian subcontinent now living in the United States are from India. Of all the Asians, Asian Indians constitute 11.8%; Pakistanis, 1.2%, and the Sri Lankans and Bangladeshis each constitute 0.2%. Other countries in the subcontinent contribute less than 0.2% to the total Asian population in the United States. It is only in the last 25 years that the Asian Indian immigration to the United States has been significant. According to the 1990 census report, the Asian Indian population in the United States is 815, 447. Of this total number, 76.3% entered the United States after 1975. Mostly for this reason, 75.4% of Asian Indians in the United States are foreign born (United States Department of Commerce, 1993a, 1993b).

Like other Asians, Asian Indians tend to live within a two-parent family structure. While married-couple families constitute 78.6% of all families in the United States, Asian American married-couple families is 89.2%. At 10.8%, the percentage of families headed by a single male or female parent is the lowest of all ethnic groups. This compares with the national percentage of single-parent headed families of 21.4 (U. S. Department of Commerce, 1993a, 1993b).

LINGUISTIC AND EDUCATIONAL BACKGROUND OF ASIAN INDIANS IN THE UNITED STATES

As noted previously, India is a land of multiple languages. English is still commonly taught in schools and colleges. For the most part, the medium of instruction in colleges and universities is English. Therefore, college-educated Indians across different states understand each other only by English. For this reason, and also because a majority of Indians who migrated to other countries are college graduates, most Asian Indians in the United States have better English proficiency than immigrants from other countries. For instance, 31% (the lowest figure) of Asian Indians in the United States do not speak English "very well," compared to 60.4% Chinese, 57.7% Japanese, and 78.1% Hmong (the highest) (U. S. Department of Commerce, 1993a, 1993b). Though specific figures are not available, most Asian Indians in the United States are bilingual. Besides English, they speak at least one other Indian language—usually their native tongue. Many Asian Indians are multilingual to various degrees of proficiency.

The educational attainment of Asian Americans is higher than that of the United States general population. Asian Indians in the United States have the highest educational attainment of all ethnic groups. Nationally, 20.3% of the total population holds a bachelor's degree or higher; among the Asian Americans, 36.6% have comparable education. However, 58.1% of Asian Indians in the United States have a bachelor's degree or higher. The group with the second highest percentage with similar educational attainment is Chinese at 40.7%. At 48.7%, Asian Indian females who hold a bachelor's degree or higher are the highest of all females in the country (U. S. Department of Commerce, 1993a, 1993b).

OCCUPATION AND INCOME OF ASIAN INDIANS IN THE UNITED STATES

Compared to those in the general population of the United States, more Asian Americans tend to be in the labor force. In 1990, 65% of all Americans were in the labor force compared to 67.4% of Asian Americans. Among the Asian Indians in the United States, 72.3% were in the labor force. The highest percentage in the labor force was among the Filipinos at 75.4%. Also, compared to women in general (56.8%), more Asian women (58.6%) were in the labor force. The unemployment rate for the Asian Indians was 5.6%, compared to 6.2% for the general population (U. S. Department of Commerce, 1993a, 1993b).

Asians generally, and Asian Indians in particular, tend to hold technical, managerial, professional, and sales positions. Nationally, 26.4% in 1990 were in managerial and professional positions. Among

Asian Americans, 31.2%, and among Asian Indians, 43.6% were in similar positions. Although 31.7% of all Americans were in technical, sales, and administrative support employment, 33.3% of all Asian Americans and 33.2% of Asian Indians were in those kinds of employment.

Mostly because of their higher educational attainment, Asian Americans in general and Asian Indians and Japanese in particular, have higher income than the general United States population. In 1989, the median *household* income in the United States was $30,058. But for all Asian Americans, it was $37,007. Among the Asian Americans, the Asian Indians had the highest median household income of $44,696. The Filipinos ($43,780) and the Japanese ($41,626) had the next highest levels of household income. The Japanese, however, had the highest median *family* income of $51,550 as compared with the Asian Indians' $49,309 (U. S. Department of Commerce, 1993a, 1993b).

卐

CLINICAL IMPLICATIONS

Speech-language-hearing professionalists who work with Asian Indians with communicative disorders face a formidable linguistic diversity. The number of speech-language pathologists in the United States who speak one of the languages of India is negligible. A majority of speech-language pathologists of Asian Indian origin are university faculty members or researchers, not clinical service providers in public schools. Also, a speech-language pathologist who speaks one of the languages of India is more likely to face a client of Asian Indian origin who does not speak his or her language. It should be remembered that even in India, the medium of communication between different linguistic communities is English.

Unlike some other culturally diverse groups such as the Hmong or the Mexican Hispanics, Asian Indians have greater English proficiency. Their children tend to learn English as their strong second language and, in many cases, as their first language. Therefore, because of the way Asian Indians use English in India and abroad, assessment and treatment of communicative disorders for many Asian Indian clients may be appropriately done in English. However, as with any other culturally and linguistically diverse group, the clinician should find out the dominant language of the client and his or her family. If

English is not the dominant language, the clinician faces the same challenges as he or she would in working with a linguistically different client. In such cases, the clinician should follow the guidelines of the American Speech-Language-Hearing Association (1985). A general understanding of the cultural and linguistic background of the client is essential in all cases, including those that receive assessment and treatment services offered in English. It is hoped that this chapter has served the purpose of giving an introduction to the cultural and linguistic heritage of India.

⊓

REFERENCES

American Speech-Language-Hearing Association. (1985). Clinical management of communicatively handicapped minority language populations. *Asha, 27,* 57–60.

Basham, A. L. (1975). *A cultural history of India.* Oxford: Oxford University Press.

Basham, A. L. (1967). *The wonder that was India.* London: Sidgwick & Jackson.

Bright, W. (1990) *Language variation in South Asia.* New York: Oxford University Press.

Chatterji, S. K. (1965). *Dravidian.* Annamalainagar, India: Annamalai University.

Mahajan, V. D. (1970). *History of India: From beginning to 1526 AD.* New Delhi: S. Chand & Co.

Majumdar, R. C. (1968). *Ancient India.* Delhi: Motilal Banarsidass.

Maps and Publications Ltd. (1991). *Statistical handbook on India.* Madras, India, TT: Author.

Spear, P. (1966). *A history of India* (2 vol.). New York: Penguin.

Smith, D. E., & Karpinski, L. C. (1911). *The Hindu-Arabic numerals.* Boston: Ginn & Company.

Steever S. B. (1993). *Analysis to synthesis: The development of complex verb morphology in the Dravidian languages.* New York: Oxford University Press.

U. S. Department of Commerce. (1993a). *We, the American Asians.* Washington, DC: Author.

U. S. Department of Commerce. (1993b). *We, the Asian and Pacific Islander Americans.* Washington, DC: Author.

Whitney, W. D. (1967). *A Sanskrit grammar.* Cambridge, MA: Harvard University Press.

Zograph, G. A. (1982). *Languages of South Asia, A guide* (Vol. 3). London: Routledge & Kegan Paul.

CHANDRA SHEKAR, PH.D.

Dr. Shekar is a Lecturer in Linguistics in the Department of Linguistics at the California State University-Fresno. He received his master's degree in 1986 from the University of Ottawa and his doctorate in 1994 from the University of Washington. Dr. Shekar has specialized in syntactic theory within the Government Binding theory, especially of Dravidian languages of India. He has made a thorough analysis of the syntax of Case assignment in Kannada, a Dravidian language. He has extensive experience in teaching linguistics to both linguistic and non-linguistic majors.

M. N. HEGDE, PH.D.

Dr. M. N. Hegde is a Professor of Communicative Sciences and Disorders at the California State University-Fresno. He received his master's degree in 1961 from the University of Mysore and his doctorate in 1974 from Southern Illinois University at Carbondale. Dr. Hegde has specialized in language and fluency disorders and in treatment efficacy research. He has published numerous articles in scientific and professional journals. Dr. Hegde is the author of several highly regarded and widely adopted textbooks in speech-language pathology and audiology.

CHAPTER 6

"THE CRYING FATHER" AND "MY FATHER DOESN'T LOVE ME": SELECTIVE OBSERVATIONS AND REFLECTIONS ON SOUTHEAST ASIANS AND SPECIAL EDUCATION

KENJI IMA, Ph.D.
PHINGA-EVELYN KHEO, M.S.

Tri Tran, an 8-year-old Vietnamese student, pushes another student during story time. This is one of a many disruptive behaviors the teacher has come to expect from Tri. Not only is he a behavior problem, but Tri has not progressed in reading skills from the previous year. The teacher is uncertain about how to interpret Tri's disruptive behaviors and slow academic progress, and she wonders about whether or not to have him tested for special education. In spite of the public accolades about model Asian students, many teachers have students like Tri in their classrooms and they are puzzled over how to deal with them.

When approaching such students as Tri, teachers face a problem of ascertaining the source of the troubles: Is it linguistic, cultural, traumatic, or neurophysiological in origin, or perhaps a combination of these factors? If one observes heightened anxiety, confusion in the "locus of control," withdrawal or unresponsiveness in a language minority student, can the teacher confidently determine whether or not the child is suffering from acculturative stress, depression, a learning disability, or all of these conditions? And underlying those considerations is the cultural gap issue—how does one ask Tri the proper questions? How should one interpret Tri's responses, given cultural differences between teacher and student? How should one talk to Tri's father and mother regarding his behavior and lack of progress? How does one determine whether or not Tri should be placed in a special education program? If the educator determines Tri belongs in a special education program, how does one convince his parents?

Manifestations of learning problems may have their genesis from a wide variety of factors. Most practitioners are ill-equipped to diagnose the source of these problems, thus leaving untended a large number of students who either remain underserved in the corner of a regular classroom or are moved to a special education program that may not have the resources or skills to deal with the child's linguistic and cultural background. In light of the traditionally low prevalence of such students from Asian groups, many teachers are surprised to see "difficult" children from Southeast Asia and are puzzled about solutions.

We explored these concerns through qualitative observations and interviews with teachers, counselors, aides, and Southeast Asian students. Based on these observations and participant comments, we constructed cultural views of Southeast Asians and the consequences of differing views between Southeast Asians and American professionals. As with all qualitative work, we verified our interpretations by having our informants evaluate them. We remain open to other interpretations and invite others to investigate the gap between service providers and newcomer Southeast Asian refugee students and parents.

Although this chapter explores concerns based on observations and interviews in one school district, we believe the findings are commonplace in districts dealing with Southeast Asian students. Furthermore, we believe these issues to be generic to youth who come from newcomer cultural and language groups. For this chapter we will address mainly Vietnamese refugee students, keeping in mind that although they may share some of the same problems experienced by Cambodian, Hmong, Lao, and Mien refugee youth, we cannot assume that they should be analyzed and interpreted in precisely the same manner. Thus we are cognizant of the dangers of over-generalizing to all Asian newcomer groups and are alerted to the cultural diversity within the larger Asian newcomer pool. In spite of these cautionary remarks, these stories provide a probe into the problems facing Southeast Asians in special education. As an initial step, let us examine two background stories of Southeast Asians.

⊓

THE CRYING FATHER AND MY FATHER DOESN'T LOVE ME: TWO BACKGROUND STORIES

This chapter anecdotally discusses the special educational needs of Southeast Asian youth, particularly the high at-risk student who not only may drop out of school but also may be underserved for special educational needs. Ima (1991) observed delinquency-prone Southeast Asian youth and has concluded that not only are they likely to be underserved in general, but perhaps more tragically their dropping out of school turns out to be a major factor in a delinquency career. School is one of the few institutions that links such youth with the larger society. The severing of that link has major consequences on the life chances of these youth and may influence their participation in the criminal world. Thus, the attempts to keep youths in school leads to special educational services. The first story is about a crying Vietnamese father that highlights an unexpected cultural theme. The second story is about an acculturated refugee youth and her response to her unacculturated parents.

A Vietnamese father is asked to visit the school as part of the procedures for informing parents about children requiring special education services. As the father did not speak English, a Vietnamese translator was provided and the father listened to an array of educational specialists discuss his son's problems. The label "special education" has no real equivalency in the Vietnamese language, as the concept does not exist in that language. The translator could not think of a proper word except to suggest that his son had a "mental problem." This comment was more than the father could stand and he burst into tears. What he had heard was a litany of "criticisms" of his son. Everyone felt sorry for the father and one teacher, out of sympathy, put her arms around him.

The Vietnamese translator was caught off guard by the teacher's actions and immediately knew that this was a most inappropriate action. He would have preferred that the educators leave the man alone. One might ask, why should the educators have left the room when it seemed so evident that the father was upset and "needed" comfort. What would you prefer if you were the man? Many American-born teachers may not have put their arms around the man, but surely most would see this as a generous effort to give comfort an upset parent. For the Vietnamese man, this was the worst action the teacher could have taken—the gesture reinforced the parent's loss of face and made the situation far worse for him. Walking out of the classroom would have been seen as a sign of respect in the Vietnamese culture, as it would have given the man time to recover his composure without further humiliation and reduce the possibility that he might withdraw his child from school.

This case illustrates a problem of conflicting cultural expectations. The relationship between teacher and parent presents a problem of face that can be handled by the use of a knowledgeable go-between. In the above example, it would have been preferable to prepare the parent for the teachers' comments by having a Vietnamese-speaking aide or interpreter discuss the various notions of special education with the father before the meeting. Generally speaking, Vietnamese parents see a child as an extension of themselves and, therefore, judgment of the child is also considered as a judgment of the parent. In this case, the parent viewed his son's "mental illness" label as a judgment of what he did as a parent—hence, his feeling that he was being criticized. One can imagine the concerns running through his mind as he listened to the enumeration of the various special education assessment terms: "I didn't hit my child. I feed and clothe him. What could I have done to make him have mental illness?" For many refugees who are struggling to survive, such a session can be devastating, as such events threaten their rationale for fleeing Vietnam to make a better life for their child. The crying was probably uncontrollable, but the gesture of the teacher putting her arms around him only served to increase his loss of face. Further, it made him feel as if he had no control over his life or that of his son.

This is probably an exceptional case in terms of the father breaking down as he did. One Vietnamese teacher hearing of this story said, "He probably loved his son very much." Other Vietnamese parents are less likely to express emotions so openly. Some parents will react with anger over the implication that their child is not "normal," expressing words like "It's not true." Or if they are embarrassed, they may say "He's lazy" or "He's always been that way." And some even feign giving up, saying that nothing can be done. Nevertheless, the underlying cultural themes (face, close identity of child and parent, protection of face through the use of go-betweens, the cultural strangeness of special education and all of its associated terms) is commonly shared by most refugee parents.

The crying father story emerged in a discussion among Asian teachers dealing with communication between Asian and non-Asian individuals. This concern about communication arose over conflicts between persons from different ethnic groups at schools. A common educational response is to seek "conflict resolution," but this approach raises questions about the cultural appropriateness for Asian individuals. One proposed resolution strategy is to have the conflicting individuals face each other and "clear the air," with each side expressing its viewpoint while holding in abeyance one's views until each party has had sufficient time to air a view. We asked Asian individuals about this strategy and a common response was "Don't muddy the water" or "Don't do it." They regarded such a strategy as a losing proposition, as it would be likely to result in someone losing face. They considered it too great a gamble and suggested having a mediator negotiate a mutually agreeable solution. This might take several conversations with each side until the go-between could find a mutually agreeable solution. This strategy preserves the respect for the conflicting sides and provides a cooling-off period. Additionally, if the go-between could have some position of authority in the parent's culture, it would give added legitimacy to the negotiation.

The problem lies in a fundamental difference in cultural notions regarding honor and dignity (Berger, Berger, & Kellner, 1981)—representing traditional and modern views. Most Southeast Asian adults would subscribe to the notion of honor while the American counterpart would emphasize dignity. Honor means acting according to traditional cultural norms. For example, traditional views of men and women emphasize strong morality codes and rigid social distinctions between the sexes. By contrast, modernization enhances concern for people as individuals, which is expressed in the concept of dignity.

Whereas various categories of people have distinctive codes of honor, the modern notion of dignity is seen as a universal human trait, originating in the inherent value of everyone. We recognize the dignity of others when we acknowledge our common humanity by overlooking social differences. Though these reflections may seem remote from the concern over special education, they are central.

Special educational questions, puzzling to most Southeast Asian parents, are more than likely to generate negative reactions from them, particularly as the queries imply negative judgments of parents in the parents' minds. This raises the issue of face, central to the crying father story, which may seem unreasonable to American-born professionals, but nevertheless can create extreme difficulties for the home-school relationship. The solution may take several hours rather than 10 minutes. That time can be used to reassure the parent of the propriety of the parent's values and that the process is not an implicit judgment that the parent's values are wrong. A preliminary briefing can also give the parent time to absorb the concepts of American education. Above all, it is important to emphasize facts and solutions rather than emotions or speculative interpretations of states of mind. In the end, if the authority figure or go-between has brought concessions from each side, then the final solution often involves the invocation of authority as the final stamp of resolution. Even if there are some reservations on one or both sides, the problem will have been solved. This example illustrates the complexity of approaching Southeast Asian parents. As one Vietnamese professional stated, "You have to be flexible." Let us look at another story, but now from the view of an Americanized child and her Vietnamese father.

An Asian school counselor saw a Vietnamese special education student who cried every time they had a conference because the youth felt her father did not express love for her. She wanted sweet words from her father and hugs of affection. Instead, what she experienced was rejection through the parent's continual negative assessment of her accomplishments, such as her grades were never discussed as adequate, her parents mentioned publicly to others in front of the girl that she was not doing all that well. She reacted negatively to these comments and even felt so frustrated that she considered not trying as hard in the future as she had in the past.

The counselor observed that Vietnamese parents do not praise their children in front of them, fearing that the words might reduce their motivation to achieve. The parents actually wanted nothing but the highest academic performance and would not accept anything less. The counselor suggested that many parents believe that saying positive things might reduce their child's motivation. If the parent is going to say something positive, it will be said out of earshot of the child. Thus, if the child wants to know what the parent feels, it is possible to discover this by asking an intermediary who may have heard positive comments. Beyond not receiving spoken praise, the counselor asked the student whether or not her parents prepared special foods for her. To this question she replied yes. The Asian counselor told her that this was the parents' sign of affection and love and not to expect spoken expressions of love. The student was still unhappy, but came to accept this interpretation. Although food indulgence is a common sign of affection, parents also express their emotions through generous gift giving to the child, even if the parents are short of money.

What does this story tell us about understanding Vietnamese parents? Making bridges between a child and a foreign-born parent is a critical issue. As typically experienced by all newcomer groups, Southeast Asian youth face a gap between parents born and raised in Southeast Asia versus those children reared largely in the United States. The gap affects not only families but whole communities. An obvious solution is for all to learn to talk to each other, but it is easier said than done—especially given the face issue. As parents wish their children to succeed, we know that parents have to be an integral part of the solution in developing that communication between generations. The older generation faces the shock of losing its authority, especially when there is role reversal. This occurs when children talk to authorities on behalf of families because they are more fluent in the English language. The rapid acculturation of American ways by the Asian youth creates even a larger gap. In short, there often develops a deep silence between parent and child.

Educators wishing to reduce the at-risk behavior of youth—truancy, dropping out of school, poor test performance, drugs and other substance abuse, and delinquency—will have to address differences between Asian and American parental approaches. In America, we are taught that positive reinforcement is the best strategy and we justify this on our assumption that positive reinforcement leads to a higher level of self-concept that in turn leads to greater behavioral compliance. In other words, we presume youths who think well of themselves are better students. By contrast, Vietnamese and other Asian parents, particularly those from Confucian-based cultures, are less likely to praise their children and instead practice "negative" reinforcement as we noted above, such as when a child brings home a report card with four As and one B grade, the parent will dwell on the B grade asking why it too was not an A grade.

From the American view, that traditional approach is likely to create anxiety and possibly a future reluctance to try to achieve—thus the preference for praising the four A grades and possibly encouraging an improvement on the B grade, instead of emphasizing that the B should be an A grade. As mentioned above, from the Asian parent's perspective, the overly generous praising would likely reduce the motivation for effort for future academic endeavors, quite the opposite of the American cultural assumption. As a Vietnamese proverb states, "When we love our children, we give them a beating; when we hate our children, we give them sweet words." Another version of this same idea are these words: "Fish will be rotten without salt; children will always be rotten if they have disobeyed their parents" (Freeman, 1989, p. 28). These proverbs suggest that parents must be hard on children to instill discipline in them and to do otherwise suggests that parents do not love them. In other words, their issue is one of creating a child who is self-disciplined with little regard to the notion of feeling good about oneself. The assumption they make is that through experience the child will come to appreciate the wisdom of this approach. This Asian parenting approach raises criticism from teachers and even from students who have accepted the American way. The Americanized student would like praise, as experienced in classrooms, and he or she would like spoken reinforcement rather than silence. They want to talk, but find parents unreceptive. From the Asian parent's view, their world is based on authority and, in this case, the relations of parents to children, there is an inherent power difference between parent and child—leaving no room for initiation from child to parent. To even suggest that the parent listen to the child challenges that fundamental belief. Having to listen to the child implies giving up one's authority.

On the other hand, Asian parents feel a strong obligation to provide for the material well being of their child, especially noted above in the special food preparation and indulgence of the child's food appetite. This is their expression of love. One Vietnamese parent said he would be willing to sell his house to finance his son's education— that is his sign of love. Few expect the overt expression of love as we know it as Americans and thus both American-born teachers as well as Americanized children interpret silence as not showing love. The extent to which Asian parents will make large sacrifices for their children is commonplace. Stevenson and Stigler (1992) document the

Asian parent's willingness to sacrifice. The researchers asked if the parents of fifth grade students had bought their children a desk—in Taipei, Taiwan, 95% of parents had, in Sendai, Japan, 98%, and in Minneapolis 63%. They also found that Chicago parents were 50% more likely to have children do chores than Beijing parents. One Chinese parent said, "My child is too busy. All she has to do is her duty as a student." These observations may surprise Americans but they document a fundamental difference in parenting between American and Asian cultures.

Southeast Asian parents have the same attitude toward their role as parents. Among the numerous stories of parental self-sacrifice we have heard, we offer a case of a Vietnamese refugee family. Both mother and father were professionals in Vietnam, but decided to leave their homeland to give their two children a better life, beyond the traditional Vietnamese rationale of seeking freedom. They arrived in the United States while still in their forties and could not find professionals jobs comparable to their Vietnamese positions. Instead, the father found work in a kitchen and the mother worked as a seamstress. They found that "Life in America is harder than expected." They experienced physical problems as a result of their hard work—the father developed a visual problem and the mother had a heart problem, but they accepted their health degradation as part of the price for making a better life for their children. Both children matriculated to prestigious colleges. Thus, in spite of the deterioration of their health, the parents are proud and see full justification for their sacrifices. This is a story of parental love.

Among Vietnamese people, parents feel they have the right to tell the child what to do, but the child has little if any rights to communicate feelings back to parents. Instead, if the child wishes to communicate back to the parent, he or she will talk to older siblings about his or her feelings, expressed in the form of a complaint that does not overtly suggest to the sibling that the message be passed on. Then that sibling communicates the feeling to the next older one and so on until the oldest talks to the mother. This is a classic instance of the Asian reputation for being indirect. This is how to say something without appearing to say it. This method preserves authority and avoids endangering face. Beyond this mechanism is the common phenomenon of people talking behind each other's back in the form of extensive gossiping. Eventually, it is hoped that the news will get to the intended recipient who, in turn, makes alterations in his or her behavior, if it is deemed to be appropriate. This approach violates the

American sense of being direct and frank about one's feelings whether between parent and child or teacher and student.

When an experienced Asian counselor counsels parents, she or he often separates parents from children, giving each side plenty to time to air grievances and views, thus avoiding direct confrontation and the potential loss of face. However, when Asian newcomer parents are confronted by typical American professionals, they are told to communicate directly with each other. For example, when American courts deal with Asian parents who are charged with child abuse, the parent is often assigned to a therapist whose job it is to teach the parent how to avoid further physical abuse and how to use alternative forms of parental control. Those therapists emphasize not using physical means and learning to use various techniques of assertive discipline—invoking time-outs, removing privileges for unacceptable behavior and using positive reinforcement. Asian newcomer parents resist trying such parenting strategies and argue that traditional physical discipline is more effective. Counselors have to teach them step-by-step about alternative strategies, introducing each strategy with lavish encouragement to try out the new methods. Asian counselors mention that though these alternative approaches may violate the parents' sense of cultural appropriateness, there is an effective way to convey the message. They begin by reinforcing and validating the value of traditional Asian culture, while at the same time telling the parents that the traditional methods do not work in U.S. society and that they need to invent a new way to implement traditional values. Then, counselors discuss the alternative strategies without judging the parents culture and by emphasizing that alternative methods produce results. The demonstration has to be concrete and slowly introduced. This approach takes the edge out of the implicit negative judgment of the parent and focuses on solutions and on "what works."

The two cases, the crying father and my father doesn't love me, address cultural agendas Asians carry to school that teachers need to address. Although teachers view the potential special education student as an individual, Southeast Asian parents treat their children as extensions of themselves with de-emphasis on overt expressions of affections. Next, we look at the schooling context affecting the relationship of teacher to students and their parents. In the following section, we describe the context within which Tri's teacher makes her decision on what to do about Tri and how to effectively communicate with his parents. Should she refer him or not for special education? If yes, how should it be done? What are some issues in getting a proper assessment and placement for Tri? What are the broader implications for Asian newcomers? Overall, these questions point toward the need for institutional inclusion—or how Asian newcomers can and should be treated with equity and respect.

⊓

THE SCHOOLING CONTEXT

Although all school districts have resources to solve Tri's problems, most schools have a series of barriers that exclude language minority students such as Tri. Let us examine the schooling context in which Tri and his teacher face each other. Bilingual students, such as Tri, are theoretically eligible for all educational services, in addition to second language instruction. Nevertheless, it is difficult to get the full range of services for a newcomer student, because most districts have yet to develop procedures to deal with the overall needs of these students. For example, in the district studied, there is little coordination between special education and English as a second language departments. Theoretically, if parents insist on services, their child is likely to receive services, because laws support such requests. However, most newcomer parents are unaware of their rights and, even if they are aware, they are more than likely to be afraid of asserting their rights, resulting in the lack of services to newcomer students. In effect, most newcomers are ill equipped to deal with the politics of requesting and receiving school services.

A central issue facing Vietnamese and other newcomer Asian students is the language barrier. Although there are bilingual personnel, in this district there is a pervasive assumption that translation needs should be provided by the English as a second language program (ESL). Were they to accept all requests for translation, the bilingual staff would have little time left for their main responsibilities, including in-service training and guidance for primary language and ESL classes. Therefore, ESL administrators have attempted to persuade other divisions to hire bilingual personnel to handle translation needs. Administrators of other divisions argue that they do not need a full-time translator or that their budgets are too limited to hire bilingual personnel. Those divisions having administrators who can speak two or more languages are more likely to agree on the need for bilingual personnel. An example is the new head of the community relations division who, himself, is a Spanish-English bilingual speaker. He has taken on the responsibility of district translation needs. The previous administrator, a monolingual English speaker, though sensitive to the needs of ethnic minority students had only one translator on his staff.

Most administrative heads are reluctant to address the translation issue in large part because of their lack of understanding of the bilingual student. Typically they place higher priority on other issues. The response to the needs of bilingual students is characterized by a crisis management approach of attempting to retain existing programs while dealing with the increasing numbers of non-English speakers. Their response has been to assign LEP (limited English proficient) students to the second language program rather other programs—defining a student's problem as second language learning rather than special learning problems.

Even if translators are made available, they usually have little special training. To shift from the reactive stance to a proactive one requires administrators, other decision makers, or community organizations to employ special political pressure, which few are willing to apply. The shift in thinking requires a fundamental shift in the educator's paradigm. For example, when educators think of language minority students in terms of color, they use their experience with African Americans as the model for intervention, such as hiring teachers as role models, for example, a monolingual English-speaking Chinese American teacher for bilingual Vietnamese students. However, addressing the needs of language minority students requires an understanding of language differences and associated cultural differences between teacher and student. Simply using existing English language documents does not address cultural curriculum needs nor does hiring a person of the same race/ethnicity automatically address language and cultural differences.

Even if a Vietnamese person is hired, language and cultural problems are not automatically solved. At several schools that have had long-time employed Southeast Asian aides, the principal identifies these individuals as the school's response to the needs of language minority students; however, those aides have established a special niche for themselves as extensions of the principal and other staff. This process results in "rubber stamping" what administrators and other monolingual English speaking staff believe, such as the desirability of English submersion classes versus primary language classes. From the community viewpoint, these aides protect existing practices and prevent changes that might benefit language minority students. Refugee personnel make frequent comments about the employee's responsibility to support his or her supervisor as the first priority and only secondarily to consider the student's needs. This reflects their traditional expectations of a patron-client relationship that makes the personal relation of subordinate to supervisor their prime consideration.

The special education department does not have a staff member who speaks an Asian language, other than an aide who speaks Tagalog. When they find a student who is identified as a potential special education candidate, they search for a translator and rarely locate a person familiar with special education terminology. When the division had special funding for parent contact, they hired bilingual personnel. But, when that funding ended, they eliminated bilingual personnel except for Spanish speakers. In place of the bilingual staffing, they hire contractors for translation services. One consultant, a Chinese-English bilingual translator, who also worked for the courts, complained that this division paid a paltry sum—less than $7 per hour, much less than the court rate of $20 to $70 per hour. For those who are unfamiliar with the translation issue, one should note that many English words are extremely difficult to translate, requiring considerable expertise to find the right words. Therefore, specially trained and experienced translators are mandatory for professional quality translations. Given this district's ad hoc translation policy, special education translations are likely to be uneven, at best, and faulty for most encounters between special education specialists and language minority students and their parents, especially those who speak a language other than Spanish. In an interview with a Vietnamese student who was identified as a potential special education case, the resource teacher called on a site-based Vietnamese aide to do the translation. According to a Vietnamese observer, the translation was of poor quality, resulting in a poor evaluation.

Beyond the translation issue is a general problem of access to special education by language minority students. First, teachers wishing to have a LEP student identified as a special education case must get the approval of the second language department. According to school counselors, the special education counselor is not responsive. Recently, a Vietnamese student was referred for special education because he was acting out. The counselor was unhappy with the testing because of the poor translation. The student was refused admission to special education and so the counselor requested another test, but has been refused. She requested the test in September, but it was not until January that a response was issued. The student's ESL teacher claims the student needs special education because he was behind seventh grade students and should have been at the ninth grade level. Compared with other newcomers, he was doing poorly.

He had no schooling in Vietnam and his father said his Vietnamese vocabulary is limited. At 15 years of age, is he simply immature or really in need of special education? The site counselor is frustrated over the refusal of the special education department to respond more proactively.

Although the ESL program is developing guidelines for testing LEP students, there remains a need for improved student assessments. Students are either misplaced or are not given instruction appropriate for their level of literacy and academic competence. This results in students who "drown" in overly difficult materials or are "bored" by watered-down materials. Refugee teachers and other personnel comment about students who either complain about filling out meaningless assignments and other "Mickey Mouse" work or are lost by their lack of understanding the English language. Both extremes result in underserved students who often skip classes. This inadequate monitoring of the English language level of students feeds into the confusion over whether or not to test students for special education.

To document the general inequitable integration of Southeast Asian students, let us look at the Gifted and Talented Education (GATE) department, which has made concessions to language minority students by increasing the identification of Filipino students and creating a special program for Spanish-speaking students. They have recently begun to create a general strategy for increasing gifted placement of language minority students through the adoption of a nonverbal identification test, but, as a general practice, there remains a less than full effort to identify Southeast Asian students. Recently, for example, a teacher asked for assistance in dealing with a Cambodian limited-English-proficient student who received very high math scores, yet scored far below average on reading scores. It did not occur to the teacher, until an outsider made the suggestion, to place him in an advanced math class while keeping him in ESL classes. Furthermore, despite his high math scores, the teacher did not consider him as a candidate for gifted education. Although the GATE program is not directly responsible for this teacher's ignorance, it illustrates a pervasive lack of concern or perhaps ignorance that results in the under representation of language minority students in the GATE program. Millet (1993) estimates the Southeast Asian under-representation level to be about 25%.

Finally, still to be addressed are the reclassification criteria of LEP students and assessments that accurately measure the academic progress of LEP students. Exited students remained unmonitored, even though teachers at every site mention the continuing need to provide those LEP students with continued language assistance. The problem of reclassification also affects newcomer students who transfer to another school. Even though their previous school may have reclassified the student as eligible for regular English-language-based courses, the receiving school may reverse the reclassification and place them in ESL classes, which students consider a demotion. This problem of inconsistent classification remains unsolved. Recently, 15 Vietnamese students who had transferred from a middle school to a senior high school were rejected for regular English language classes and were reassigned to ESL classes, even though the middle school ESL teachers considered them prepared for regular classes. Part of the problem is the use of different tests and criteria for reclassification. These students were frustrated and felt they were being placed behind by this decision. A Vietnamese staff person interviewed these students and was told that part of the problem was the possibility that the senior high would lose an ESL position if they did not fill up those classes. Perhaps it is a reflection of internal politics of teachers attempting to retain their class assignments, but it is also clear that the inconsistency of reclassification creates problems for newcomer students and their morale.

Then, the general lack of primary language knowledge and cultural understanding of Southeast Asians among American-born teachers and allied professionals results in problematic referral of Southeast Asian students to special education programs—partly because these are seen as programs with smaller student-teacher ratios. However, precisely because of the lack of clarity about the source and nature of refugee students' learning problems, questions might be raised about the appropriateness of assigning them to special education classes. If there are no bilingual services available, then this may be a reasonable placement, if only because those students may be apt to receive more individual attention from teachers. This can be all the more true if the specialist is informed about the range of possible sources of learning difficulties faced by refugee students (e.g., second language acquisition, acculturation, trauma) and makes allowance for these as part of the services rendered. If teachers operate on the assumption that they are dealing with linguistically disordered or special education students as traditionally defined, then there is cause to be skeptical of such a placement, for all of the reasons earlier mentioned.

Given this larger organizational context, teachers cannot make decisions in the best interests of the child without considering the practical ramifications—simply put, the reality which means that commonsense proposals will fall short of feasibility. Resources, staffing, special programs, assessment/placement practices, and the general programs have yet to be made equitable for Southeast Asian youth, reflecting the traditional inertia of organizations to retain the familiar and to resist change. We have cited the following litany of problems facing special educational assessment for Southeast Asian students: (1) parents who are unprepared and even unwilling to invoke their rights as parents to be advocates for their children, (2) organizational conflicts between second language and special education programs, (3) the lack of knowledge and misplaced attitudes of professionals, (4) the lack of training among translators, (5) confusion of cultural and linguistic needs with misuse of racial identification, (6) misuse of aides, (7) inadequate assessment/placement practices, and (8) the lack of coordination between grade level placement. The district in this study is probably no less behind in their ability to incorporate Southeast Asian students than most districts having these students. Nevertheless, this institutional resistance to change means that ultimately the responsibility rests on the shoulders of individual classroom teachers. Teachers have to make decisions under trying conditions and, if they can catch the attention of specialists teams, then they have to become advocates on behalf of their students. Surely one step toward a solution, beyond their concern for their students, is the teacher's understanding of the cultural/linguistic gap between the teacher and student that was addressed in a prior section. Recognizing this, let us now examine some stories from the encounters between Southeast Asian students, parents, and teachers.

⌐

CULTURAL MISUNDERSTANDINGS AND SPECIAL EDUCATION: OBSERVATIONS OF DISCOVERING AND ASSESSING VIETNAMESE STUDENTS FOR SPECIAL EDUCATION

In San Diego, as one travels from one community to another, one notices shifts in parent attitudes toward their own children. In the lowest income area, Vietnamese parents speak little English but demand traditional behavior from their children. In a working class neighborhood, about half of the parents speak English, and in a mixed to affluent suburban area, most speak English. As the Viet-namese parents move up the social ladder, which is reflected in the social standing of the neighborhood, their children are more Ameri-canized—often getting out of hand, lacking discipline, and talking back to teachers. In spite of these variations, a persistent preoccupa-tion among parents is the expectation that children will assist fami-lies, particularly by doing well in school, which will position them to have access to better paying jobs. Ideally, all parents have high expec-tations for their children as suggested in the previous stories about Vietnamese parents and their children.

In the first area, where most parents speak little English, many reeducation camp survivors live. For example, an ex-Vietnamese sol-dier who arrived with his family found himself too old (around 45 to 50 years old) to make the adjustment of learning English and getting a job. As is often the case, the wife took over as the supporter, learning English and entering the world of work. As a result, the father was not only frustrated about being impoverished, but also with a feeling that he could do little to overcome poverty. Currently, he is receiving $600 per month and collects cans for money through recycling. His wife works as a hairdresser. He wonders whether or not he made the right choice in coming to the United States. Nevertheless, he is here and sees no choice but to struggle. He prays that his son will succeed in school.

As a result of these conditions, the children are placed under great pressure to help their family. The children often are withdrawn and keep their problems to themselves. They are required to take care of siblings and handle many of the responsibilities of their parents. Under these conditions of stress, if they find the strength to endure, they may even end up becoming high achievers. On the other hand, if they buckle under these pressures, they may be suicidal or seek alter-native self-destructive ends such as gangs and drugs. Females are under greater family pressure, which results in depression, suicidal tendencies, running away from home, but rarely joining gangs. On the other hand, the males are under less pressure but get into more delinquent troubles. If they have problems with English on entering the sixth grade, then they are at-risk of school failure. If one tracks an unsuccessful Vietnamese student at the K-5 level, by middle school one will notice the youngster having school problems frequently reflected in absenteeism and possibly dropping out of school. Most Vietnamese students will show up in school, but if they have prob-lems with academics, they will eventually have attendance problems (Ima, 1991).

The pressure to succeed is extremely strong, and whenever students find themselves failing, they suffer the consequences as manifest in depression, fighting, emulating "wannabe" gang behaviors, ditching school, showing disrespect to teachers, and dropping out of school. Among Southeast Asian juvenile delinquents, school failure is strongly associated with antisocial behaviors. For the teacher, these are signs to notice and to consider whether or not the lack of progress may reflect a learning handicap.

The emphasis on academic success is so deeply rooted that the student's major self-concept rests on school success or failure. Often parents do not communicate with their children nor do they understand the school system in this country, as found in the "my father doesn't love me" story. Among Vietnamese parents, the unrelenting pressure to succeed is reflected in the comparisons made between children in front of "everybody." A mother might say, "His sister is getting all As," or "Oh, do you know that 'so-and-so' was accepted at a famous university." Both statements are made with the implications that the less successful child is supposed to try harder. In one Vietnamese family of three children identified as gifted, parents made ongoing invidious comparisons between them, resulting in the "putting down" of a lower performing child. The only way a child knows what his or her parent thinks is through indirect means, such as overhearing comments between parents discussing their pleasure in knowing their children are doing well.

Given the preoccupation to do well in school, if a teacher raises questions about special education, parents are likely to be negative. As mentioned in the story about the crying father, many parents interpret the term "special education" as a label for being "dumb" or that "something's wrong with the child." Most often they do not understand the label. One case illustrates how to deal with Vietnamese parents. A Vietnamese male student had shown no progress for 2 years and was considered for assignment to a special education class. The Vietnamese-speaking counselor interviewed the child and parents separately. She discovered the student had difficulty expressing himself; he could not make complete sentences and could not combine sentences in his native language. After a conversation with the parents, she discovered that he had had to repeat classes at both the first and second grade levels in Vietnam, leading her to believe the child had learning problems beyond the second language issue. This information was combined with his U.S. school failure to justify his placement in a special education class. The special education teacher used visual materials and the students had one-to-one contact with the teacher's aide. Both measures produced results that pleased the student and parents. After seeing the progress, the parents accepted the program. This example illustrates the importance of emphasizing factual matters with Asian parents.

A trained and sensitive translator can elicit an appropriate life history to ascertain facts about a student's life that may help to explain difficulties in a student's school performance. Another Vietnamese case further reinforces this view. In this instance, a Vietnamese student entered U.S. schooling in kindergarten and despite having much difficulty acquiring the English language was advanced from grade to grade. Finally, one teacher wondered why the student was still at ESL level 2, 1 being the most basic level, rather than participating in regular English-speaking classes. Teachers defined the problem as discipline, because the youth would act out and hit other children. Furthermore, he wore clothes of the "wannabe" gangsters, which further reinforced the teachers' interpretation of discipline as the problem. However, a Vietnamese-speaking counselor examined his spelling tests and found that he only used consonants and rarely vowels. This was a clue, not about discipline and the lack of English language development, but about a potential special education case. The father was then invited to a school meeting and interviewed by the counselor. She discovered that the mother had a difficult childbirth with this child. When the child came out of the womb, the father described the son as having black and blue coloring, an indication of a lack of oxygen, a potential retardation case.

This father did not consider the information about childbirth important, but rather dwelled on how much better his other children were doing in school. The other children were doing A-level schoolwork, and the father was very frustrated over this child's slow progress and on occasions hit his son. This situation was especially difficult for the father who said his wife had been left behind in Vietnam as a sacrifice so that he and the children could come to America. However once here, the father became alcoholic, leaving his daughter to take over the role of mother to the troubled student. Although the particular learning problem does not stem directly from the home circumstances, those conditions exacerbated the youth's school problems, particularly his emulation of gang clothing and behaviors. Why, after 6 years of schooling, did this youth's teachers continue to treat him as an ESL student rather than as one having learning disabilities? Why, given his troubled behaviors, would teachers pass him from grade to grade, even noting that he had not been progressing in the English language? Although the teachers were not trained to discover special education students from among non-English speaking students, they were preoccupied with getting rid of a troublesome student by passing him through the system.

A seventh grade teacher wondered why his Vietnamese student was reading at the first grade level, especially as the student had attended American schools since he was 5 years old. The student could not read all of the words in a Sesame Street book, was behind in his homework, and he had trouble copying words—copying by the letter rather than by the word. The teacher noticed these deficiencies, but did nothing about them until another teacher challenged him about this student's low performance. Because the student was not a behavior problem, the teacher was happy to have him in her class. The student had been graded for his good behavior and efforts rather than performance. An examination of the student's elementary folder revealed comments which documented a history of being promoted for good behavior, despite the student's low level of literacy—typical comments included "cannot read or write but cooperative." In both this and the previous case, we have contradictory assessments (good and bad students) but the same outcome—movement of language minority students from grade to grade without someone saying "The emperor has no clothes" or "This student is not progressing."

In yet another case, a Vietnamese student had neurological problems identified by professionals from an Asian health clinic. He was assigned to a special education class and still had problems making academic progress. Nevertheless, he was passed from grade to grade because his teachers considered him too old for his grade level. He also was a behavior problem, disrupting the classroom and even showing disrespect towards his teachers. In interviews with his parents, educators discovered that when he was 3 years old, this student had fallen into a well and was unconscious for 3 to 4 hours. In tests, he showed a mild level of retardation. When he was finally transferred to a high school, teachers continued to emphasize his behavioral problems and overlooked his retardation status. According to a Vietnamese counselor, "They just kept promoting him." Finally he reached such a high level of frustration that he dropped out of school. The parents were uneducated, but rarely do any Vietnamese parents associate early childhood problems with current low performance. "As a child he was always sick." "You know when he was 3 years old he was involved in an accident and then he was slow. But that's fate."

Though there is a critical problem of treatment, the importance of this case is the process of gaining information about the student's background that led to the retardation assessment. First, in this case as well in the above mentioned cases, Vietnamese parents are not likely to volunteer information such as the difficulty of childbirth or early childhood injury. To elicit such information, interviewers have to ask specific questions about childbirth or incidents that may have damaged the child's neurological condition. The interviewing skills which this Vietnamese counselor brought to these assessments were based on training in a health agency. This training emphasized an intensive intake interview, including the use of probing questions regarding the child's health history and an emphasis on ascertaining the sources of the child's behavioral problems before looking into the cognitive and emotional sources of difficulties. The counselor suggests a process of first addressing the language issue—for the newly arrived, interviewing in Vietnamese and for those who have lived here for 6 or more months, English may be used. Then one investigates discipline and related issues. Approaching the Vietnamese child's medical history is difficult, requiring development of a good rapport with the parents. This means spending much time with them before asking sensitive questions. Then one searches the child's life history for neurological factors, such as traumatic experiences in the home country and then more recent family disturbances. Lastly, Vietnamese parents will be open to solutions if they are desperate. What they want is evidence of change. Once they see results, then they will be more cooperative.

In the above cases, the issue was the discovery of special education need for students in addition to their limited English condition. However, it is also possible to misidentify a special educational need among the newcomer students. Usually, when a refugee child has difficulty speaking in English, one would assume that one might use the child's primary language. But what if the child speaks neither language well? One teacher had such a Cambodian child in her classroom and assumed the child was a candidate for special education. The counselor observed the child and interviewed her mother. She found that during birth the mother had a mental health problem and as a result did not bond with the child. The father was missing. The mother could not communicate well, probably the result of some trauma experienced during the Pol Pot years. At any rate, there were many unanswered questions about the immaturity of the child. The interview was conducted in English, as a Cambodian translator was unavailable. The counselor debated whether to test the second grade child at that time or delay testing, fearing that the child could be labeled prematurely as retarded. The teacher interpreted the child's lack of expression as reflecting a disability, but the counselor felt it was necessary to get the child's viewpoint. The counselor recommended waiting for a year to see whether or not the child would improve. To everyone's surprise, the child did show marked improvement. After investigating the case further, the counselor discovered that the child was a witness to her mother's beating by her boyfriend, resulting in her withdrawal, hence her lack of expression. After the boyfriend left, the child began speaking normally and does not now require special educational services. Very likely, nurturing teachers made a difference beyond the positive effect of the departure of the abusive male. Although it is not absolutely certain that it completely explains the improvements, the change of home environment remains the best explanation thus far. Additionally, this experience suggests the complexity of dealing with potential special education children involving factors outside of the school setting. Even though the counselor did not speak the Cambodian language, her familiarity with Southeast Asian cultures gave her the additional insights and skills to ferret out the nonschool factors.

The next case, "a hyper Vietnamese child," illustrates a case of misidentification. A second grade Vietnamese student was seen by the teacher as "hyper" and thus was referred to a local Asian mental health agency. Drugs were prescribed for him, but his father did not follow the instructions. Instead of two pills he gave his son one pill. The youngster is now in the fourth grade, but he still cannot read or write. A new Vietnamese-speaking teacher was assigned to his class who was unaware of the student's prior history. The teacher discovered that the child sees a "sh" as a "s" and began helping him to make the proper distinctions. Following a course of naiveté about the child's history, he began to teach the child how to read. The question raised by the teacher was why the student had not been taught to read in the first place. The ESL program did not teach reading. In contrast, the student's experiences while actually learning to read was associated with relative calmness. In fact, the new teacher did not see him as a discipline problem. Furthermore, the teacher noted that the student was particularly quick in math. This case suggests that the rapid diagnosis of having a "hyper" problem based on chemical imbalance circumvented the student's need to learn how to read in the first place. According to the new teacher, the student had been frustrated by not knowing how to respond to the teacher. This case raises questions about the confusion between language acquisition and special educational needs. The youngster's kindergarten teacher had defined him by a negative label that had then been transmitted to the next teacher who then transmitted the same image and so on until the "naive" teacher broke the labeling chain. He simply saw a child who could not read rather than one who was a behavior problem. In retrospect, the child had been seen as giving up too easily on his English language assignments (e.g., stuffing his English materials in his desk), while at the same time doing well on his math assignments and handing them in on time. This case also illustrates a problem in assessing the child in the English language while ignoring his performance in mathematics, which probably provides a better estimate of the child's cognitive skills and progress. Although these are anecdotal individual cases, the process for identifying special education needs among newcomer students can be examined case by case. Let us examine some examples of the identification process.

A tester asked a Vietnamese student to describe the book of Genesis and he replied "Go to hell." The tester's initial reaction was anger over the vulgar words and their implied insult. However, after thinking about the student's remark, the tester asked, "Are you telling me to go to hell or that the book is about hell?" The student replied the latter. In this situation, the student with less than full fluency in English, used a shorthand statement that he thought answered the question and was not intended to insult the teacher. Can you imagine what a less sensitive tester might have done with such a response?

Or take yet another example of testing a Vietnamese student. The tester asked, "What is a young cow?" expecting the response of "calf." Instead the student responds "a young cow." This student did not have a word for calf, so the tester scored him in error. In Vietnamese, this is a correct answer—in Vietnamese a cow is "con bò" and a calf is "con bò con" or "young cow." Therefore, if one uses the Vietnamese rule, "young cow" is correct. This is an example of how the Vietnamese student may be seen as having limited comprehension in English, but competency in Vietnamese.

These stories reflect a larger issue of misassessment of students. Let us examine a placement test using a student's story-telling skills. This instrument, the *Observation Assessment Instrument*, is used to assess a student's language development. The student is shown a picture and is asked to comment on the picture at three levels—*observation of objects* (student is asked to list people and objects in a picture: What do you see in the picture? Name the objects you see in the picture. Do you see anything else? Point to it.); *description of action* (student is asked to tell about the picture using sentences or phrases: What happens in the picture? What else? What else happens? Tell me about that. What makes you think that way?); and *interpretation* (student is asked to expand conversationally from the picture and is expected to express ideas other than those in the picture, such as experiences and feelings: When you look at this picture, what are you thinking? Tell me a story about this picture. If you were in the picture, what would happen to the story? What will you do? Why? If you were in the picture, how would you feel? Why? Why do you think that way?).

Based on the experiences of a Southeast Asian counselor who used this instrument with Southeast Asian students, three issues arose—the use of short prompts, appropriateness of requesting response to unfamiliar objects, and feeling expression. An American teacher will ask "Tell me what happened in the picture?" and expect an answer. However, when one translates that sentence into Vietnamese, you must say "What do you think is happening in the picture? What do you see in the picture? Is there something you can tell me about the picture?" The extra prompts are culturally necessary. In a related issue, Vietnamese students are not inclined to respond to unfamiliar pictures. If the picture is unfamiliar, then the student will say little. One student said in response to an unfamiliar picture, "I don't understand what story you want me to tell." In other words, if the picture is unfamiliar, then one might expect a limited response, thus "reflecting" a poorer vocabulary.

Finally, there is the issue of appropriateness of expressing feelings. Are students going to risk looking foolish or not? There is a difference between going beyond or staying with the familiar. These students are trained to use "tried and true formulas." The prompts in this instrument ask them to speculate about the picture. They will reject this request, especially if the figures are unfamiliar. In the United States, we ask students to be spontaneous and to speculate, leaving them the notion that almost anything goes, mistakes and all. This is production without judgment, commonplace in the newer pedagogies, which encourage production and, thus, development of language skills, as in the whole language approach. On the other hand, the foreign-educated Vietnamese students, along with most other newcomer Asian students, have not been encouraged to be so expressive.

The prompt asking for the student's feelings and personal interpretation creates tension among Vietnamese students who look for clues on how they are "supposed" to answer. By contrast, Asian pedagogies elicit productions that are critically judged. Thus, students are encouraged to reproduce explicated standard productions, such as singing, speaking, drawing. Requesting a response to personal interpretation questions is seen as strange for these newcomers, because in their home schooling they never would have been asked these questions. The questions appear too unstructured—a search for creative thinking. Traditional Vietnamese pedagogy would encourage teachers to ask specific, familiar questions. Students would not be expected to invent something new and surely nothing that strayed too far away from the subject at hand. In the United States, it is acceptable to express one's feelings, but in Vietnam, one is expected to give a more narrowly defined set of acceptable answers. One is not expected to respond about feelings and motives, but demonstrate signs of sophistication and vocabulary. In Vietnamese there are at least two types of vocabulary words, the informal and the formal. The formal vocabulary is mainly based on Chinese origin words called "hán Hiêt" which means "double words" that have subtle meanings. Vietnamese teachers look for those formal words. In the *Observation Assessment Instrument* testing situation, these students are likely to score more poorly than might be the case if the pictures were familiar and the methodology for asking questions more culturally appropriate.

After scoring poorly on a picture identifying test, one refugee looking at a picture on the wall showing Cambodians in a refugee camp commented that they were not really refugees, but Khmer Rouge because they were "too fat" for a typical starving refugee, and, besides, she also noted that one was wearing a Khmer Rouge scarf indicating that they were Khmer Rouge taking advantage of the refugee camp. This rather sophisticated comment reflected the respondent's cultural familiarity with the picture and also displayed a sophisticated analysis of who the people were based on their appearance. Though this comment was not used to calculate the student's score, it clearly displayed a high verbal competence that was not revealed in the regular testing situation. In comparing U.S. and Vietnamese (and other Asian cultures) styles of learning, one finds U.S. pedagogy emphasizing oral language performance especially in ESL classes whereas Asian schools are more likely to emphasize reading and writing in earlier grades.

In this section we began our observations noting the pressures placed on Southeast Asian, especially Vietnamese, students to perform well in schools. At the same time parents resist attempts to have their children labeled as special education students, given both their preoccupation with high academic placement and unfamiliarity with the terms of special education. More than likely, they interpret special education placement to mean their children are mentally unhealthy. We reviewed strategies to circumvent parent resistance including the use of go-betweens and approaches which address parental resistance. Then we reviewed case materials on school- and teacher-based barriers and provided strategies for circumventing cultural barriers to an appropriate assessment and placement of refugee students. Strategies included developing better rapport with parents who can supply additional information regarding a child's life history that may provide clues to the child's learning difficulties. Finally we concluded with the plea for more understanding of the cultural gap between American educators and Southeast Asian parents and students requiring a rethinking of how teachers ought to approach students and parents.

ㅁ

CONCLUSION

Our primary goal was to alert educators to the need to address the cultural differences between themselves and Southeast Asian students and parents, which accounts for the title of this chapter. We explored two primary cases and ancillary observations on both the parents' and students' views revealing that the core of the cultural differences is the parent-child relationship. The discussion of school context illustrated institutional practices that delay or undermine services to newcomer students, complicating the process of addressing the education needs of individual students. Finally, we examined case materials used to identify and assess Southeast Asian, particularly Vietnamese, students for special education services, based on the original theme of addressing cultural differences between teacher and newcomer.

Although newly arrived Southeast Asians are now fewer in number, the problems exemplified in dealing with the population is instructive for thinking about dealing with newcomer populations in general. More than ever, teachers and schools are confronted with students who do not speak the English language and whose home cultures are dramatically different from school culture. Although the particulars of a culture may vary with others in the region, the overall set of challenges remains the same—learning the culture and applying that understanding to special education practices such as assessment, plus reorganizing school practices to deal with a changing student population.

An alternative to the direct referral of Southeast Asians to special education programs is a prereferral process that sorts out the various temporal and social factors (including second language, acculturation, and traumatic refugee experiences) that may shape their learning problems—*prior* to a decision to trigger the typical referral process into special education. The necessary ingredients are a bilingual and bicultural staff capable of dealing with the communication problems—preferably a professionally trained individual or at a minimum a paraprofessional bilingual specialist—and the availability of alternative services. In the prereferral stage, the individual student can be diagnosed, and if his or her problem does not clearly require a language disorder or special education specialist, then the student can be sent to alternative placements, thus obviating the need to rely on special educational programs that may lack appropriate resources or expertise.

ACKNOWLEDGMENT

We give special thanks to Charles Hwang and Quoc Tran who gave us sterling examples and insights into cultural differences between Southeast Asians and American professionals.

REFERENCES

Berger, P., Berger B., & Kellner, H. (1981). *Sociology reinterpreted: An essay on method and vocation.* Garden City, NY: Anchor Books.

Freeman, J. (1989) *Hearts of sorrow: Vietnamese-American lives.* Stanford, CA: Stanford University Press.

Ima, K. (1991). *A handbook for professionals working with Southeast Asian delinquent and at-risk youth.* (Available from Social Advocates for Youth, 3615 Kearny Villa Rd., San Diego, CA 92123)

Millett, S. (1993). *Annual report of GATE student achievement outcomes, 1992–93* (report #690). San Diego, CA: San Diego Unified School District.

Stevenson, H., & James S. (1992). *The learning gap: Why our schools are failing and what we can learn from Japanese and Chinese education.* New York: Summit Books.

KENJI IMA, PH.D.

Dr. Ima is a Professor of Sociology at San Diego State University. He received his doctorate from Northwestern University and has written about Asian Americans on schooling, child abuse, delinquency, professional development, and Southeast Asian refugee adjustments. He is a member of advocacy organizations at the local, state, and national levels dealing with Asian American youth.

PHINGA-EVELYN KHEO, M.S.

Phinga-Evelyn Kheo is the head counselor at Wilson Academy of International Studies in San Diego. She earned her bachelor's degree in French, with a minor in accounting. In 1990, she earned her master's degree in counseling from San Diego State University. Phinga-Evelyn Kheo left Vietnam in 1975 with the first wave of refugees. She found a place for herself in America by seeking higher education. While attending college, she worked as a teaching aide in an elementary school, and this experience led her to a career in counseling. As an advocate for Southeast Asian and other outsider youth, she wants them to have what she, herself, wants—the opportunity to be the best one can be.

PART III

A thorough understanding of cultural and linguistic backgrounds provides a solid foundation to explore the challenges presented by the diversity of students and their families that educators encounter within educational and clinical settings.

A series of challenges lie ahead for educators. The first is the inability to understand the native language of the people they serve; the second is finding reliable interpreters; and the third is the lack of diagnostic skills due to no standard data. Perhaps the biggest challenge is working with the family. Additionally, providing and maintaining an optimal environment for a student to learn a language keep educators honest and earnest.

Part Three discusses the needs for pre-assessment, strategies for assessment, and intervention. Cheng, in Chapters 7 and 8, presents in-depth case studies to illustrate the significance of culture in shaping a person's thoughts and decision making and critical consideration in pre-assessment and assessment. Chang, Lai, and Shimizu, in Chapter 9, provide some helpful strategies to ensure educational success. Since the goal of education equity is to provide education that leads to success in school and in life, and since the goal of education is to develop life-long learners and critical thinking skills, educators need to be vigilant in properly diagnosing, maintaining optimal instruction, and maximizing all of the students' potentials. Finally, in Chapter 10, Cheng provides a framework for reframing the paradigms of service delivery.

CHAPTER 7

ESL STRATEGIES FOR API POPULATIONS

LI-RONG LILLY CHENG, PH.D.

Kenyon Chen (1983) notes that many disabled ESL/LEP students have three strikes against them—limited English proficiency, poverty, and language or learning disability—which may dispose them to setback or failure. Lack of parental support also complicates learning for these students. Although three strikes usually constitutes an "out," any number of disadvantages can impede academic success.

Lack of attention to the particular language or learning difficulties of immigrant or refugee students is no longer acceptable. In *Lau v. Nichols* (1974), the Supreme Court established a rudimentary standard for the treatment and instruction of students of all backgrounds, ruling that public schools must take "affirmative steps" to compensate for a child's lack of English skills "There is no equality of treatment merely by providing students with the same facilities, textbooks, teachers, and curriculum; students who do not understand English are effectively foreclosed from any meaningful education" (Crawford, 1992, p.190). Teachers are now expected to address the special needs—no matter how complex these needs may be—of *all* students.

Along with investigating the social, familial, and personal factors that influence ESL learning, education researchers are advocating optimal learning and language learning environments (OLE and OLLE) toward improving the quality of ESL education (Cheng, 1994; Figueroa, 1989). Furthermore, teachers are examining their own world views, values, beliefs, habits, and learning and cognitive styles in hopes of understanding what cultural and linguistic "baggage" their students carry to school with them (Cheng, 1989).

This chapter explores the means through which educators may better understand students' risks and needs and how to provide effective, meaningful education. The chapter also present ways for school professionals to collaborate with community experts and families of ESL students to create optimal language learning environments.

ㄴㄱ

EDUCATIONAL PROFILES OF ESL STUDENTS

ESL students come from diverse cultural/linguistic backgrounds and speak various home languages. Despite their different immigration or refugee experiences and socioeconomic statuses, they share many of the following characteristics (Cheng, 1990, 1993):

1. Insufficient overall communication skills in English;
2. Lack of social knowledge and experience;
3. Varying degrees of world knowledge;
4. Varying degrees of home-language literacy;
5. Varying degrees of English reading proficiency;
6. Varying degrees of English auditory comprehension ability;
7. Lack of metalinguistic awareness in English;
8. The presence of a "foreign accent" in spoken English;
9. Mild to moderate difficulty with written English;
10. Problems completing requirements of "traditional" American education;
11. Depression and emotional instability (possible experience of trauma);
12. Identity crisis;
13. Social isolation and alienation; and
14. Different prior knowledge based on cultural, social, religious, personal, and educational background.

Some refugee and immigrant groups adapt more readily to the American way of life than others. According to Spindler and Spindler

(1990), adjustment reflects the nature of cultural conflict. Some immigrants affirm native traditions by reviving them and rejecting mainstream culture. Many refugees from Southeast Asia remain non-English speaking, read newspapers in home languages, enjoy foods from their countries of origin and associate only with individuals from the same language and cultural background. They exist essentially away from the primary cultural community, except for a few who learn to negotiate within both mainstream and native-oriented cultures. These individuals become cultural/linguistic brokers (Mura, 1991; Takaki, 1989), combining selected aspects, such as religion, from both cultures. Still other immigrants or refugees withdraw, rejecting both conflicting cultures, choosing to hover in a transitional stage, remaining noncommittal toward both their native culture and American culture.

A large percentage of LEP students are being excluded from the special education programs they need in order to succeed. For example, in 1993, the Alhambra (CA) School District was 46.34% Asian in ethnic origin; languages included Cantonese, Mandarin, Chiuchow, Hakka, Taiwanese, and Toishan Chinese, as well as Khmer, Vietnamese, Japanese, Korean, Lao, Tagalog, Hindi, Ilocano, Indonesian, Punjabi, Urdu, Visyan, and Thai. Despite this, only 22% of special education recipients were Asian, revealing a discrepancy between school policy (providing equitable treatment to all language minority groups) and practice (Dung, Viernes, & Mudd, 1994).

ESL/LEP students' school experience is a key to their future success. We must investigate linguistic, intellectual and social codes, conflicting cultural beliefs and assumptions, and deeper issues of affective personal, emotional, and educational implications for successful school, community, and home discourse (Cummins, 1994; Ripich & Creaghead, 1994). Educators should heed the results of tests for language and learning disability. Allowing students to slip through the cracks can result in their emotional imbalance, disenfranchisement, and delinquency.

⊐

TRIALS AND ERRORS IN THE ESL CLASSROOM

Many factors should be considered during the education and evaluation of ESL students. ESL aims to elevate students to native or near-native-level proficiency and prepare them for mainstream classes as quickly as possible. School districts such as Fairfax (VA), Montgomery (MD), Los Angeles (CA), Dade (FL), and Chicago (IL), as well as New York City, have dealt with LEP/ESL students for many years. Other districts have yet to develop programs. Garden City (KS) (pop. 24,600), for example, had a boom in its meatpacking industry during the 1980s. The town has since attracted workers of Mexican and Southeast Asian descent and in 1993 out of 3,666 elementary school children, approximately 700 required special help because of limited English proficiency.

ESL classroom dynamics include personal difficulties, large-scale group conflicts, and everything in between. Before problematic conditions and relationships can be modified to benefit school, family, and societal discourse, they must first be recognized.

ESL CLASSROOM CASE STUDY

The following observations were provided by a school psychology student of Chinese descent who devoted 2 weeks to a summer ESL classroom in a California middle school while conducting an independent study of Asian students. The class consisted of 11 Japanese, 4 Chinese (2 Chinese, 2 Taiwanese), 2 Vietnamese, 2 Polish, 1 Korean, and 1 Mexican student. Although the observer spoke both Mandarin and Cantonese, she interacted on an equal basis with students of all cultural and linguistic backgrounds. Also present were a teacher, a paid ESL aide, and two volunteers.

Students were variously experienced with ESL. Some had been in the program for 4 years and others had just arrived. Although the teacher provided encouragement for improvement of grammar, reading, overall English, and study skills, she instructed at a single level of difficulty, which appeared to block the progress of the higher level students. She expressed dismay at having to overlook skill-level and age differences, but blamed the district for withholding facilities and general support.

Chinese students were notably polite, maintaining a disposition that characterizes Chinese students from overseas. Extensive work with one of them revealed increasing despondency and symptoms of unhappiness. Other students, particularly those of Japanese descent, offered minimal response to inquiries and instruction. The Vietnamese students were most animated and responsive.

Dismaying patterns of disorganization and high levels of noise made the class's group dynamics nightmarish. Students worked collaboratively together and played during recess exclusively with others from their own cultural-linguistic background. Of the two students without ethnic counterparts (Korean and Mexican), one sat with the Japanese students and the other by herself. Students spoke in their native languages when speaking to others in their groups and limited their interactions to just those individuals within their group. Only three students attempted and succeeded at interacting with students of other groups.

The Japanese students took Japanese-language movies, sports and comic magazines with them to class. They also took homemade videos modeled on American game shows, such as "Jeopardy." Some of the Chinese students commented that the productions were cheap imitations of American shows, and this caused a minor outbreak of hostility. More problems were revealed when one student demonstrated prejudice against another in regards to her skin color, which was darker than most Asians', and her larger-than-usual size.

Intragroup conflict also occurred, but its sources were unidentifiable because of the different languages being used. Conflict was most frequent among Japanese students, but the Chinese students showed a lack of interest and interaction amongst themselves. Common nationality did little to unite them, as they spoke different dialects; reticence, solitude, and alienation from family seemed to characterize their unhappiness.

Via its curriculum, this ESL class explored cultural values, trends, health, hygiene, school survival skills, sports, geography, landmarks and symbols, food, ecology, weather and seasons, neighborhoods, communities, holidays, famous Americans, and fine arts. Although its coverage of American life was fairly comprehensive, its approach to history was racially limited. The curriculum emphasized the historical role of African Americans, but ignored those of Japanese-, Mexican-, Chinese-, and native Americans as well as other Americans of recent foreign descent.

The teacher's compliance with her students' tendency to memorize rather than analyze incurred a general indifference toward subject matter among them. For example, she told students to learn the following sentence: "B.H. Middle School is in the County of S., in the State of California, in the nation of the United States, and in the northern hemisphere." Instead of trying to understand meanings of the words "county," "state," "nation," and "hemisphere," they memorized the sentence in raw form and later simply filled in the blanks. When this disparity was pointed out to the teacher, she said she would make sure her students understood material conceptually in the future.

Other than depending on rote memorization, students also made many spelling errors, even when copying from the chalkboard. Verb tenses, prepositions, and agreement between subjects and verbs also presented difficulty. This is understandable, as many languages lack verb tenses, agreement rules, articles, prepositions, and distinctions between singular and plural. Chinese words are monosyllabic; hence, Chinese students found it difficult to pronounce polysyllabic words. Furthermore, the Chinese language has no alphabet, so using one to create spellings and pronunciations in English came as a brand new concept to these students. Finally, words with more than one meaning caused a great deal of confusion.

Despite these inherent difficulties in teaching an ESL class, a firm grasp of ESL methods, cultural characteristics, and learning styles empowered the teacher to improve communication and instruction and to benefit the students. The following list encompasses many of the methods and theories that the ESL teacher successfully applied and that should be considered as part of ESL curriculum and extracurricular interactions with ESL students (Chow, 1994).

- *Individualized lessons:* These should be tailored to students' varying levels and proclivity for language acquisition. Some students possess mastery in their native tongues and are fully literate, with others not able to recall what languages they think or dream in, let alone demonstrate literacy in.
- *Positive interpersonal, intergroup and intragroup dynamics:* These can be initiated through games or exercises in which students of different ethnicities and languages by necessity intermingle.
- *Open confrontation of racial prejudice:* Appreciation of diversity and awareness of prejudice must be heightened throughout schools and districts, not just in ESL classrooms.
- *Immediate welcoming into "school family":* This can be an introduction or informal interview based on the following questions: How long have you been in the United States? Did you come with your family? What grade were you in your native country? Will you tell us a little about school there? What are your hobbies and favorite subjects? Do you feel homesick? An

interview such as this may cause some discomfort because of limited English or general shyness. As a ritual of welcome, it helps to break the ice and, for the student, marks passage into the new environment. It also bolsters confidence, emotional well-being, concentration, and overall success. Using an interpreter is invaluable in these interactions.

■ *The natural language approach:* Speech production comes slowly, progressing in natural stages, and cannot be forced. Beginner learners of English should receive gradual introduction to vocabulary and be expected to only minimally participate verbally. Those of more advanced proficiency should respond in short phrases, with those of high proficiency encouraged to speak and write in complete sentences.

■ *Minimal error correction:* Over-correcting causes inhibition. Choose students' most serious errors, discuss them carefully, and apply proper usage. Invite patience, enthusiasm, and successful learning by providing reinforcement and feedback.

■ *A literate, multicultural classroom environment:* Students should be allowed to choose from multicultural books, dictionaries, and booklists according to their interests and skill levels. They should read during designated reading times. Also, audiovisual equipment such as tape recorders, headphones, televisions, and computers can offer valuable supplements to standard instruction.

■ *Shared reading:* Reading out loud to and with students can improve their comprehension and pronunciation. This approach entails more personalized teaching.

■ *Students as authors:* Short stories, essays, cultural memoirs, illustrations, and maps may be bound into books to encourage students and to emphasize the importance of their achievements. Work should be valued and displayed.

■ *Respect for diversity:* Encouraging students to keep their first languages while learning English conforms with the concept that ability to learn a second language correlates with proficiency in a primary language. Keeping native language dictionaries in the classroom ensures continued contact and exposure to primary languages.

■ *Keeping names:* A name is an important part of one's identity; using students' native language names shows sensitivity and respect for their cultures.

COMPLICATIONS FROM GENERAL TO SPECIFIC

Although many ESL students succeed academically and go on to college, others experience impossible difficulties with English. This section will address some of the complexities that can arise in ESL classrooms.

LANGUAGE SOCIALIZATION

Language use varies widely among bilingual families (Grosjean, 1982; Langdon & Merino, 1992; Vihman & McLaughlin, 1982). Kuo's study of 47 preschool Chinese children in the Twin Cities (MN) area (1974) reveals not only that family plays a key role in children's bilingual socialization, but that there are two significant variables. The first is behavioral; parents speaking Chinese at home will influence their preschool-aged children to speak Chinese. The second variable relates to national identity: a family's duration of residence in the United States and the family's status of naturalization tend to influence the use of English at home. Furthermore, as children age and find themselves more fully satisfied by extrafamilial activities and contacts, their families' impact tends to decline.

AFFECTIVE FILTER

This concept refers to a language learner's subconscious attitude toward the second language (Krashen, 1981, 1982). It includes three components: motivation, self-confidence, and anxiety. The lower the anxiety, the higher the motivation and the smoother the process of language learning. To create an effective language learning environment, teachers and peers must work to foster the learner's self-confidence in an effort to reduce anxiety.

LANGUAGE LOSS

Language loss is a common problem encountered by bilingual individuals. Hakuta (1993) contends that language is not lost, but simply dormant until called on. However, it appears that frequent shifting from home language to English coincides with loss of home or native language proficiency. Social or peer pressures may reinforce this shift (Langdon & Merino, 1992).

LEARNING STYLES

Some students study alone, others in groups; some study in quiet environments, others amidst distractions. Teachers and practitioners should recognize the diversity of legitimate learning styles and attempt to identify these styles. In this way, teaching materials and strategies can be designed according to individual preferences (Nellum-Davis, 1993; Ramirez, 1990).

HIGH-CONTEXT ORIENTATION

Cultures may vary the amount of information that is explicitly transmitted through verbal channels as opposed to information that is communicated through the context of the situation, the physical cues present, and the person's body and facial language. API cultures reflect high-context orientation. In this situationally centered, or context-bound, orientation, most meaningful information is conveyed in the physical context or internalized by the person who receives the information. Little information is contained in the verbally transmitted part of the message (Clark, 1993). In API cultures in which "children are to be seen and not heard," youngsters learn communication within an adult cultural milieu. As API cultures' verbally transmitted messages contain less information than others, API children will closely gauge nonverbal interactions (Hall, 1976). API verbal interaction is circular rather than linear resulting in seemingly lengthy discussion that may not be central to the topic of discussion (Kaplan, 1966), setting it apart from expectations held by the American mainstream educational system. In general, mainstream cultural patterns pertain to minimal context orientation and convey information in a precise, linear, and straightforward manner (Cheng, 1993). Educators should be prepared for differing degrees of context orientation among culturally and linguistically diverse students.

HIDDEN AGENDAS

ESL/LEP students from diverse cultural and social backgrounds must attain and master crosscultural competence in all areas of life, including and especially education (Cheng, 1990). Academic success in a crosscultural environment not only requires literacy but "comprehensible input." ESL students who find classroom discourse and its oral/written and nonverbal rules incomprehensible and difficult are at a constant disadvantage (Krashen, 1981). Tacit cultural rules exist both in and out of the classroom in what might be called the "hidden agenda."

Hidden agendas, or hidden curricula, exist throughout schools and in all social encounters (Taylor, 1986). In *Life In Classrooms*, Jackson (1968) defines the hidden curriculum as: "The praise and the power that combine to give a distinctive flavor to classroom life . . . which each student and teacher must master if he is to make his way satisfactorily through the school." Immigrant students must reconcile their agendas to American culture as well as to their teachers' personal values (Tran, 1991). Mastering hidden agendas demands that students not only understand but share their teachers' educational values. And ESL students must incorporate these agendas into their education in order to attain crosscultural competence (Cheng, 1990).

Pang (1988) reported that although some students actively engage in verbal discourse with their teachers, others remain detached. At the same time, teachers interact with students on the bases of responsiveness and personal dynamics. Barba and Pang (1991) report that high dropout rates among minority students might be attributed to disengagement (being ignored in classroom verbal interactions)resulting from a failure to master the hidden curriculum or to share the same values and beliefs as their teachers.

INCONGRUENCIES OF CLASSROOM DISCOURSE RULES

Major differences exist between discourse at work in American classrooms and those operating in other cultures. For example, there are major difference between American and Chinese modes of class interactions. Cheng (1991) explains that American teachers expect students to be interactive, creative, and participatory, yet Asian parents have trained their children to be quiet and obedient, and not to challenge or question their teachers. Similarly, a study of Vietnamese children (Bishop, 1988) reveals that the children were using English along with home culture discourse rules, simultaneously engaging two different codes, one linguistic and one pragmatic. As many Asian-American children feel ambivalent and confused toward class participation, we must recognize the conflicting messages they are receiving from teachers and parents. We must also provide them some understanding of "hidden curricula" and "classroom discourse rules."

LINGUISTIC AND CULTURAL CODE-SWITCHING

Normal Chinese women's voices are strong and bossy. We American-Chinese girls had to whisper to make ourselves American-feminine. Once a year, the teachers referred my sister and me to speech therapy, but our voices would straighten out, unpredictably normal, for the therapists. We invented an American-feminine speaking personality, except for one girl who could not speak up even in Chinese school. (Maxine Hong Kingston, *The Woman Warrior*, 1976, p. 172)

ESL/LEP students must develop both linguistic and cultural code-switching strategies to succeed within American schools. They must learn nonverbal communication cues and codes such as hand-raising, eye contact, facial expressions, and so on as means of showing interest, enthusiasm, and participation. Teachers should encourage and assist this type of learning by modeling the accepted codes of behavior as often as possible. Furthermore, teachers should examine the relationship between language and culture, affirm differences and similarities between cultures, and demonstrate acceptance.

Given the diversity of child rearing, family living, religion, medicine, and education practices they bring to the United States, API immigrants provide pertinent examples of behavioral and linguistic code-switching (Cheng, 1991). Particular among them are Nisei and Sansei, second and third generation Japanese, who share their parents' and grandparents' values (Kitano & Daniels, 1988; Mura, 1991). Mainstream culture conflicts with their world views, identities, and styles of interaction. At the same time, these individuals consider themselves thoroughly American and experience frustration when regarded as strangers or outsiders (Mura, 1991; Takaki, 1989).

NONVERBAL COMMUNICATION

Nonverbal cues, such as eye contact, physical contact, and body language, are embedded in sociocultural contexts. Immigrant students usually alter these cues once they have become entrenched in the American educational system.

For most API cultures, nonverbal communication or "reading the eyes" takes precedence over verbal communication; the Chinese say, "examine the face and observe the overall expression." Indeed,

Knapp (1972) suggests that only 35% of social meaning is transmitted through words and the rest by nonverbal means. Facial expressions, gestures, physical proximity, spatial arrangements, postures, and silences convey a great deal in the process of communication.

In discussing the intricacies of attempted communication between individuals from two different linguistic and cultural backgrounds, Taylor (1986) suggests that educators need to learn about cultural characteristics that might contribute to the quality of communication with ESL/LEP students. Students' linguistic functions are not the sole determinants of communicative competence. Therefore, teachers and clinicians must investigate home cultures and discourse rules. They must recognize the legitimacy of minimal eye contact, infrequent physical contact, and reservation in expressing open praise among API students (Cheng, 1989).

LEARNING CULTURE

Children learn a great deal through experience. But although experience-based information is essential for school success, most schools exclude it from their curricula. For instance, most American children associate Thanksgiving with turkey, stuffing, dressing, pumpkin pie, and cranberry sauce, but a Hmong child who has never even seen a turkey would be at a loss. By inviting children into an American home for Thanksgiving dinner, educators can expose such children to a significant cultural experience. Likewise, holding dinners or lunches at school during which children can sample unfamiliar ethnic foods provides direct cultural experience and learning. Such strategies can improve classroom interactions for all students.

ESL/LEP students must adjust their world views, values, beliefs, habits, and learning and cognitive styles to accommodate school culture. Teachers can ease this adjustment by nurturing appreciation of cultural and linguistic diversity (Cheng, 1989). They can also expand their own knowledge of immigrant cultures and unique discourse patterns within the English language. Related topics include turn-taking and allocation, silence, and interruption, plus topic initiation, shift, and maintenance (Prutting & Kirchner, 1983). Understanding these subjects beyond intuitive use improves communication.

ESL AND ESL: ENGLISH AS SCHOOL AND SECOND LANGUAGE

Many ESL/LEP students speak native languages at home and only use English to negotiate outside the home. Most use limited English in school and have difficulty acquiring cognitive academic linguistic proficiency (CALP)(Cummins, 1982). They find school activities—including communication with teachers, administrators, peers, and staff—incomprehensible, threatening, and foreign, going home to non-English-speaking environments likely with only home language television programs, newspapers, books, and magazines available. Lack of practice in English can lead to disenfranchisement and school failure; thus, intensive English language training is crucial for students at risk.

LITERACY ACQUISITION

Caplan, Choy, and Whitmore (1992) describe how some Asian families collaborate in literacy acquisition and support school success. Children of such families show proficiency in their home languages and put forth rigorous effort to improve their school language. In the course of assisting these children, parents learn about the school, its curriculum, and its language.

Other LEP students lack such support. In a study of 16 Cantonese LEP students with learning disabilities, Chang and Lai (1992) remarked that:

1. Home language stimulation (in the subjects' native language) was limited to simple verbal exchange that included explanation of rules and disciplines, meeting basic needs for food, drink, and clothing, and doing routine chores.
2. Exchanges excluded exploration or discovery learning for cognitive and linguistic development.
3. Children spent excessive time watching television, playing video games, and helping with household chores. They seldom visited friends, attended public events, or played sports. They experienced little in the way of social interaction.
4. Subjects read very little at home. Parents were busy with housework and offered limited literacy support.

In situations such as this, LEP students and their parents need constructive suggestions and encouragement. Taylor (1986) assert that "only when children have had the opportunity to inventively construct literate language uses which make sense to them will they be able to participate fully in the literate society." Literacy lays the foundation for school and future success. Teachers cannot assume LEP students are receiving home literacy support; rather they must attempt to understand what a day at home holds for these students and, from this, form strategies to aid in the process of literacy acquisition.

BICS AND CALP

LEP students often demonstrate minimum level basic interpersonal communication skills (BICS) but less competency in cognitive academic linguistic proficiency (CALP) because of lack of exposure to printed texts and home literacy support (Chang & Lai, 1992). In California, for example, students who fall below the 36th percentile in CTBS reading comprehension and math application are classified as LEP (Dung et al., 1994). Once they score higher than the 36th percentile on both language comprehension and math application, they are reclassified as FEP. By law, they must undergo testing every 3 years; most students continue this for 3 to 4 years. As a result, many are fluent in oral English communication, but still classified as LEP. As major differences exist between competencies required by BICS and CALP, those who are LEP may continue to lag behind.

Most students residing in non-English-speaking ethnic enclaves such as Monterey Park, CA (Mandarin), Fountain Valley, CA (Vietnamese), and San Francisco (Cantonese) will experience difficulty developing CALP, which first requires grasping the fundamentals of written English. Students lacking this proficiency are at-risk for academic failure.

⊓

PURSUING THE AMERICAN DREAM: MYTH OR REALITY

Trueba, Cheng, and Ima (1993) describe numerous success stories of Chinese Americans. Three factors seem most powerful in determining school success: parental knowledge of access to resources, home teaching by parents or tutors, and auxiliary learning, including music, sports, and travel. Many parents borrow this framework from other parents and assume it will guarantee success. They are apt to meet with failure. Those who "abandon" their children, entrusting them to other guardians or surrogate families will probably find the above strategies not only ineffective but detrimental to their children's overall balance and well-being. The fundamental importance of parental input and support should *never* be forgotten or overlooked.

The following case illustrates how parents' offhand application of "frameworks for success"—without whole-hearted support or presence—can harm a child's school performance and, more importantly, the child's emotional well-being. This case study was provided by a female American-born university graduate who regularly tutors and interacts with nonnative English speakers and first generation Asians.

UNACCOMPANIED MINORS:
THEIR DESPAIR, HOPELESSNESS, AND LOSS

Jason is a Taiwanese ninth grader attending the La Mar School District. His parents brought him to the United States in 1992 with tourist visas and two primary motives: to establish a base for their lucrative manufacturing business and to settle their son into a school where he might profit by a relatively strong education. Their business entailed residing in Taiwan and occasionally visiting the United States. They left their son with nonfamilial guardians and, at times, even alone. After about a year, they offered him the option of returning to Taiwan. However, his illegal status in the United States excluded him from the possibility of future re-entry. Visiting Taiwan—for whatever length of time and for whatever reason—meant never coming back.

Jason was immediately accepted within a group of peers in his first ESL program, as the program was experiencing an influx of Taiwanese-speaking students. At that time, his guardian was a young man from China who had essentially taken the position in exchange for room and board and who only minimally attended to Jason's needs. Jason felt frustrated with English and, hence, with school, but he enjoyed the lighter homework load associated with American schools as well as plenty of time for video games.

To date, Jason socializes with other Taiwanese whose parents live elsewhere, but leave their children with great amounts of pocket money to play video games, eat in restaurants, and shop. These children's fixations on video games and sleeping at each others' houses attest to the fact that their need for comfort, company, and general support are left largely unfulfilled.

Jason's parents have not hesitated to spend money on their son's education and "roundedness." For example, when he expressed a desire to move after his first year, his mother sought a new school and registered him despite her own lack of English communication skills. Then his parents bought him a $600,000 house and left him there with a new guardian, who was Chinese like the previous one. They also hired a tutor to help Jason progress with English and gain in academic motivation.

Jason's parents scheduled their son with back-to-back sports, music, homework, and tutoring activities once he arrived at the academically stronger public school in a more affluent district. Still, his new life granted him academic exemptions based on limited English proficiency, more lenient grades, and a plush lifestyle. In these respects, it offered consolation for cultural alienation and parental abandonment.

Like other ESL students, Jason lacked English proficiency. But in 1 year of school he learned basic reading, writing, and conversation skills. Areas of academic difficulty resembled those of other ESL students, particularly those of Chinese and Taiwanese descent, although his life situation posed challenges entirely unique and personal.

Before initiating lessons, Jason's tutor administered diagnostic testing in grammar, spelling, phonetics, reading, reading comprehension, and writing. His strengths included reading, pronouncing words previously encountered, reading comprehension, and basic punctuation. His weaknesses were verb conjugation, subject-verb agreement, use of pronouns and articles, plurality, and formation of complete sentences, as well as his general attitude. At that time, however, his despondency caused no alarm.

Tutoring sessions took place at Jason's house on week nights, just after dinnertime from 7 to 9 p.m. The tutor started Jason with lists of words—some common, others unusual—to be articulated aloud. The tutor took special care to include words with double or triple consonant blends and multiple syllables, bearing in mind that Chinese speakers tend to have particular trouble with these aspects of English. Any words mispronounced were check-marked and retested the same evening or during subsequent sessions until correct pronunciation was achieved. During this exercise, Jason repeated the same mistakes, groaned when asked to try again and said, "forget" as a general response.

Grammar exercises were excerpted from textbooks, first at the sixth grade level and later at adult ESL levels. Jason's cooperation improved with the switch to more advanced material. Other exercises were devised by the tutor beforehand or on-the-spot. These included page-long stories in which Jason was asked to provide correction for punctuation and spelling, having been given a total number of errors to be found. He wrote stories and essays of his own, which the tutor corrected. The tutor then explained each mistake and had Jason write sentences demonstrating proper usage.

Reading lessons were derived from elementary-level materials, but were abandoned when Jason first complained, asking for more advanced ones. "This for babies," he remarked about an eighth-grade-level novel that had been chosen to match his ability. Starting with basic fundamentals proved to invite distraction and undermine enthusiasm and cooperation. During reading, tutor and pupil read out loud for 10 minutes each. Discussions followed, wherein the tutor posed questions for essay response and Jason put in writing. He showed minimal effort during these routines, making more mistakes than demonstrated during diagnostic testing.

Jason had a slouching posture and munched high sugar foods, such as cookies and chocolate, indicating a low-energy level, and the tutor found it difficult to pep him up. He groaned at every request and snapped at corrections, lagging most noticeably on evenings when he particularly mentioned fatigue. Mistakes and mispronunciations stunted his reading, with misspellings, incomplete sentences, and surface-level statements characterizing his writing. Progress *did* take place when he made an effort and was reinforced through notation and praising, but his effort seemed to depend on rare resurgent energy.

After a month, Jason and his tutor began meeting in a coffeehouse where a public social environment was expected to stimulate responsiveness and provide exposure to an American cultural scenario. At first, his performance improved. He commented that he enjoyed the new environment more than the old and ventured to make jokes with people at neighboring tables and behind the counter.

Lesson content remained largely the same, but sports magazines and drawing were introduced as media for enjoyable learning, as Jason had indicated these as interests. Drawing activities took place during 5- to 10-minute breaks and illustrated assigned subjects, such as family and cultural events. After both tutor and pupil had drawn, they exchanged pictures and wrote stories or explanations for each other's work. Jason seemed to enjoy this activity, because it allowed imagination, artwork, and teacher participation. Sessions were completed with 10-minute Scrabble games, which Jason clearly enjoyed and sometimes won.

At this writing, Jason's track and field season has reached full swing, and he has arrived at nighttime sessions exhausted and recovering from multiple-hour naps. He has repeatedly flopped onto his seat and slouched at a 2-foot distance from the table until his tutor has asked him to sit up and scoot in. This he has done reluctantly, saying, "tired." Apart from track practice and competition, he appears at a loss for motivation in all areas. When asked what he does with weekend time or on a certain day, he replies, "nothing." When asked what he especially enjoys, again: "Nothing."

Several factors may account for Jason's lack of motivation, cooperation, and sense of hopelesssness. Depression is the obvious poison, but beneath that is the cultural and familial situation, which is wholly unsupportive of his current pursuits and goals. How can Jason's parents support their son from across the sea? How can he possibly support *himself* during such a culturally and individually formative time of life? The few adult role models made available to their son by Jason's parents have little capacity to pull him out of his despair. One such role model is his guardian, a Taiwanese man in his late 20s with little sympathy for Jason and a financial motive for living in the house. The second is his tutor, a young woman whose cultural background, gender, and age at once eliminate his confidence in her. The third, a family friend of Taiwanese descent, is busily entangled in roles as mother, university professor, and multicultural advocate. None of these people replace Jason's parents.

Jason's tutor has sustained Jason's cooperation by initiating lengthy discussions of his feelings about his home situation, school in America, progress with English, and the possibility of returning to Taiwan. In his brief responses to her questions (which aim at sensitivity), he shows equal discouragement toward all facets of life and particular confusion regarding whether to stay in America or return to Taiwan for good—these choices being the only options his parents have given him. Jason has fashioned another option for himself: moving out to live alone.

Alongside such discussions (in which Jason has repeatedly approached breaking down), his tutor has continued recreational activities in place of more challenging grammar and phonetics exercises. Reading from magazines, drawing, writing stories and playing Scrabble have become primary teaching avenues. His direct attitude has improved, making for less resistance. But his energy has remained consistently low and his progress minimal. Furthermore, his drawings have displayed an alarming theme: violence.

Under the circumstances, it is questionable whether Jason's unleavened engagement in after-school activities is helping him. His parents have overextended him (and left him little time for friends) in an effort to keep him too busy to feel lonely, alienated, and depressed. Contrary to their intentions, he feels tired, unmotivated, and in no mood to learn a complicated foreign language, even if doing so could improve his life tremendously. As noted in similar case studies, ESL students' progress with English correlates to home support and emotional well-being. Jason's status with both of these factors will have to improve before he can find within himself an incentive to try harder.

It is clear that English serves as a school language for Jason, and its limited context is resulting in complications extremely common for LEP/ESL students. Three strikes against Jason include LEP status, deprivation of parental support, and the consequent lack of motivation. His home situation has complicated school performance largely in ways school personnel cannot remedy. Schools must offer children like him counseling and guidance, but more importantly, they must notify parents of the consequences of their absence in a child's life and its potential long-term harm. Although parents' initial intent may be to educate and ultimately benefit their children, they are neglecting the most important ingredient to human development: sustained, caring, nurturing relationships between parents and child.

ᄂ〒

MANAGING NEEDS: SUGGESTIONS FOR PARENTS AND EDUCATORS

Today's ESL classrooms must deal with demands pertaining not only to students' diverse backgrounds and learning situations, but to broader issues involving entire school systems and communities. The following important issues must be addressed if we are to improve the quality of ESL education:

In the ESL Classroom

- Ever-increasing class sizes;
- Wide variance of languages and proficiency levels;
- Identification of learning disability limitations;
- School day length;
- Service provision in dominant languages.

Parent Involvement

- Promotion of meaningful involvement;
- Availability of district and community resources;
- Specific parental services, such as literacy training;

■ Families' "comfort level" in attending school functions and teacher conferences.

Staff Awareness

■ Health care, as "sick kids cannot learn": taking partial responsibility for students' knowledge of personal health maintenance;
■ Workloads are increasing because of more students;
■ Health care professionals and educators' understanding of normal progress in second-language acquisition.

Resources

■ Budget reduction and subsequent lack of materials;
■ Scant recruitment and retention of bilingual staff of many language backgrounds (not just Hispanics), including translators and qualified special education teachers;
■ Lack of basic multicultural materials;
■ Inadequate assessment materials in languages other than English;
■ Poor public awareness of needs for funds and other contributions;
■ Lacking primary language speech therapy.

Collaboration Among Parents, Educators, Administrators, and Related Professionals

■ Developing partnerships with universities willing to contribute resources;
■ ESL teacher involvement at students study team (SST) meetings;
■ Building outside support for ESL programs (interagency collaboration);
■ Integrating special and regular education programs;
■ Conferring between schools, parents, and outside agencies;
■ Sustaining consistent strategies for fulfilling student, class, and school needs.

Limited-English Proficiency

■ Attempting to communicate with families of non-English speaking students;
■ Promoting preschool acquisition of English proficiency: need for providing a smooth transition into kindergarten for children arriving without English language experience;
■ Attention to older children entering school with little or no previous schooling and/or English proficiency;

- Provision of language assessment in both primary and second languages;
- Identification of connections between LEP and learning disability.

Understanding Cultural/Linguistic Backgrounds

- Extent of previous schooling;
- Degree of acculturation;
- Parents' socioeconomic and immigrant/refugee statuses, access to family histories, education in English or primary language literacy, attitudes towards education;
- Cultural beliefs and practices in discipline, child-rearing, parent involvement, and health care;
- Child abuse: recognizing any legal obligation to report;
- Natural (gradual) acquisition of second language: identifying students' needs for special education;
- Integrating transient populations into general and special education classrooms;
- Progress in language acquisition as students mature;
- Evolution of values and standards within school systems and families;
- Cultural stereotypes: teachers observing and questioning their own beliefs and assumptions;
- Students' efforts as they relate to parent/teacher expectations.

SUGGESTIONS FOR EDUCATORS

Cummins (1982) proposes a framework for the classification of language and content activities in ESL classrooms. In it Cummins classifies activities such as "developing survival vocabulary" and "following demonstrated directions" as "undemanding context-embedded" and activities such as "developing an academic vocabulary" and "understanding academic presentations accompanied by visuals" as "demanding context-embedded." Within the same framework, "engaging in predictable telephone conversations" and "writing answers to lower level questions" were labeled "undemanding context-reduced," with "understanding academic presentations without visuals or presentations" and "solving math word problems without illustrations" labeled "demanding context-reduced." Most questions concerning ESL/LEP demands point back to the need for optimal learning environments, (OLEs) (Figueroa, 1989), or better yet, optimal language learning environments (OLLEs) (Cheng, 1994). The inclusive OLE concept promotes learning and empowerment among educators and children and their families, with OLLE dealing more specifically with language learning/teaching. Because language serves as the primary tool for exchange of information, teachers must recognize its contextual learning base and the *reduced* nature of the school context may not be part of the students' life experiences (Cummins, 1994). In creating OLLE, educators must start from their students' embedded language learning contexts and move gradually to reduced contexts such as that of the school classroom—going from personal life stories to biographies. Alongside this transition, cognitive tasks should graduate from simple to demanding.

The concept of optimal language learning environment and experiences for English (OLLEEE) should be understood by all ESL educators. As English is perceived as a language of authority and power, LEP students may find it threatening and feel shy about practicing. Their parents may be NEP or LEP, meaning home practice of English will be nonexistent or minimal. Here are some questions to consider: How can we make English learning more enjoyable? How can we create natural and stimulating English learning environments? How can we reduce learners' anxiety? Means include:

1. Promotion of language use in school and social contexts: Arrange high-interest cultural activities such as origami demonstrations by Japanese students or calligraphy by Chinese students. Invite students to home- or school-based food potluck meals in which food from traditional menus can be sampled.
2. Provision of low-risk, low-anxiety language learning contexts: get to know students. Approach them with questions about their likes and dislikes and strengths; request to see some work from subjects in which they excel.
3. Creation of experiential, relevant language activities: learn about students' experiences by asking them to tell stories. In Hawaiian classrooms, this "talk story" approach has been remarkably successful by allowing students to reveal preexisting cognitive and linguistic repertoires (Au & Jordan, 1981). It improves classroom comfort and creates a positive climate for understanding.
4. Promotion of language interaction in a comprehensible process, starting from least demanding tasks and progressing toward those more cognitively challenging.

5. Respect home discourse despite its conflicts with standard school discourse. Explain any hidden facets of the school agenda and express interest in students' home discourse. Ask questions and allow students to speak openly about differences and similarities between home and school experiences.

6. Allow students to self-select their support systems and cooperative learning groups. They will seek out peers with whom they feel comfortable enough to give and take mutual support and socialization.

7. Introduce cultural activities or organizations such as Scouting, YM and YWCA, PTA, Junior League, Boys and Girls Clubs, and any other programs available to students and their families.

8. Guide them into programs for which they have demonstrated interest. Plan cultural fairs where all can share ethnic/cultural activities. This powerfully reinforces school-home-child connections.

9. Identify linguistic needs through specially designed activities: During these, children are practicing English in meaningful activities.

10. Seek to fulfill the following:

■ Open communication between home and school: invite parents to school activities, including plays, luncheons, lectures, and celebrations.

■ Recruitment of bilingual volunteers to serve as escorts and liaisons during telephone calls and transportation to and from school. They serve as social bridges.

■ Home visits: Expect some families to honor your visits and others to feel threatened.

■ Utilization of bi-/multilingual personnel within agencies and organizations that provide services to ethnic communities.

Cheng, 1989; Hammond and Meiners, 1993; Harry, 1992; Langdon, 1992; and Matsuda, 1989; recommend the following when dealing with Asian families:

■ Be status conscious: Establish your role as authority figure through formal introduction when possible.

■ Try to reach consensus: View compromise as a first step toward acceptance.

- Be pragmatic: Address needs and give concrete advice.
- Respect cultural beliefs.
- Use indirect approach: Take note of personal histories, when necessary, and allow families to model rather than explain. This serves as a valuable method of investigation.
- Be patient and quiet: Consider silence a time for vital reflection.
- Be informative: Give parents all information they need, including costs and ways they can meet them.
- Pay attention to nonverbal cues.
- Create a friendly climate for parent conferences.
- Work with reliable and resourceful interpreters.

SUGGESTIONS FOR PARENTS

Parents and families should take for granted that their involvement in their children's development is of utmost importance. They should **never** expect tutors, babysitters, neighbors, or friends to replace them as role models and primary caretakers. However, parental efforts may not suffice in the face of children's academic and language difficulties. In such cases, parents must learn about special programs and resources, including assessment and intervention processes. They must become active decision makers. Parental support has become increasingly important, considering the diminishing number of certified clinicians who are able to provide services in languages other than English.

In approaching parents of ESL students, educational researchers and educators must ask themselves and discuss the following questions:

1. How do we create a friendly atmosphere that is conducive to positive interaction?
2. How do we conduct extensive interviews and leave with the necessary information, without appearing nosy or intimidating?
3. How do we query parental consent to test children and tactfully share results?
4. How do we counsel parents/families in regards to language and literacy promotion without violating their cultural norms and values?
5. How do we create a situation wherein parents *and* children feel empowered?

CASE STUDY

Su-Lin came to the United States at 14 with her parents Mr. and Mrs. C. and her younger brother. Both parents were in their forties and had resigned from work in Hong Kong to emigrate to the United States and provide a better future for their children. They shared the common fear that after 1997, the Communist takeover of Hong Kong would render life unbearable. Emigrating to the United States showed a strong commitment to their children's educational and future well being.

Mr. and Mrs. C. went to a community college to learn English and vocational skills. Within 6 months, they were both hired for assembly line work in an electronics firm. Back in Hong Kong, Mr. C. had served as the manager of a large clothing manufacturing firm and Mrs. C as a Chinese language teacher. Their new jobs required standing on their feet all day long and concentrating on meeting company standards. Their obligation to work double shifts made it difficult to be with their children.

Feeling like "social outcasts" caused Mr. and Mrs. C. to suffer low self-esteem. Back home, they had had many friends and spent weekends drinking tea, eating dim-sum, and playing games of Majong. Such luxuries were no longer possible. They had made few friends and hardly conversed with co-workers. Feelings of deep isolation and sadness were worsened by their company's financial failure. They were laid off due to lack of seniority and subsequently felt useless and insignificant.

Su-Lin attended an ESL program in her school but felt bored in math class—despite limited English proficiency—because she had acquired more advanced skills in her home country. She was quickly dubbed "genius" and asked to solve problems on the chalkboard for all to see. This recognition made her happy and proud, and her English skills improved tremendously over a 6-month period. She became the family "spokesperson," taking responsibility for phone calls and other public contacts. Later, she joined the debate team and made every effort to become a well-rounded American. Unlike her parents, she viewed herself as important and useful.

Parents can contribute immensely to their children's' education from within the home. Educators should relate to them the following suggestions—through ordinary discourse or the assistance of bi- or multilingual interpreters:

1. Speak at home in whatever language is most comfortable, not in one you struggle with.
2. Promote literacy by keeping newspapers, letters, books, and magazines around the house. Make reading an integral part of every day.
3. Conduct joint activities: household chores, eating out, shopping, writing checks, traveling, and so on, using every opportunity to share in reading and writing. Write shopping lists, read labels, choose movies by reading reviews and ratings, read instructions on new product boxes, create menus for dinner, read recipes, write out invitations, read maps. Celebrate literacy.
4. Pay routine visit to libraries and bookstores: children can borrow books and read to parents if parents are of lower proficiency. This promotes collaborative English learning.
5. Brighten parent-child discourse and strengthen cultural pride by sharing language stories.
6. Ask older siblings to work with younger ones; Encourage them to play a "teacher" role.
7. Use rented home language television programs—or anything in English—leading to substantive discussion.
8. Follow up on teachers' invitations to observe classes in session. Attend special lunches. Seek to learn more about your children's schools.
9. Have faith in interpreters and volunteers—including parents, peers, and tutors—who are offering their assistance.
10. Be aware that the PTA dedicates itself not only to parents who wish to involve themselves, but to children, whose lives benefit most directly.
11. Ask questions: Get to know your child's new school and culture by checking out what you are curious about and pressing concerns.

WORKING TOWARD SUCCESS

Confronting so many diverse needs as seen in the Asian/Pacific Islander populations can be overwhelming. ESL teachers should keep in mind that students will benefit by any and all measures improving ESL education.

HAN-HAN, A SUCCESS STORY: FROM NEP TO PEP TO FEP

Han-han came to the United States at 10 years of age when his father came as a visiting university scholar. His mother, a high school teacher, soon joined them. When Han-han first came, he was the only Mandarin-speaking child in his class. He spoke no English and the school had no ESL class in which to place him. His mother accompanied him on his first day to lessen any intimidation and explain what was going on.

Han-han's teacher not only allowed his mother to stay in the class with her son, but asked everyone to greet and welcome him. She also introduced a map of China. Over the course of the next few months, she asked other students to help Han-han, until at last he felt at ease and began going to school alone without his mother.

Han-han's teacher also went to the PTA to find other parents willing to work with the family, and went to a community church to see about religious involvement. Some parents finally introduced Han-han's parents to other families from the People's Republic of China, and they began spending weekends in other peoples' homes preparing and sharing native foods. Han-han and his family were slowly growing comfortable.

While Han-han's school was 26% African American, 33% Hispanic, and 15% Southeast Asian, he was the only Mandarin-speaking, foreign-born LEP student in his class, with his ethnicity a point to celebrate among his classmates. For the Chinese New Year, Han-han's teacher asked him to talk about Chinese customs and show pictures. His family felt proud and joyful to share their celebration, despite their limited English.

Although Han-han's mother was too shy to make use of her English, his father had become proficient. Han-han himself was able to use complete sentences such as, "I will see you on Friday" and "I like to play Nintendo" within 6 months. In class, he understood most instructions and at home took down messages such as, "The package you ordered will be delivered on Thursday." His extracurricular activities included shopping, swimming, and playing with other children in his apartment complex. Most home communication took place in Mandarin Chinese, but English books were borrowed from the library and shared between mother and son. Without any significant difficulty, Han-han learned to communicate effectively and, above all, felt good about himself.

🏛

CONCLUSION

As we can see from the above case study, the use of the home language at home did not negatively affect the success of Han-han. He used resources with the help of his parents and made progress in learning English while still retaining his home language. This is an example of a win-win situation, as he was thus able to retain the familiar connection to his native culture as well as to attain the language of his new culture, making the transition a smoother, less traumatic one. Han-han had the support of his mother in the initial stages of transition; the importance of such parental support cannot be underestimated. Additionally, the support of his teacher and classmates was crucial for his success. Finally, Han-han was self-motivated to learn. He enjoyed watching TV, participating in sports, and other culturally interactive activities. His motivation to learn made it possible for him to succeed because, the more English he learned, the more incentive he had to learn. Such a reinforcing cycle created for him an optimal language-learning environment.

🏛

REFERENCES

Au, K., & Jordan, K. (1981). Teaching reading to Hawaiian children: Finding a culturally appropriate solution. In H. Trueba, G. P. Guthrie, & K. H. Au (Eds.), *Culture and the bilingual classroom* (pp. 139–152). Rowley: Newbury House.

Barba, R. H. & Pang, V. O. (1991). *Teacher targeting behaviors in the multicultural classroom.* Unpublished manuscript.

Bishop, S. (1988). *Identification of language disorders in Vietnamese children.* Unpublished master's thesis. San Diego State University.

Caplan, N., Choy, M. H., & Whitmore, J. K. (1992). Indochinese refugee families and academic achievement. *Scientific American, 226*(2), 36–45.

Chang, J. M., & Lai, A. (1992, November). *LEP parents as resources: enhancing language and literacy development of LEP students with learning disabilities.* Luo Di-Sheng Gen: International Conference on Overseas Chinese, University of California, Berkeley.

Chen, K. (1983). *Limited English speaking, handicapped, and poor: Three threats in childhood.* New York: Teachers' College Press.

Cheng, L. (1989). Intervention strategies: A multicultural approach. *Topics in Language Disorders, 9*(3), 90–94.

Cheng, L. (1990). Recognizing diversity: A need for a paradigm shift. *American Behavior Scientist, 34*(2), 263–278.

Cheng, L. (1991). *Assessing Asian language performance: Guide for evaluating LEP students.* Oceanside, CA: Academic Communication Associates.

Cheng, L. (1993). Asian-American Cultures. In D. Battle (Ed.), *Communication disorders in multicultural populations.* Boston: Andover Medical Publishers.

Cheng, L. (1994). Difficult discourse: An untold Asian story. In D. N. Ripich & N. A. Creaghead (Eds.), *School discourse problems* (2nd ed). San Diego: Singular Publishing Group, Inc.

Chow, F. (1994). Observation of ESL Classroom. Unpublished paper. San Diego: San Diego State University.

Clark, L. (Ed.).(1993). *Faculty and student challenges in facing cultural and linguistic diversity.* Springfield, IL: Charles C. Thomas.

Crawford, J. (1992). *Hold your tongue: Bilingualism and the politics of English only.* Reading, MA: Addison-Wesley Publishing.

Cummins, J. (1982). Tests, achievement, and bilingual students. *Focus, 9.* Wheaton, MD: National Clearinghouse for Bilingual Education.

Cummins, J. (1994, March). *Bilingual Development.* Paper presented at the Teacher Of English as a Second Language annual convention, Baltimore.

Dung, I., Viernes, B., & Mudd, S. (1994, November). *Identifying language disordered Asian students: Data and implications.* Poster session presented at the annual convention of the American Speech, Language and Hearing Association, New Orleans.

Figueroa, R. A. (1989). Psychological testing of linguistic-minority students: Knowledge gaps and regulations. *Exceptional Children, 56*(2), 145–152.

Grosjean, F. (1982). *Life with two languages: An introduction to bilingualism.* Cambridge, MA: Harvard University Press.

Hakuta, K. (1993, November). *Issues on bilingual language learning.* Paper presented at the annual convention of the California Association of Asian Bilingual Education, Sacramento.

Hall, E. (1976). *Beyond culture.* Garden City, NJ: Anchor.

Hammond, S. A., & Meiners, L. H. (1993). American Indian deaf children and youth. In K. M. Christensen & G. L. Delgato, (Eds.), *Multicultural issues in deafness* (pp.143–175). New York: Longman.

Harry, B. (1992). *Cultural diversity, families and the special education system.* New York: Teachers' College Press, Columbia University.

Jackson, P. (1968). *Life in classrooms.* New York: Holt, Rinehart and Winston.

Kaplan, R. (1966). Cultural thought patterns in intercultural education. *Language Learning, 16*, 1–20.

Kingston, M. H. (1976). *The woman warrior.* New York: Random House.

Kitano, H., & Daniels, R. (1988). *Asian Americans: Emerging minorities.* Englewood Cliffs, NJ: Prentice-Hall.

Knapp, M. L. (1972). *Nonverbal communication in human interaction.* New York: Holt, Rinehart and Wilson.

Krashen, S. (1981). Bilingual education and second language acquisition theory. In Office of Bilingual Bicultural Education, California State Department of Education, *Schooling and language minority students: A theoretical framework*. Los Angeles: Evaluation, Dissemination and Assessment Center, California State University.

Krashen, S. (1982). *Principles and practice in second language acquisition*. New York: Pergamon Press.

Kuo, E. C. (1974). The family and bilingual socialization: A socio-linguistic study of a sample of Chinese children in the United States. *The Journal of Social Psychology, 92*, 181–191.

Langdon, H. (1992). Language communication and sociocultural patterns in Hispanic families. In H. W. Langdon with L. L. Cheng, (Eds.), *Hispanic children and adults with communication disorders: Assessment and intervention*. Gaithersburg, MD: Aspen Publishers.

Langdon, H., & Merino, B. (1992). Acquisition and development of a second language. In H. W. Langdon with L. L. Cheng, L. (Eds.), *Hispanic children and adults with communication disorders: Assessment and intervention*. Gaithersburg, MD: Aspen Publishers.

Lau v. Nichols, 411 U.S. 563 (1974).

Matsuda, M. (1989). Working with Asian parents: Some communication strategies. *Topics in Language Disorders. 9*(3), 45–53.

Mura, D. (1991). *Turning Japanese: Memoirs of a Sansei*. New York: Atlantic Monthly Press.

Nellum-Davis, P. (1993). Clinical practice issues. In D. Battle (Ed.), *Communication disorders in multicultural populations*. Boston: Andover Medical Publishers.

Prutting, C. A., & Kirchner, D. M. (1983). Applied pragmatics. In T. M. Gallagher & C. A. Prutting (Eds.), *Pragmatic assessment and intervention issues in language* (pp. 29–64). San Diego: College-Hill Press.

Ramirez, M. (1990). A bicognitive-multicultural model for a pluralistic education. In O. Saracho (Ed.), *Cognitive style and early education*. New York: Gordon & Breach Science.

Ripich, D. N., & Creaghead, N. A. (1994). *School discourse problems* (2nd ed). San Diego: Singular Publishing Group, Inc.

Ruiz, N. (1989). An optimal learning environment for Rosemary. *Exceptional Children, 56* (2), 130–144.

Spindler, G., & Spindler, L. (1990). *The American cultural dialogue and its transmission*. London: The Falmer Press.

Takaki, R. (1989). *Strangers from a different shore: A history of Asian Americans*. Boston: Little, Brown & Co.

Taylor, O. L. (1986). *Treatment of communication disorders in culturally and linguistically diverse populations*. San Diego: College-Hill Press.

Tran, M. L. (1991). *Hidden curriculum*. Unpublished manuscript, San Diego State University.

Trueba, H. T., Cheng, L., & Ima, K. (1993). *Myth or reality: Adaptive strategies of Asian Americans in California*. Washington, DC: The Falmer Press.

Vihman, M. M., & McLaughlin, B. (1982). Bilingualism and second language acquisition in preschool children. In C. J. Brainerd & M. Pressley (Eds.), *Verbal processes in children: Process in cognitive development research*. New York: Springer Verlag

CHAPTER 8

ASSESSING ASIAN STUDENTS FOR SPECIAL SERVICES: A PRE-ASSESSMENT CONSIDERATION

LI-RONG LILLY CHENG, Ph.D.

Asian Second language (L2) and/or potential English proficient (PEP) individuals who do not meet teachers' expectations as model students often receive inappropriate referrals to speech-language therapy and/or special education. Homeroom teachers commonly refer such students to special services when they must struggle to grasp pragmatic skills and stylistic communication differences or when they have difficulty sustaining academic progress comparable to their peers with the same background. On the basis of field observations, many Asian-language minority students may qualify for speech-language therapy for various reasons, including: (1) that the student's use of standard English has not developed according to teacher expectations; (2) that a student's level of educational performance does not warrant special education placement; (3) that there is a lack of appropriate language development or English as a second language (ESL) programs for these target students. Well-meaning teachers often suspect these learners of having speech or language disorders, language learning disabilities, or specific learning disabilities when very often this may not be the case. If Asian/Pacific L2 and PEP students demonstrate little or no academic or English acquisition progress after they have received speech or language therapy, they are definitely referred to and placed in special education service programs. Chapters 1 and 2 raise specific questions about the treatment of these learners after they have been placed in special education.

An over- or under-representation of second language learners in special education generally stems from various causes, one of which may be a lack of understanding by the field practitioner about Asian/Pacific students' socio-cultural and linguistic backgrounds. Additionally, there may be a lack of insight regarding the adjustment required by these students to meet school expectations (Trueba, Cheng & Ima, 1993). Although Asian/Pacific students vary in age, native language, degree of acculturation, country of birth, time since immigration, prior experience, and socioeconomic status, they encounter similar challenges when faced with traditional deficit-oriented beliefs and practice—they are not prepared to enter school or compete with their mainstream peers. Inaccurate perceptions and stereotypes and lack of familiarity with a specific ethnic group's culture, history, and contemporary experience may lead educators to lower their expectations and form unwarranted generalizations about the educational potentials of Asian/Pacific students (Cheng, 1993).

Assessing Asian language minority students for special education services is both complex and challenging. Assessors who do not share the same culture, language, and acculturation experiences as the students, in general, are less likely to be insightful and objective in ways necessary to make decisions about a student's placement in special education. Most anthropological studies assume that natives of a particular culture are largely unable to objectively understand and articulate the assumptions or biases of that culture. Yet, through personal life history and closer examination of one's values, one becomes initially aware of culture.

This chapter provides field practitioners with information on pre-assessment considerations for critical and interrelated variables that often influence Asian/Pacific students' school language and academic performance. Part 1 of this chapter discusses culture, language, and communication, generally and as they relate specifically to

Asian/Pacific populations. Part 2 presents and discusses variables directly relating to the assessment of Asian/Pacific learners. Finally, Part 3 is a vignette illustrating the complexities of the interplay among culture, language, and communication in the assessment of students for special education and related services.

ᄔ

PART 1
PREASSESSMENT CONSIDERATIONS: CULTURE, LANGUAGE, AND COMMUNICATION

In this section, various interrelated critical variables to illustrate the complexity and interrelatedness of culture, language, and communication as they impact an individual learner's behavior. Background information relating to the major issues raised in this section is briefly presented to assist field practitioners in further study. The interplay of culture, language, and communication greatly influences the behavior of both individual learners and of the field practitioners who come into contact with them. Most importantly, the effects of this interplay influence the perceptions and behaviors of our society at-large. Because the Asian/Pacific L2 and PEP learners are from the most recently arrived populations in many parts of the United States, American societal attitudes toward these groups as a whole influence the general and educational treatment of these groups and their families (see Chapter 1 for more on this). Hence, I have included a section on selected variables such as religions, folk beliefs, socioeconomic factors, and child-rearing practices that impact the lives of these groups, further illustrating the complexity of assessment issues for special education and related services delivery.

ᄔ

CULTURE: WORLD CULTURES AND ASIAN/PACIFIC POPULATIONS

Over the centuries, anthropologists and social scientists have studied culture and come up with numerous of definitions for it. Cheng (1991), for example, suggests that culture is composed of behavior patterns, symbols, institutional values, and other human-made elements of society. Culture is the total way of life of a group of people in a society and, as such, has its own system of standards. Most agree that culture can be studied from both etic (outside) and emic (inside) points of view (Cheng, 1991).

Each system of standards guides a society's people in their thinking, feeling, and acting. Culture is also creative and meaningful for the lives of individuals and is symbolically represented through their interactions. Furthermore, culture means more than people doing things in similar ways and sharing a common language and history; it also implies similar life experiences and world views. Lastly, it is a continuous and cumulative process that is dynamic rather than fixed or static.

Diversity exists among different cultures; behaviors considered to be valuable or desirable in one culture are often unacceptable in another. For example, in Japan, belching after a meal is considered a sign of courtesy, satisfaction, and good taste; there is no need to say "excuse me"; however, in the United States, belching without excusing oneself is considered rude.

LANGUAGES

Language for the general population and, specifically, for Asian/Pacific populations is covered in this section.

Currently, Chinese, Hindi-Urdu, Bengali, and Japanese are among the most widely spoken languages in the world (Table 8–1).

The diversity of Asian/Pacific language-minority groups presents field practitioners with a tremendous challenge. In the United States, Chinese (Mandarin and Cantonese), Vietnamese, Khmer, Lao, Hmong, Tagalog, and Hindi are widely spoken.

Familiarity with language names, origins, and general characteristics can help educators, resource teachers, school psychologists, and speech-language pathologists (SLPs) understand more about the Asian students they encounter. A brief description of major languages spoken by Asian-Pacific language minority students in U.S. public schools is presented in Table 8–2.

Language is a major function of culture; it is also the most important factor in constructing geographical communities and language communities. Asian/Pacific countries encompass hundreds of distinct languages and dialects. Not all words and their meanings within a language can be appropriately translated from one language into another (i.e., they do not have cognates) because of cultural diversity (or variations?). See Te's chapter, this volume, for examples.

TABLE 8–1

Eight major language families spoken in the United States.

Language Families	Examples
1. Germanic	English, German
2. Slavic	Russian, Polish, Yugoslavian
3. Altaic	Japanese, Korean
4. Sino-Tibetan	Mandarin, Thai, Lao, Cantonese
5. Indic	Bengali, Hindu
6. Malayo-Polynesian	Tagalog, Chamorro
7. Austro-Asiatic	Khmer, Vietnamese, Hmong
8. Romance	French, Spanish, Italian, Portugese

TABLE 8–2

Brief descriptions of major Asian/Pacific languages.

Language	Description
Bengali	Modern Indic language spoken in Bengal (East Bengal is Bangladesh; West Bengal is in the Republic of India).
Chamorro	Language spoken in Guam, Saipan, and some Micronesian islands; belongs to the Austronesian language family.
Chinese	One of a group of Sino-Tibetan languages and dialects spoken in China, including Mandarin, Cantonese, Amoy, Fukien, and Shanghai.
Hindi/Urdu	Hindustani languages spoken in Pakistan and India.
Hmong	A language spoken by the Hmong people from the mountains of Laos.
Ilokano	A language spoken in the Philippines.
Japanese	The language of Japan.
Khmer	The Mon-Khmer language of a people of Cambodia.
Korean	The language of Korea, officially unclassified, but containing many words of Chinese origin.
Lao	The official language of Laos, a Tai language of a Buddhist people living in the area of the Mekong River in Laos and Thailand.

(continued)

TABLE 8–2 *(continued)*

Language	Description
Malay	The Austronesian language of the Malays, a people inhabiting the Malay Peninsula, other parts of Malaysia, and Indonesia.
Pilipino	The national language of the Philippines.
Punjabi	An Indian language spoken in the Punjab, a region in northwest India.
Tagalog	An Austronesian language of a people native to the Philippines.
Vietnamese	The language of Vietnam, belonging to the Mon-Khmer subfamily of Austro-Asiatic languages.

COMMON LANGUAGE: LINGUA FRANCA

Not all Asian/Pacific countries share a colonial history; hence, not all have experienced or experience the imposition of an official European language. Asian regions that were colonized by European countries often have two official languages. For example, India, Indonesia, Hong Kong, the Philippines, and Vietnam use English, Dutch, English, Spanish, and French, respectively, as an additional official language. This is why some of the Asian language-minority students and/or their parents may speak one of these European languages as well as their native language. Moreover, English, Pidgin, and nonorthodox English are spoken and understood in most parts of Singapore, Malaysia, Guam, Philippines, and India.

⼖

COMMUNICATION

VERBAL COMMUNICATION

The use of social dialects is another common phenomenon in a multilingual and multicultural school environment. Features of a social dialect are "systematic and highly regular and cross all linguistic parameters, such as, phonology, morphology, syntax, semantics, lexicon, pragmatics, suprasegmental features, and kinesics. Each social dialect is adequate as a functional and effective variety of English. Each serves a communication function as well as a social solidarity function" (American Speech-Language-Hearing Association [ASHA], 1983). The issues involving social dialects are particularly important to speech-language clinicians in diagnosing API students for language disorders. Furthermore, dialects present unique and distinctive phonological, morphological, syntactical, semantic, and pragmatic features that change alongside evolving cultural needs. The following section delineates some of these changes.

GRAMMAR

Each generation of language users witnesses changes in its language's grammatical system. Throughout history, languages have undergone continual change reflecting two levels of grammatical variation: (1) the formation of words from meaningful units of the language and (2) language syntax—combination of words into larger structures, such as phrases and sentences. Variations exist in word class, sentence structure, arrangement of structure, and word placement within phrases. Verbs, verb auxiliaries, negatives, inflectional suffixes in nouns, various forms of pronouns, articles, and adverbs all undergo frequent variation (Wolfram, 1986). For example, the copula *be* has been used to mean different states of being in the Black dialect: "I be there," for example.

PHONOLOGY

Phonological differences across languages and dialects account for languages' most noticeable characteristics. Variations occur naturally in languages as they evolve through time. One source of variation comes from within a language, itself, as it adjusts and readjusts to its phonological system. For example, in the 14th century, Geoffrey Chaucer wrote:

> Soun ys noght but eyr y broken,
> And every speche that ys spoken,
> Loud or pryvee, foul or fair
> In his substance, ys but air

Written in Middle English more than 500 years ago, this passage is still comprehensible because of the phonological similarities still with us in modern English, yet the way the phonemes are read (whether they are pronounced or not) change the metre.

Other sound differences come from outside the language. For example, English-speakers have adopted sounds from languages with which they have come into contact. Conquest, imperialism, and assimilation of cultures are factors in this extrinsic change of language. The same processes responsible for the molding of English phonological structure over time into what it is today are also responsible for continuing variations in contemporary English. Differences found in current English dialects, for example, reflect the language-contact history of specific groups of speakers.

Phonological differences in dialect may manifest themselves through phonemes that are pronounced differently across different varieties of English—thus the song, "you say *toe-may-toe*, I say *toe-mah-toe*." Conversely, elimination of contrasts between basic phonemes is also common. For example, "pin" and "pen" are often pronounced the same because of regional dialect. (For more information, read Cheng, 1994a and 1994b.)

SEMANTICS

Words undergo continual change of meaning through the process of language/word construction and reconstruction. For example, "debug" comes from the word, "bug"; "bad" means "good" in certain contexts and "cool" often means a condition unrelated to temperature. Such dynamic changes occur naturally in language evolution. Some of the changes may be introduced or used by specific segments of the population (e.g., teens, young adults).

PRAGMATICS

In sociolinguistics, "pragmatics" is the relationship between signs, or linguistic expressions, and their users. Content, social setting, inflection and intonation, and suggestion play substantial roles in the transmission of literal content in communication. Distinctions between literal and nonliteral meaning, nuance, and innuendo may be lost or misinterpreted in a cross-cultural setting in which two communicators perceive a situation differently. For example, "Can you give me a second?" does not literally mean a "second."

One of language's essential roles is establishing and maintaining social interaction. The social context and relationship between participants are crucial to conversational format. Conversation involves several steps: selection of a topic, initiation of speech, turn-taking, maintenance of the topic, and closure of the conversation (Wolfram, 1986). Sociolinguistic theories can help educators decipher rules of conversation that they may encounter in dealing with speakers who are unfamiliar with a new culture.

Issues surrounding social dialects have always been complex and controversial. Two opposing views have emerged during the last few decades. In one view, Cole (1985) proposes two contrasting models: first, the *idealization model* that promotes standard English as the "linguistic archetype" with other dialects as inferior, and second, the *social reality model* that asserts that English is used in many forms, of which so-called "standard English" is but one. The latter is far less ethnocentric, given theorization in recent decades asserting that it is presumptuous to say that there is a "standard English" at all.

The American-Speech-Language-Hearing Association (ASHA, 1983) submitted a position paper on social dialectics dealing with the social reality model. The paper proposed that, "the role of the speech-language pathologist . . . is to provide the desired competency in standard English without jeopardizing the integrity of the individual's first dialect" (p. 24). Furthermore, ASHA urged that, "just as competencies are assumed and necessary in the treatment of communicative disorders, competencies are also necessary in the provision of services to non-standard English speakers, including knowledge of the particular dialect; knowledge of phonological and grammatical features of the dialect; knowledge of effects of attitudes toward dialects; and thorough understanding and appreciation of the community and culture of the nonstandard speaker" (p. 24).

NONVERBAL COMMUNICATION

Nonverbal expression plays an extremely important role in communication. We use gestures, facial expressions, pauses, different intonation and vocal patterns, and spatial arrangements to convey meaning and intent. Leubitz (1973) identifies four functions of nonverbal communication: to relay messages, to augment verbal communication, to contradict verbal communication, and to replace verbal communication. In addition, Knapp (1972) suggests that 35% of social meaning is transmitted through words and 65% through nonverbal channels. Furthermore, physical features such as body build, height, weight, skin color, and other noticeable features can communicate messages inaccurately (Gollnick & Chinn, 1986). For example, Ronald Takaki, a Japanese American from Hawaii is frequently asked about Japan and David Mura is often spoken to in Japanese although he does not know the language.

Other variables of nonverbal communication including proximity and social distance also account for varying communication styles among different ethnic groups. We begin to learn such culturally determined manners of speech and behavior within our immediate social environments from the time we are born, and pragmatics differ from culture to culture so much that someone switching cultures may be confused. Table 8–3 illustrates some pragmatic features that create confusion for interpersonal communications involving members of Asian/Pacific groups.

TABLE 8–3

Pragmatic features that may create confusion for Asian/Pacific Islanders' interpersonal communications in a mainstream American cultural context.

Turn taking	In some Asian cultures, students generally refrain from asking questions or interrupting during class. They may thus appear passive or non-participatory.
Taking leave	The response for the American greeting, "See you?" is, "You bet." This may be difficult for L2 speakers to understand.
Social distance	Culture mitigates and judges proper social distance according to such attributes as age, status, gender, place of origin, and marital status.
Questions	In some Asian cultures, the following questions are common and appropriate: ■ What is your honorable age? ■ You have gained a lot of weight, haven't you? ■ Have you eaten?
Kinship terms	In some languages, kinship terms schematically depict human relationships. Chinese speakers learning English may have trouble translating English terms such as "brother-in-law." Chinese speakers may be confused as to whether this means a sister's husband or a husband's brother.

TABLE 8–3 *(continued)*

Physical contact	In some cultures, hugging, kissing, or expressing emotion in public is frowned upon while other cultures accept and even invite such displays. Such differences may create communication problems in interpersonal relationships.
Paralinguistic rules	Facial expression is minimized in some cultures while in others it is used as a crucial part of communication.
Gazing and staring	Although young children often stare at strangers, acceptable duration and intensity of gazing and staring may differ from culture to culture.
Eye contact	In general, American educators consider sustained eye contact as appropriate classroom behavior. American teachers may perceive aborted eye contact unfavorably, while many cultures perceive this to be a sign of respect.
Response patterns	In some cultures, a giggle is a sign of embarrassment. In others, it is an appropriate response to some situations.
Gestures	Common gestures can mean radically different things in different cultures.
Politeness	What is considered polite in one culture may be considered rude in another. Assimilation into a new culture requires a shift from one standard of politeness to another. For example, in America, we ask someone at the table to pass the pepper, while in China, we reach for it without "bothering" others for it.

Taylor (1986a) presents a model of cultural interplay that takes place in everyday encounters. When people from two different cultures come into contact, conflicts and communication breakdowns may arise primarily because the conversants operate by different rules. For example, Chinese culture places great value on age, although American culture places great value on youth. Consequently, asking individuals about their age is socially acceptable in China whereas it may be considered inappropriate in the United States. Furthermore, Chinese culture views harmony as more important than confrontation. Frustration, incompetence, alienation, rejection, confusion, and ambivalence may rise from such disparities.

Conflict occurs when language is learned without adequate familiarity with the cultural values that accompany it.

In addition to insufficient fluency in English communication, many Asian L2 and PEP students who lack social knowledge and cultural literacy of mainstream Western culture can be perceived as less competent in communication. Many of them often lack experience communicating in American social contexts and feel like strangers or outsiders. Younger students may be unfamiliar with specific social rules. For example, they may not know that speaking in class is acceptable and even expected in certain situations.

Having knowledge about a group's cultural and pragmatic characteristics can dramatically improve interpersonal and cross-cultural communications. Field practitioners need to collaborate with interpreters in assessing students' native language competence and identifying possible speech or language disorders or other academic difficulties, particularly in the areas of literacy learning. Interpreters can often help clarify cultural or pragmatic characteristics and linguistic inferences that may be misperceived as deviancy without an understanding of the cultural context.

"Accent" exhibited by multicultural/multilingual populations presents yet another rich and diverse area of linguistic variability.

⅂

CULTURE AND LANGUAGE INTERACTIONS

In this section, I will describe the relationship between culture and language, particularly the interplay between Asian and Anglo-American cultures and languages and how it may impact on Asian L2 and PEP learners.

CULTURE AND LANGUAGE FORM

Within a language group, native speakers utilize their language's rules and customs *unconsciously and automatically*, having acquired them through daily interactions; however, new language learners have to learn these new rules and customs and how to follow them. For Asian/Pacific language minority students to develop English language proficiency, they need to first comprehend and master the complexities—both explicit and implicit—of the English language and of American socio-cultural customs. Given the diversity within the family of Asian/Pacific languages, themselves, the relative degrees of transferability—meaning qualities already shared with English/American language and culture—between Asian/Pacific and English languages cannot be easily generalized across Asian language and ethnic boundaries.

Differences in language are directly related to the varying needs of each culture. Words and vocabularies emerge to express concepts or products that have infiltrated into that culture; until then, they do not exist. For example, only after the invention of modern technologies, such as the Xerox photocopier, did many modern languages have a word for photocopier. Borrowing and incorporating words into a language—thus changing it—ultimately reflects changes in a given culture.

Because culture is an adaptation, or way of survival (Banks, 1990), it is often developed to accommodate certain environmental conditions and available natural and technological resources (Gollnick & Chinn, 1990; Hilliard, 1992); subsequently, specific concepts and/or languages are developed to reflect such an adaptation. For example, the Inuits, who live in northern Canada where there is ice, sea, and extreme cold, have developed a culture very different from the Marshallese of the Pacific Islands where there is plenty of fish, coconut, and other types of tropical vegetation and fruits. The culture of a metropolitan city is different from that of a farming community, just as that of the tropics, where there is extreme rainfall, heat, and humidity, is different from that of the desert, where there is extreme heat but little rainfall.

Such ecological variation also has a direct influence on the development of language. The Inuits have many words for snow and the Chamorro have many words for coconut. The Chinese language contains many words to describe cooking and many to represent rice products. Similarly, American English utilizes many words to describe baked goods (bran muffin, English muffin, corn bread, bagel, kaiser roll, biscuit, etc.); it also has many words for food or liquid containers, such as plates, saucers, dishes, bowls, platters, and so on. Each of these serve a specific, albeit similar, function. In Vietnamese, one word is used to represent all kinds of containers.

Different words represent various cultural orientations because cultural values permeate the vocabulary of a language. In Japanese, there are approximately 83 different ways to say "I," while in Samoan, the word "I" does not exist. English has only a few words to represent cousins, aunts, and uncles; yet Chinese has a very elaborate list of terms to illustrate specific relationships of aunts and uncles from each side of their family as well as from specific generations. In English, many kinds of bread are used to make a sandwich, thus the specificity in the words kaiser roll, sourdough, pumpernickel, bagel, and so on. In both Chinese and Vietnamese, "cousin" is represented by many words differentiated by gender, age, and family hierarchy. The emphasis on specificity of these terms provides Chinese and Vietnamese children with more precise concepts of family relationships and hierarchies.

CULTURE AND LANGUAGE CONTENT

By their very nature, implicit elements of a culture are difficult to define. Nonetheless, these inherent parts of a person's being are demonstrated through actions and thoughts and are unconsciously acquired, molded by significant others and personal experiences. For example, in some Asian cultures, adults may maintain emotional and economic dependence on their parents throughout their lifetimes. If a family member is born or becomes handicapped, the Asian family takes full responsibility. Other cultures may have very different attitudes about dependence and independence. There are even nomadic cultures that still "leave the weak behind." Cross-cultural studies and attempts to understand attitudes toward handicapping conditions, and life itself, make it possible to observe some implicit cultural elements (Meyerson, 1990; Strauss, 1990; Weddington, 1990).

CULTURE AND LANGUAGE USE

Knowledge of a common language mitigates nearly every social encounter. Conversely, a lack of cultural language or knowledge can result in misunderstanding and communication breakdown. For example, in a Chinese greeting, an old friend may say "Ni fa fu le," "You have gained weight." The intention is to imply that the person is doing quite well: eating well and feeling good. The same phrase in an American setting would probably have a very different, negative connotation. Also, the Chinese often greet neighbors and colleagues by asking, "Have you eaten?" This may strike Americans as peculiar, as such a greeting conveys care and familiarity, sentiments that Americans normally reserve for friends or family.

⊔

INTERPLAY OF CULTURE, LANGUAGE, AND COMMUNICATION

The complexity of language and literacy development and learning processes demands a closer examination of the interplay among the three interrelated variables that affect Asian/Pacific learners' achievement in school: culture, language, and communication.

COMMUNICATIVE COMPETENCE AND CULTURAL COMPETENCE

The notion of communicative competence, introduced by Hymes (1974), refers to an individual's capacity to use language, perhaps best described as the ability to say the right thing in the right way at the right time in the right place. Its two major characteristics are (1) the ability to analyze the listener's role, and (2) the ability to use linguistic resources in appropriate communication strategies (knowing when to use terms of politeness or respect such as "Sir" or "Ma'am"). Studying communication and the acquisition of communicative competence from the functional view, Halliday (1978) concludes that learning language is the progressive development of a number of basic functions of language (including negating, protesting, commenting, describing, etc.) and the construction of meaning potentials.

COMMUNICATIVE COMPETENCIES AND MULTICULTURAL COMPETENCIES

Like most speakers trying to explain their native language and culture, few American researchers or field practitioners can delineate "effective" communication from an American perspective because of the complexities of the values and beliefs that implicitly dictate communication behaviors. For example, the American aspiration to be a "classless" society leads to a more informal communication style than is typical of other cultures. Also, because Americans are highly time- and result-oriented, they expect quick responses, find silent periods uncomfortable, and may view more reflective communicators as slow or dull. The American belief in rugged individualism and competition likewise corresponds to a direct and assertive communication style. By American standards, communication styles of other cultures may be judged as evasive or socially incompetent (Cheng 1991). Social competence, the ability to interact appropriately in social situations, is critical for successful adjustment in life. According to Gresham (1986), social competence is "an evaluative term based on judgments (given certain criteria) that a person has performed a [social] task adequately." Individuals who are not able to surmount the obstacles of social competence may find success or even survival in the American culture to be impossible.

Similarly, what African-American, Latino, or Asian/Pacific Americans consider to be effective communication within their peer groups may be very different for each minority group. For example, increasing evidence shows that many Latino children learn best in a "cooperative" environment (Merino, 1991), whereas Asian children may prefer to receive information directly from the teacher. Also, certain Mexican-Americans retell a story in simplified terms because they view it as shared information between both participants in the exchange. These tendencies, like those of the Asian/Pacific cultures, may lead to dysfunctional learning in typical U.S. classroom settings (Heath, 1986).

To make life in school even more of a problem, the concept of cultural literacy (Hirsch, 1988) reveals the complexity involved in Asian/Pacific L2 and PEP learners' achieving cultural and communicative competencies. Although the notion of cultural literacy is controversial, as it is extremely difficult to define what should be included in as crucial in our culture, it does provide Asian/Pacific students with a key to improve their acquisition of cultural knowledge about parts of American history and a guide from which to function successfully within mainstream American culture. However, given an increasingly and widely professed acceptance of cultural pluralism in our society, Hirsch's (1988) attempt to make all Americans more literate about their own culture raises a critical need to include important facts about some of the major contributions to America's pluralistic society and tapestry made by culturally and linguistically diverse populations. This necessity is particularly important for multicultural- and multilingual-school contexts and many workplaces.

LANGUAGE STYLES

Virtually every English speaker prefers to imbue some individual style along a continuum of formality. However, styles and conditions for adjusting them along this continuum vary considerably. Early sociolinguistic studies have reduced the critical variable defining the dimension of formality and informality in language style to a single "principle of attention" paid to speech (Labov, 1972). The more attention paid to speech, the more formal the style. Formal styles were defined as those used in situations in which speech is the primary focus; whereas informal styles are used in those in which speaker audio-monitoring is minimal (Taylor, 1986a, 1986b). Classroom discourse is generally formal and language styles vary from teacher to teacher. However, discourse outside of the classroom tends to be informal and casual. Children who are not exposed to this variety of discourse style may appear serious and formal at all times and in all situations.

Education is viewed as a formal process by most Asian cultures and reading factual information is considered valuable study. Orderliness and obedience are important to Asian students, and students learn to attain these characteristics through observation and memorization. Asian/Pacific students prefer pattern practice and rote learning over discovery learning and consider teachers to be carriers of knowledge or transmitters of information (Cheng, 1991). American education, on the other hand, stresses critical thinking and discovery in a less stressful, more open atmosphere. Such incongruencies in educational practices can result in communication difficulties and academic setbacks.

WRITTEN DISCOURSE

Writing is another major vehicle for communication. Teachers may encourage certain styles of writing and expect all students to conform to them. In Kaplan's comparison of writing styles among members of different language groups, he found that some students write in an oral narrative rather than expository or "standard" academic writing (Kaplan, 1966). Anglo-American writing typically requires sequential organization: beginning, development, and conclusion. Asian writing may be non-sequentially coordinated in structure, beginning **without** an introduction, but replacing this with a recitation of a variety of ideas without apparent connections and without apparent endings. Lessons learned from such Asian writing are not to be extracted directly from the writing but inferred by the reader. The Analects of Confucius or the writings of Lao Tzu, for example, often seem cryptic to Westerners because of the open-ended nature of the writing. Emphasizing inference and open-endedness, Asian writing concepts differ greatly from most American school-based writing which most often calls for explicit conceptual development.

Teachers should recognize and appreciate stylistic differences from U.S. writing conventions, rather than lead students to think that their own culturally influenced writing style is "incorrect" or "inadequate." They should allow opportunities for their students to explore both narrative and expository writing as a means of styles enhancing student self-esteem and literacy. At present, license to write in diverse ways is an unpopular concept and not tolerated. Students who receive remarks such as "awkward," "unclear," or "unacceptable," often become discouraged and avoid writing; such discouragement may even result in complete failure in school.

In addition, selection of culturally appropriate topics is also a challenge for educators of multicultural classes. A few examples illustrate this point. For instance, asking students to develop connections for what appears to be unconnected or to use a component of imagination demands conceptual processes which are not generally stressed in Asian schools. Rather, the Asian rote-learning process requires that a writer draw on conventions and repeat formulas of the past. In Asia, deviations from this sort of writing imply attitudes of challenge and individualism, which, although encouraged in American schools, are unexpected in the Asian system. Another example is that a teacher asking students to write on the topic, "What will you do if your parents die suddenly?" breaches a cultural taboo prevalent in most Asian cultures. Even if a teacher may intend such an assignment merely as an exercise to encourage students to explore hypothetical possibilities, to students from Asian/Pacific cultures, to talk about their parents' deaths is to invite a curse on the parents.

🖵

PART 2
PREASSESSMENT CONSIDERATIONS: RELIGIONS, FOLK BELIEFS, POVERTY, AND ABUSE

In this section, relevant variables that influence Asian/Pacific students' behaviors, attitudes, and school achievement are explored. Additionally, guidelines for the clinician's initial encounter with a multicultural client are provided in Appendixes 8A and 8B.

RELIGIONS

Among the great variety of religious and philosophical beliefs practiced in the United States by its culturally diverse populations are Animism, Buddhism, Catholicism, Confucianism, Islam, Shintoism, and Taoism. As clinicians and educators, it is our responsibility to sensitize ourselves to traditions followed by various cultures. By learning more about them, we will broaden our own scope of understanding and help bridge gaps between cultures as all exchanges of cultural traditions encourage beneficial openness and acceptance.

The primary religion in China, Vietnam, Laos, and Cambodia is Buddhism. This religion began around the fifth century as an offshoot of Hinduism. Buddha preached kindness, nonviolence, and attainment of a state in which human desires, which cause misery, would be nonexistent. The Laotians and Khmer practice Theravadic Buddhism while the Hmong and the Vietnamese practice Mahayana Buddhism. Many Japanese practice Zen Buddhism as well as Shinto, an indigenous religion that has intermingled with Buddhism.

Confucianism maintains a strong influence in China and Vietnam. Rules that dictate relationships between father and son, teacher and student, husband and wife, and so forth—as voiced by Confucius—direct this religion. The influence of Confucius extends all the way to Vietnam, Japan, Thailand, Singapore, Korea, and other Southeast Asian countries.

Taoism is derived from the doctrines of Lao Tzu, with the basic principle being non-interference with nature. One must follow nature's course rather than overcome it. Taoism promotes passivity and non-intervention, principles that could be deleterious when parents are asked to approve interventions for remediation of language or learning disorders. Sometimes parents need to take action to intervene but do not because of their Taoist beliefs.

Animism is another common religion in Southeast Asia. It holds that demons and spirits exist in everything, including one's body. Baci is a commonly practiced form of Animism among Southeast Asians. It is performed when someone is ill or has to go away on a trip (Cheng, 1987). Mysticism is also in practice in many parts of Asia and the Pacific. Other folk practices such as rubbing, pinching, and so on may seem abusive to an uninformed service provider.

Islam (Moslem faith) is practiced in the Philippines, Malaysia, Indonesia, some parts of China and the Middle East. There are two branches of Islam: Sunni and Shiite. Catholicism is practiced in the

Philippines, Micronesian Islands, many parts of Asia, Mexico, Haiti, Central/South America, Western Europe and North America. Mormon missionaries from the United States have founded churches throughout Asia and the Pacific Islands.

What organizing principle might explain the cultural relevance of our world's diverse religions? The Hmong present a good case study. Although they have adopted many religions, their central preoccupation remains the family and its continuity. Their practice of Animism involves propitiating ancestral spirits. Conversion to Christianity is undergone in family units so that forming of family alliances relates strongly to the adoption of new religions.

FOLK BELIEFS

Folk beliefs influence an individual's perception of illnesses, disabilities, and treatment. The Haitian practice of Voodoo has spread to many parts of the world whereas Southeast Asian Animism is exclusive to its part of the world. (For a more complete description of these beliefs, see Cheng [1989].) Furthermore, many cultures have integrated folk belief in spirits with religious beliefs introduced to them by Western missionaries. For example, Pacific Island and Puerto Rican cultures blend spiritualism and Catholicism (Cheng & Scheffner-Hammer, 1992; Scheffner-Hammer, 1990). Cheng (1989) reports that birth defects are often viewed as "curses." Such a folk belief has tremendous impact on the treatment of children born with such defects. For many centures, the Chinese have believed that "curses" are caused by one's ancestors' "bad deeds." These "bad deeds" cause the descendants to have bad luck, to die, or to experience birth defects. Although most contemporary Asians do not believe in this, many continue to; these people often go to temple to pray for forgiveness from the goddess of mercy.

POVERTY AND ABUSES

To adequately assess Asian/Pacific students, particularly among L2 and PEP learners, field practitioners need to have a broad knowledge about the current statistics regarding children in poverty. A large number of language minority students, particularly some groups of recent immigrants from Southeast Asian countries, live in inner cities and their families have little financial and social support.

⌐

PREASSESSMENT CONSIDERATIONS: CRITICAL VARIABLES RELATING TO INDIVIDUAL LEARNERS

In this section, critical variables that impact individual learners as they work at school are presented. Based on field observations, we've selected variables that have direct impact on Asian/Pacific L2 and PEP learners' school performance as they strive to become literate in English and advance in formal American scholastic programs.

ELEMENTS REQUIRED FOR ADJUSTMENT AND ACCULTURATION

Further examination and discussion of the multifaceted challenges faced by individuals of lower socioeconomic background is needed. Many are from underrepresented ethnic groups and experience great difficulty in adjusting to mainstream U.S. culture. The following are some critical elements of adjustment.

ADJUSTMENT/MAINSTREAMING

Acquiring English language proficiency is one step in achieving mainstreaming. Most non-English proficient (NEP), limited-English proficient (LEP), and fluent-English proficient (FEP) students require assessment of their English language comprehension and production before there can be mainstream placement. There are a number of critical variables to be considered:

1. ESL classes: Number of years in ESL; These students usually spend 3 years in addition to 1 transitional year in an ESL program.
2. No ESL classes: Many schools lack ESL classes. What types of language classes have PEP students in schools without ESL been getting?
3. PEP forever students: Some students never exit an ESL program.
4. Home language(s) proficiency: Proficiency in home language(s) is another critical element. Some have limited pri-

mary language proficiency, although others have had a strong foundation from which to build.

PERCEIVED BARRIERS TO EDUCATIONAL SUCCESS

Interviews with 100 high school Southeast Asian refugee students disclosed the following barriers to educational success (Ima, personal communication):

- Lack of supervision after school: Many students go home after school without parent or guardian supervision. Some are required to help with cooking, cleaning, and other jobs—leaving them little time to study. Others are unaccompanied minors or detached youths who require special attention and care. Still others join gangs, or drop out of school, altogether.
- Lack of opportunity to practice English outside of school: In many homes, only the native home language or languages are spoken. Schools provide PEP students with an English-speaking environment, but these students tend to group into small circles without English-speaking peers. Students with speech and language disorders suffer a greater disadvantage because of their inability to communicate effectively with teachers and peers, in either home or school language.
- Impact of cultural/social expectations: Cultural groups pressure their children differently than mainstream U.S. customs in terms of school and marriage. Hmong girls are expected to marry while still young; boys are to start providing for their families in early youth as well. Such pressures and expectations can lead to students dropping out of school (Lewis, Vang, & Cheng, 1989).

Professionals need to redesign curriculum materials and develop strategies for learning packages that respond to students' complex social and economic needs. Indeed, we must infuse multicultural and pluralistic perspectives into overall service delivery. We must also empower students by providing them with opportunities to adapt to their new culture/language and by respecting their differences, eventually leading them to successful integration into the society as functional bicultural/multicultural individuals.

Cheng (1993) surveyed adult ESL students and found that they felt "stupid" and "less intelligent" when they could not express themselves well in English. Interestingly, English-speaking adults relate the same feelings of embarrassment and stupidity during their attempts to learn Spanish as an auxilliary language.

EXPERIENCES IN HOME COUNTRY

Educational systems vary from country to country. Some have compulsory education of varying lengths and some do not. Preliminary understanding of educational practices in PEP students' home countries can prepare professionals for assessing these students (refer to Chapter 1, this volume). Furthermore, teachers can work more effectively with parents who were educated outside of the United States even though the children were born in the United States.

After accepting the inadequacies of testing materials and possible unreliability of interpreters, an assessor must take a long hard look at any available comprehensive, reliable information. Assessment is more than just testing. It requires the mindful gathering of background information on PEP students' development and health, family, language development, cognitive skills, and social-emotional histories. The following are suggestions for collecting comprehensive and reliable information regarding the individual; furthermore, what follows provides an exemplar for the preassessment process.

DEVELOPMENTAL AND HEALTH HISTORIES

This information should be gathered from interviews with parents and studies of medical reports. Monolingual assessors need fairly reliable interpreters to obtain valid necessary information from parents and families. Straight translation of medical terminology about childhood diseases usually is not adequate, as diseases contracted in rural areas so often have lacked professional medical care or diagnoses. Interpreters should ask parents to describe the symptoms of ailments their children have had. They should ask parents to demonstrate through gesture, symptoms such as ear-pulling, eye-rolling, and body-stiffening.

FAMILY AND CULTURAL-LINGUISTIC HISTORIES

Inquiries regarding both the immediate family members and extended family members living within the same household contribute to effective assessment. Assessors and their interpreters should query information from students' primary caregivers (often the child's grandparents). Here are some vital questions:

- How does the child spend his or her free time?
- Who takes care of the child?
- How is the parent-child/caretaker-child interaction?
- What kinds of stimulation and experiences is the child receiving?
- What languages and dialects are spoken at home?
- What television program or programs does the child watch?
- What are some of the child's chores and responsibilities?
- What is the caregiver's attitude toward the child's contribution to the home? (Keep in mind that some cultures—middle-class Chinese, for example—typically exclude children from household chores.)

Assessors and interpreters should consider the following characteristics of adaptive behavior when suspecting cases of cognitive delay in Asian-Pacific Islander children:

1. A parent may feel torn between allowing their child to develop typical U.S. independence and taking on a normal, nurturing role. Note that a good Asian parent takes complete responsibility for his or her child's needs.
2. A parent may be able to best provide accurate information on areas of delay by comparing developmental rates of several of their children.
3. A child from another culture may have been toilet-trained or introduced to solid food much earlier or later than a typical American child.
4. An Asian-Pacific Island child may have limited opportunity for independent and assertive behaviors.
5. A student from a predominantly Asian/Pacific Island background may show "absurd" results on adaptive behavior scales—for example, seldom drinking from water faucets or ordering meals in restaurants. A student may also use chopsticks more readily than forks and knives.

LANGUAGE DEVELOPMENT HISTORY

When interpreters are not adequately trained, they may ask very general questions when, for example, they are solely responsible for finding out about a child's proficiency in a native language. Parents often reply that there are no problems, that their children understand what the parents are saying and can express themselves. Such answers are clearly useless to the assessment process. Questions that may be helpful in obtaining more specific information about a child's language use include:

■ What language is used at home and with what frequency?
■ Do children initiate conversation?
■ What do they talk about?
■ How often do parents and children converse?
■ How much time do children spend in passive activities such as watching TV or playing video games?
■ Do parents value their children's silence?

Interviews should provide assessors clear ideas about the quality of language used in homes. Appendix 8C provides a sample of how native speech materials can be developed.

Also beware of indiscriminate citing of "auditory processing" problems. PEP children generally have little difficulty with auditory discrimination tasks. They can usually perform digit series successfully in English and native languages. After a couple of years of American schooling, they show little preference as to which language to use during such tasks. On the other hand, they usually show below age-level ability with sentence memorization and grammar.

COGNITIVE SKILLS HISTORY

Nonverbal tasks provide the only valid indicator of ability in cognitive skills. But translated test answers only provide an impression of ability. Problem-solving tasks such as inference explanation and determination of cause-and-effect can be effective tools. On the other hand, results from one-word basic concept, classification, and antonym tests will reflect limitations due to lack of English proficiency.

SOCIAL/EMOTIONAL HISTORIES

Note that characteristics mentioned under "Adaptive Behaviors" apply here as well. Chinese children, for example, generally do fewer household chores than they will in their early teens. As an exception, children from very poor Chinese families may take responsibility for younger siblings, meal-cooking, and housework—even when they are very young.

PEP students rarely have friends visit their homes, go to others' homes, or spend time on the telephone like their American peers. Large apartment houses with multiple units, such as those inhabited by many Indochinese PEPs in San Francisco, limit peer interaction to what takes place in school.

Parents often say that their children "play (with) toys," rather than play video games or watch television. Assessors should ask specific questions regarding the kinds of toys their children play with and how they play with them, as well as asking about any "pretending" games being played. Parents may indicate that they help their children with studies rather than play with them. This doesn't mean they don't love their children, but that parents may fail to recognize the vital connection between playing and learning.

TEAMING WITH INTERPRETERS

Keep in mind that, in general, it is difficult to work without interpreters. Speech-language clinicians should request that their interpreters ask specific questions that clearly pertain to their primary SLP intentions. Interviews, observations, and tasks should be used rather than standardized tests, and testing should be undertaken by teams of collaborators, including psychologists, speech/language clinicians, learning specialists, and social workers. Ideal assessment takes place as a collaborative effort.

⊔

PART 3
VIGNETTE: A HMONG
EXPERIENCE WITH ASSESSMENT

This final chapter section provides an in-depth study of the theoretical and practical difficulties faced by the Hmong as they enter the American educational system. It suggests ways of bridging cultural and communication gaps and achieving educationally functional and pluralistic classrooms.

Sometimes referred to as "Miao" or "Meo," the Hmong, originally native to China, are among many Southeast Asian refugee groups that have arrived steadily in the U.S. since 1975. Their long struggle for survival provides the key to their culture and identity, as they have lived at odds with or isolated from existing powers for a long time (Walker, 1988). The Hmong have moved from place to place to look for land and other Hmong, both of which are prerequisites for the concept of a future to the minds of older individuals of this group (Walker, 1988).

The Hmong moved from China to the mountainous area of northern Laos in the 19th century. Most of them farmed and few went through schooling. Those who moved to cities received more education and engaged in business or other urban occupations. Most Hmong children received education at home through generations-old oral history lessons. Everyone took part in teaching them about Hmong culture.

Between 1960 and 1975, the U.S. Central Intelligence Agency recruited thousands of Hmong to conduct clandestine maneuvers in their region against the Vietcong and the Communist Pathet Lao (Cheng, 1987). Years of conflict originating during the closing days of World War II led to this involvement with the CIA. This connection not only implicated mercenary arrangements, but also involved a history of conflict between various Hmong (and Lao) factions.

By March 1970, Hmong populations in Laos had dropped in number by about 100,000 from war, massacre, hunger, and disease. Under their patrilineal system and a belief that fathers serve as key figures to their families' survival, deaths threatened the family continuity of Hmong. After the fall of the noncommunist Laotian government in 1975, approximately 100,000 Hmong fled Laos to escape retaliation for their support of the defeated government. Most were illiterate and had never before been outside their mountain homeland. The average education level of their male refugees was first grade (Rumbaut & Ima, 1987).

Most Hmong children in American schools do not remember the war or Laos, but some were born and grew up in refugee camps in Thailand. These children were influenced by "camp culture" which refers to influences—modern and old, local and global—that dominated children's lives in refugee camps (Moffat & Walker, 1986). More than 25% of Hmong children now in the United States were born here after their families arrived as refugees from Laos. A Hmong child in elementary school in 1989 might have been born in the United States or in a Thai refugee camp.

Although these children rarely come from "usual" Laotian life experiences, knowing about their parents' backgrounds can facilitate: (1) assessing whether or not children are functioning within the expected range of the home context, (2) looking for clues as to possible trauma and/or physically handicapping events, and (3) communicating to parents all of the information they might need to make informed decisions about their children's education (Lewis et al., 1989).

The Hmong are from widely spread locations, encompassing a variety of traditions and customs, which makes it difficult to generalize about them. Most Hmong know how things were done in their own region but cannot speak for those of other regions. Indeed most documents on the Hmong are written by non-Hmongs, despite a recent trend to the contrary (Bliatout, Downing, & Yang, 1988). Their year of arrival permits a rough characterization of the families' educational and vocational histories and socioeconomic status. The evacuation of U.S. troops from Saigon in April, 1975 marked the beginning of the first wave of Southeast Asian refugees to the United States. After the Hmong leader General Vang Pao fled to Thailand in 1975 to escape the Pathet Lao takeover of Laos, the United States accepted approximately 5,000 Hmong for resettlement.

The first refugee wave, therefore, had strong connections to Vang Pao and the U.S. government. Xeu Vang Vangyi (1980) identifies the Hmong who came in 1977–1978 as the second wave, and the majority of Hmong refugees who came in 1979–1981 as the third wave. According to Vangyi, the first and second waves of Hmong had at least some education, but the third wave brought soldiers, peasants, farmers, and other working groups who had no formal education, no language training, and no experience with Western societies.

Some researchers assert that Hmong arriving since 1986 constitute a fourth wave. The fourth wave has brought those individuals least willing to give up hope of returning to Laos. They have been the most exposed to war and spent the longest time in refugee camps. The fourth wave may resemble the second wave in that its adults once held relatively privileged positions. But its younger generation's education and exposure to technology reflect the limited range of opportunity available in refugee camps. However, more fourth-wave children will have attended primary school than in previous waves. They have been internationalized by the camp experience (Moffat & Walker, 1986). The Hmong who come during the fourth wave are more prepared for the transition and have received educational programs designed for refugees.

When the first Hmong groups came to the United States in 1975, they were scattered in groups to small communities of several hundred people across the United States. They were settled in California, Colorado, Hawaii, Minnesota, Montana, Pennsylvania, and South Carolina. Following a massive influx between 1979 and 1980, major changes occurred in their distribution. Hmong communities began appearing in a number of new states, and some who had been placed in specific communities through government resettlement programs undertook secondary migrations. This raised the Hmong population in California to over 47,000 by the end of 1986, the largest in the country. In all, more than 60,000 Hmong from Laos resettled in the United States between 1975 and 1987. An estimated 25,000 or more Hmong children have been born in this country.

CRITICAL QUESTIONS

Important questions about the Hmong are:

- Is there a Hmong alphabet?
- Is it the same or similar to the English alphabet?
- Are Hmong language materials available in the United States?
- Are most Hmong literate or not? (According to Lewis, personal communication, May, 1990, only 10% are literate.)
- What kinds of activities can regular classroom teachers give Hmong children during reading time to enhance their English skills, assuming they cannot keep up with classmates because of lack of English proficiency?
- Of Hmong children born outside the United States, do most come from refugee camps?
- What is life like in refugee camps?
- Are children in camps taught English?
- What kinds of interaction do these children have with their teachers?
- Do they consider it disrespectful to contribute to discussions or directly ask questions?

CHARACTERISTICS OF THE HMONG LANGUAGE

ORAL LANGUAGE

Understanding structural rules of oral Hmong is important to avoid misdiagnosis. This language has 56 initial consonants, seven tones, and one final consonant, /ng/. It has two major dialects: White (Hmoob Dawb) and Green (Hmoob Ntsuab). And it has four series of stopped consonants, voiced and voiceless fricatives, nasals, liquids, and a single voiced glide. Its sounds were developed and represented in letters of the romanized alphabet by missionary linguists in the late 1950s. (For more information about the Hmong language, see Cheng, 1987; Lewis et al., 1989.)

STRESS AND INTONATION

Hmong speakers may have difficulty with final consonants, and particularly consonant clusters in seeking to attain English. They learn polysyllabic English words with correct primary and secondary stresses with relative ease once they can regard syllables as individual Hmong words with tones. A Hmong learner may place too much importance on vowel sounds in unaccented syllables, not understanding that these are often "schwa" sounds in English (similar to the Hmong vowel represented by "w" or /i/).

Hmong words are essentially monosyllabic and compound words are di- or polysyllabic. Hmong script has no universally accepted standards. Unlike English, Hmong is noninflectional and lacks homonyms, homophones, and synonyms, causing difficulty for Hmong English learners. Hmong, like other Asian languages, uses classifiers with nouns. These reveal attributes of the nouns in ways that English does not (Bliatout et al., 1988). Knowledge of linguistic differences provides professionals necessary background for accurate assessment.

ORAL TRADITION

The Hmong, like Native Americans, have always emphasized oral skills and had no written language until recent years. They achieved high social status not because of wealth or education but because of speaking skills which are considered extremely desirable for social functions, religious ceremonies, group meetings, and other events. In traditional Hmong society, one learned how to speak well from elders. In addition, people could become community leaders only if they possessed formal speaking skills.

Learning how to create verses is considered an important part of Hmong culture. Children begin this at an early age, creating verses at social functions such as weddings and namings, as well as religious and funeral services (Bliatout et al., 1988).

The Lao school system emphasizes the traditional belief that life success depends on the ability to communicate well on social occasions in front of family, clan, village members and government authority. It also places great emphasis on rote memorization.

What do these observations imply for teachers or clinicians? Language form, content, and use give rise to a style unique to Hmong culture. These students will perform well in preparing speeches, reports, letters, or essays if given memorizable samples of varying topics and contexts. Although this technique may run counter to American teachers' approach to encouraging creativity in that it doesn't provide structure, it will provide assessors a proper view of children's abilities to learn the school language, whether oral or written. It will provide a context for success and form a scaffolding to be gradually withdrawn as children become more proficient in English skills.

This same strategy can be applied to other kinds of learning. Auditory, tactile, and visual modalities should be included when designing classroom activities for Hmong children. Facts, verses, and figures can be taught by assigning recitation. Any kind of patterned, rhyming, or rhythmic speech will complement the Hmong traditional ways of learning information. Visual aids are also helpful. Shapes, symbols, and colors from traditional Hmong costumes may aid in discrimination and memory when paired with visual material (Bliatout et al., 1988).

Recognizing the Hmong reliance on oral tradition is especially important, as Americans generally rely on written communications. Note, for example, the common use in schools of printed notes that many parents largely ignore. Knowing the Hmong reliance on oral communication, teachers and school personnel can identify individuals in the community with access to the local Hmong oral network and use it to communicate with Hmong parents.

LEARNING STYLES

All immigrant children carry cultural experiences based on their parents' economic and social environments into schools. Youngsters from an essentially preliterate, pretechnological culture bring unique behavioral patterns, belief systems, attitudes, emotions, learning styles, and communication styles to the American classroom. These styles differ greatly from those of mainstream American culture. Understanding and appreciating the unique culture of the Hmong provide educators proper perspective on vast observable differences.

Hmong behavior patterns also differ from those expected in American schools. For example, teachers symbolize "authority" and "wisdom" to the Hmong. They are not to be questioned or challenged. To show respect and deference, Hmong students are taught never to sustain eye contact with their teacher. Hmong and other major Asian groups identify themselves per group, not per individual. They always respect group priorities. In Merced, California, for example, first- and second-grade teachers found that Hmong girls in their classes were better students than Hmong boys and expected the girls to continue to compete as aggressively as other students. This, however, runs counter to the traditional cultural expectations facing Hmong children at home.

Although the Hmong are very lenient with their younger children and may allow those of elementary school age to play and compete, Hmong females are considered adults at puberty. At that time, they are considered ready to marry and have children (Walker,1988). In fact, many drop out of school to do so. Those who finish high school get married very soon afterwards and rarely go on to college.

FOLK PRACTICES

Hmong males also marry early, but their age of marriage is several years older than that of females. The Hmong concept of early adulthood versus extended adolescence creates problems for both Hmong youth and American teachers. The American ideal of "delayed" marriage and childbirth is rationalized by youths needing additional years to prepare for job markets requiring extensive educational backgrounds. Hmong youth in the United States often change both their age of marriage and first childbirth to fit the American norm. Teachers may be asked for advice and support during the transition period, risking undermining culture and families. It is best to find ways to bridge tradition with contemporary American customs.

Although there are great differences with American norms to overcome in acculturating, the Hmongs' adaptability continues as characteristic of their culture. American researchers who have studied the Hmong in the United States tend to view Hmong culture as static, although literature dealing with Hmong living in China, Laos, and

Thailand stresses their dynamic and flexible nature. One reason for the survival of the Hmong through thousands of years of change—and from ancient China to the contemporary United States—is their strong desire to preserve their ethnicity and culture.

HMONG STUDENTS IN THE AMERICAN CLASSROOM

Goldstein (1985) maintained that "Hmong youth have been socialized to a world view in which the group took precedence over the individual and the personal well-being was dependent on the health of the family or kin group" (p. 261). Along the same lines, Hmong students may help one another with workbooks and answer sheets, at times violating school rules designed for individual testing and achievement.

The Hmong learning style may provide a good basis for teachers interested in developing methods of cooperative learning. In her study of learning among Hmong adults in Madison, Wisconsin, Hvitfeldt (1986), found cooperation, noncompetitiveness, and group support "central to the Hmong students' interpretation of student role" (p. 70). Students often feel embarrassed about being praised personally by a teacher, so teachers should refrain from this method of reinforcement, using group praise instead.

Hmong students constantly interact with their peers through verbal and nonverbal communication. Weaker students look around for assistance, with stronger ones maintaining a constant check on the slower students' progress. Help is freely given, even when not requested; it is accepted as a matter of course (Hvitfeldt, 1986). Perhaps this is true for any student, but most Hmong students soon learn what is expected of them in the classroom (Cheng 1994a).

Although Hmong students in the United States no longer live as villagers, teachers should allow them an appropriate learning strategy—that is, seeing and doing. Demonstrating what is to be done, letting students try, correcting their errors, and permitting them to try again will enhance their learning and quite possibly the learning of all students in the classroom.

BARRIERS FOR HMONG

Hmong culture creates barriers for Hmong students in American schools. Sonsalla (1984) found that their home culture sets priorities for them that vary from those encouraged by their American teachers.

Despite their own lack of schooling, Hmong parents consider education a key to their children's future. Foreign language literacy (such as in Lao or French) is considered very desirable. Because most Hmong parents are illiterate and speak little or no English, they cannot assist their children with homework. They entrust their children's education to the school and teachers. Very few attend parent-teacher meetings or understand the details of American schooling.

OVERCOMING BARRIERS: ATTAINING A SENSE OF PRIDE IN CULTURE

Native language literacy encourages a sense of pride in students. It provides a positive sense of personal identity and enhances adjustment to their ethnic group. It reflects acceptance and knowledge of their culture. Like most children, by age 5 or 6, Hmong have acquired interpersonal communicative skills in their home and community language, Hmong. Unless taught through a planned program, however, these students will never proceed to cognitive or academic language proficiency in their native language. Educators should encourage these students' parents and older siblings to undertake various activities with younger students—geared toward maximizing communication skills in their native language.

WORKING WITH PARENTS AND FAMILIES

Teachers sometimes advise parents of language minority children to use English at home. But because many parents have extremely limited skills in English, this can result in poor communication between them and their children. Parents speaking broken English in a telegraphic manner actually limit the quantity and quality of verbal interaction between children and parents. As an alternative, teachers should encourage parents to verbalize with children in their strongest language in ways that build language comprehension and facilitate communication.

Many parents—especially those without formal schooling—are unfamiliar with rituals and activities that go on in mainstream homes: sitting with children to look at books, pointing to pictures and asking questions, reading a few lines, and letting youngsters fill in the rest; reading bedtime stories; doing coloring books; singing nursery rhymes;

playing word games; and letting a child retell a familiar story. All these activities enhance the children's reading skills and can be done in any language. Unfortunately, the most frequent verbalization consists of commands or instructions: close the door; watch your sister; time to eat; wash up before you eat, and so on (Bliatout et al., 1988).

Bliatout and colleagues (1988)suggest that to work effectively with Hmong parents, "Teachers can help parents understand what their children are bringing home by using a consistent symbol, word, or color of ink to indicate how well work has been done. To get a sense of their children's school performance, non-literate parents may rely on such cues as 'if there's a lot of writing on the paper by the teacher, then it's bad; if there's a short word, then it's good'" (p. 37).

Parents may not know that teachers customarily send materials home to parents on a regular basis. If they know when to expect an envelope from school, then they can ask to see it. In the United States, there is a great volume of written communication between school and home, including permission slips, announcements, and advertisements and information about optional activities. Parents may not know that they need to respond or know how to follow through. One helpful approach is to have teachers mark a red X signifying importance or a need for feedback. They might also ask a bilingual aide to call parents and explain handouts procedures.

"An important part of the parent education program is explaining grades, observed behavior and performances, homework policy, and expectations of the teacher and the school. As part of parent education, school personnel should aptly explain what they assume to be true for children in their classes. This way, parents will know when to come to school for meetings and conferences, and they will more or less understand what is being said" (Bliatout et al., 1988, p. 37). Along with relaying information through active community grapevines, Hmong paraprofessionals can contact heads of households directly and encourage them to attend school meetings.

School personnel should be careful not to impose their opinions on parents. Although most Hmong parents lack experience with the U.S. school system, they take interest in their children's progress and rely on schools to keep them up to date. Many parents are uncomfortable when asked for precipitous decisions. Sometimes, they offer consent for special placement and such only after having consulted with a respected member of their Hmong community. The most appropriate approach is to have such an individual or a trusted paraprofessional present information in a format familiar to the parents and then wait for parents to decide for themselves. Schools must accept negative answers, even when they relate to special education referrals from Individual Education Plan meetings (Bliatout et al., 1988).

HMONG IN THE UNITED STATES TODAY

Hmong refugees in the United States continue to undergo lifestyle changes alongside social, economic, and educational development. Within a decade, a new generation of literacy has arisen from a culture formerly low in literacy. But most efforts toward mastering English have been geared toward surviving in this society. Evidence shows that Hmong literacy has not been systematically developed amongst children and teenaged Hmong students. Adult and teenaged students literate in Hmong will probably succeed at transferring their literacy skills to English.

"Hmong children born in the United States are not refugees, and therefore do not qualify for special programs funded under U.S. refugee programs. Children born here may have received little contact with public health nurses, and may not have received all their childhood immunizations" (Bliatout et al., 1988, p. 9). Those born in Laos possess either immigration documents or alien registration cards, referred to as green cards. Dates of birth cited on these cards are often inaccurate because they were arbitrarily assigned by officials in camps. And age-based decisions often necessitate birthdate verification. "Sometimes the closest accurate time may be something like 'after the corn harvest in the year before we escaped to Thailand'" (Bliatout et al., 1988, p. 9).

Most Hmong families in the United States have moved many times. Programs designed for migrant education—with clear criteria for entry placement and short term objectives that transfer to many basal programs—may help overcome the negative affects of frequent moving. Educating parents about differences between school districts and how family decisions affect children's school success is also extremely important.

Many teachers do not know what can be done to promote bilingualism. Can Hmong parents provide needed resources for public schools? Do any districts hire bilingual Hmong speakers? Although some publications on the Hmong exist (Lewis et al., 1989), we lack comprehensive information. Meanwhile, teachers working with Hmong will be on the cutting edge of seeking information to help them understand this often misunderstood population. The Hmong's lack of preparation and knowledge about the U.S. school system presents an extreme challenge for service providers. Only through consistent inquiry about expectations, lifestyles, world views, cultural ways and learning styles can they strengthen their understanding of Hmong behavior. U.S. public schools are feeling a desperate need for cultural sensitivity on the part of teachers and specialists in striving to equalize these students' chances for academic success.

⊐

CONCLUSION

Multiple factors must be taken into consideration in our preassessment process for Asian/Pacfic Island students. These include linguistic, social/cultural, and educational factors that contribute to successful communication. Each case must be evaluated with care and an understanding of the individual's family background—personal history, natural support system, language learning history, cultural imperatives, and other relevant factors that influence education and learning outcome.

⊐

REFERENCES

Aikman, D. (1993, Fall). Not quite so welcome anymore. *Time* [Special Issue], 142(21), 10–15.

American Speech-Language-Hearing Association. (1983). Position paper on social dialect. *ASHA, 25*(9), 23–24.

Banks, J. A. (1990, November). *Transforming the curriculum*. Conference on Diversity. California Teacher Credentialing Commission, Oakland, CA.

Bliatout, B., Downing, B., Lewis, J., & Yang, D. (1988). *Handbook for teaching Hmong-speaking students*. Folsom, CA: Southeast Asian Community Resource Center (Folsom Cordova Unified School District).

California State University. (1984). *Fall 1983 non-citizen enrollment*. CSU Analytic Studies (Statistical Report #10). Long Beach, CA: Author.

California State University. (1988). *Enrollment by ethnic group*. CSU Analytic Studies (Statistical Report #3). Long Beach, CA: Author.

Cheng, L. (1987). English communicative competence of language minority children: Assessment and treatment of language "impaired" preschoolers.

In H. T. Trueba (Ed.), *Success or failure: Learning and the language minority student*. (pp. 49–68). New York: Newbury House Publishers.

Cheng, L. (1989). Service delivery to Asian/Pacific PEP children: A cross-cultural framework. *Topics in Language Disorders, 9*(3), 1–14.

Cheng, L. (1990). Recognizing diversity. *American Behavioral Scientist, 34*(2), 263–278.

Cheng, L. (1991). *Assessing Asian language performance: Guidelines for limited English proficient students* (2nd ed.). Oceanside, CA: Academic Communication Associates.

Cheng, L. (1993). Faculty challenges in the education of foreign-born students. In L. Clark. (Ed.), *Faculty and student challenges in facing cultural and linguistic diversity*. Springfield, IL: Charles C. Thomas Publisher.

Cheng, L. (1994a). Difficult discourse: An untold Asian story. In D. N. Ripich & N. C. Creaghead (Eds.), *School discourse problems* (pp. 155–170). San Diego, CA: Singular Publishing.

Cheng, L. (1994b). Asian/Pacific students and the learning of English. In J. E. Bernthal, & N. E. Bankson (Eds), *Child phonology: Characteristics, assessment and intervention with special populations* (pp.255–274). New York: Thieme Medical Publishers.

Cheng, L., & Ima, K. (1988). The California Basic Educational Skills Test (CBEST) and Indochinese teacher interns: A case of a cultural barrier to foreign-born Asian professionals? In G. Y. Okihiro, S. Hune, A. A. Hansen, & J. M. Liu (Eds.), *Reflections on shattered windows: Promises and prospects for Asian-American studies* (pp. 68–79). Pullman, WA: Washington State University Press.

Cheng, L., & Scheffner-Hammer, C. (1992). *Cultural perceptions of disabilities*. San Diego, CA: Los Amigos Research Associates.

Children's Defense Fund (1992). *Leave no child behind: The state of America's children 1992*. Washington, DC: Author.

Cole, L. (1985). *Nonstandard English: Handbook for assessment and instruction*. Silver Spring, MD: Author.

Darter, A. (1991). *Culture and power in the classroom*. New York: Bergin & Garvey.

Dung, I., & Mudd, S. (1994, November). *Position paper: Social dialects and implications of the position of social dialects*. ASHA Annual Convention. New Orleans, LA.

Goldstein, B. (1985). *Schooling for cultural transitions: Hmong girls and boys in American high schools*. Unpublished doctoral dissertation, University of Wisconsin.

Gollnick, D. M., & Chinn, P. C. (1986). *Multicultural education in a pluralistic society*. Columbus, OH: Charles E. Merrill.

Gollnick, D. M., & Chinn, P. C. (1990). *Multicultural education in a pluralistic society*. Columbus, OH: Merrill.

Gresham, F. M. (1986). Conceptual issues in the assessment of social competence in children. In P. Strain, M. Guralnick, & H. Walker (Eds.), *Children's social behavior: Development, assessment, and modification* (pp. 143–186). New York: Academic Press.

Halliday, M. A. (1978). *Language as a social semiotic: The social interpretation of language and meaning*. London: Edward Arnold.

Heath, S. B. (1986). Socio-cultural contexts of language development. In *Beyond language: Social and cultural factors in schooling language minority students* (143–186). Los Angeles: California State University, Evaluation, Dissemination and Assessment Center.

Hilliard, A. (1976). *Alternatives to IQ testing: An approach to the identification of gifted minority children*. (Final Report). Sacramento: California State Department of Education.

Hilliard, A. (1990, February). *Validity & equity in curriculum and teaching*. Multicultural lecture series. San Diego: San Diego State University.

Hilliard, A. (1992, October). Facing diversity: Challenges in assessment. Cross Cultural Conference, San Diego County.

Hirsch, E. D. (1988). *Cultural literacy*. New York: Vintage Books.

Hvitfeldt, C. (1986). Traditional culture, perceptual style and learning: The classroom behavior of Hmong adults. *Adult Education Quarterly, 36*(2), 65–77.

Hymes, D. (1974). *Foundations in sociolinguistics*. Philadelphia: University of Pennsylvania Press.

Kaplan, L. (1966). Cultural thought patterns in intercultural education. *Language Learning, 16*, 1–20.

Knapp, L. (1972). *Nonverbal communication in human interaction*. New York: Holt, Rinehart & Winston.

Labov, W. (1972). Some principles of linguistic methodology. *Language in Society, 1*, 97–120.

Leubitz, L. (1973). *Nonverbal communication: A guide for teachers*. Skokie, IL: National Textbook.

Lewis, J., Vang, L., & Cheng, L. (1989). Identifying the language-learning difficulties of Hmong students: Implications of context and culture. *Topics in Language Disorders, 9*(3), 21–37.

Merino, B. J. (1991). Promoting school success for Chicanos: The view from inside the bilingual classroom. In R. Valencia (Ed), *Chicano school failure and success: Research and policy agenda for the 1990's* (pp. 119–148). New York: The Farmer Press.

Moffat, C., & Walker, C. (1986). Ban Vinai—A changing world for Hmong children. *Cultural Survival, 10*, 4.

Meyerson, M. (1990). Cultural considerations in the treatment of Latinos with craniofacial malformations. *Cleft Palate Journal, 27*, 279–288.

Ruiz, R. (1989). Orientations in language planning. In S. L. McKay & S. L. C. Wong (Eds.), *Language diversity: Problem or resource?* (pp. 3–25). New York: Newbury House Publishers

Rumbaut, T., & Ima, K. (1987). *The adaptation of Southeast Asian refugee youth: A comparative study*. San Diego: San Diego State University.

Scheffner-Hammer, C. (1990). Special education services in the Chamorro and Carolinian cultures. Unpublished manuscript.

Sonsalla, R. (1984). *A comparative case study of secondary programs for Hmong refugee students in the Minneapolis and St. Paul Schools.* Unpublished master's thesis, University of Minnesota, Minneapolis.

Strauss, R. (1990). Cultural considerations in the treatment of Latinos with craniofacial malformations. *Cleft Palate Journal, 27,* 275–278.

Takaki, R. (1989). *Strangers from a different shore: A history of Asian Americans.* Boston: Little, Brown & Co.

Taylor, O. L. (1986). *Nature of communication disorders in culturally and linguistically diverse populations.* San Diego: College-Hill Press.

Taylor, O.L. (1986). A cultural and communicative approach to teaching standard English as a second dialect. In O. L. Taylor (Ed.), *Treatment of communication disorders in culturally and linguistically diverse populations* (pp. 153–178). San Diego: College-Hill Press.

Trueba, H. T., Cheng, L., & Ima, K. (1993). *Myth or reality: Adaptive strategies of Asian Americans in California.* Washington, DC: The Falmer Press.

Vangyi, X. (1980, October). *The needs for the education for Laotian refugees.* First National Indochinese Conference. Santa Ana, CA.

Vang, L., Lewis, J., & Cheng, L. (1989). Identifying the language-learning difficulties of Hmong students: Implications of context and culture. *Topics in Language Disorder, 9*(3), 21–37.

Walker, C. L. (1985). Learning English: The Southeast Asian refugee experience. *Topics in Language Disorders, 5*(4), 53–65.

Walker, C. (1988). *An introduction to the Hmong.* Unpublished manuscript.

Weddington, G. (1990). Cultural considerations in the treatment of Latinos with craniofacial malformations. *Cleft Palate Journal, 27,* 289–293.

Wolfram, W. (1986). Language variation in the United States. In O. L. Taylor (Ed.), *Nature of communication disorders in culturally and linguistically diverse populations.* Austin, TX: Pro-Ed.

Wolfram, W. (1993). Research to practice: A proactive role for speech-language pathologists in sociolinguistic education. *Language, Speech and Hearing Services in Schools, 24,* 27–35.

APPENDIX 8A

The following outline lays out steps for speech-language pathologists and related professionals to follow with the culturally and linguistically diverse population. With this system, the clinician follows a step-by-step process to appropriately work with the multicultural population.

STEP 1: UTILIZING LITERARY RESOURCES

The following texts are useful literary resources:

Battle, Dolores E. (1993). *Communication Disorders in Multicultural Populations*. Boston: Andover Medical Publishers.

Cheng, Li-Rong Lilly. (1991). *Assessing Asian Language Performance*. Oceanside: Academic Communication Associates.

Taylor, Orlando. (1986). *Treatment of Communication Disorders in Culturally and Linguistically Diverse Populations*. San Diego: College-Hill Press.

Source: From Perry, H., & Martin, K. (1994, November). *Guidelines for the clinician's initial encounter with a multicultural client.* Poster session presented at the American Speech-Language-Hearing Association Annual Convention, New Orleans. Used with permission.

STEP 2: ENTERING A COLLABORATIVE MODEL WITH OTHER PROFESSIONALS WHO SERVE AS REFERENCES (ALSO SEE APPENDIX 8B)

SLP
Assessment of language performance
Speech modification
Accent reduction
Increase awareness of communicative factors

REGULAR EDUCATION TEACHER
Observation of client in classroom setting
Program variation to enhance language learning

ESL TEACHER
Observation of client in classroom setting
Evaluation of communicative competence in Language 1
Identification of possible communication disorders in native language

PARENT AND/OR STUDENT
Awareness of language goals
Motivation

LANGUAGE ARTS TEACHER
Observation of client in classroom setting
Target specific skills needed in Language 2

OTHER PROFESSIONALS
Specialists to provide information on specific topics that cannot be answered by any of the other professionals mentioned.

CULTURAL INFORMANT
Providing sociolinguistic information
Providing information about cultural values, beliefs, customs, etc.

STEP 3: CHECKLIST TO ASSURE ALL RELEVANT FACTORS HAVE BEEN CONSIDERED

SOCIOLINGUISTIC FACTORS
Percentage use of native language as compared to percentage use of Language 2
Language of conversational partners
Age of second language acquisition

LINGUISTIC FACTORS
Ability to learn and utilize language
Proficiency in first language
Interferences from the first language

EDUCATIONAL FACTORS
Value of education in the native country
Educational level of client and parents

PSYCHOLOGICAL FACTORS
Reason for learning the second language
Motivation to learn the language
Self-esteem of learner
Ability to assimilate to the environment

CULTURAL FACTORS
Native country, region of origin
Native country's perceptions of second language learning
Importance of second language for individual success

IMMIGRATION AND FAMILY FACTORS
Reason for leaving native country
Date of arrival in new country

STEP 4: PROFESSIONAL COLLABORATION TO CHOOSE APPROPRIATE MEANS OF ASSESSMENT

Steps 1, 2, 3
Taken into consideration for

Ethnographic
Interview

A
P
P
R
O
P
R
I
A
T
E

means of ASSESSMENT

STEP 5: COLLABORATIVE INTERVENTION THAT ADDRESSES SOCIOLINGUISTIC DIFFERENCES

Long-Term Objectives

Short-Term Objectives

Lesson Plans

Activities

APPENDIX 8B

THE PROFESSIONAL MODEL

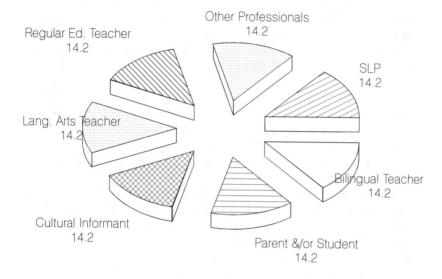

Source: From Perry, H., & Martin, K. (1994, November). *Guidelines for the clinician's initial encounter with a multicultural client.* Poster session presented at the American Speech-Language-Hearing Association Annual Convention, New Orleans. Used with permission.

APPENDIX 8C

CANTONESE SPEECH MATERIALS (Whitehill, 1994)

The Cantonese Speech Materials consist of four sections: Section 1: a list of one-hundred words; Section 2: ten sentences; Section 3: a reading passage; and Section 4: instructions for a 1-minute monologue. Only Section 1 is included here, but the following information provides an overview of all of the materials.

The materials were adapted from several sources. The word list was adapted from Kam, 1982. The sentences were developed by Mavis Hui and Christina Chan, two final-year students in the Department of Speech and Hearing Sciences, University of Hong Kong. The reading passage ("Barbra Streisand Passage") was adapted from Edwins Yiu's 1991 adaptation of a passage originally developed by Leung Man Tak.

The materials are designed to provide a good sample of the speech sounds of Cantonese. No attempt was made to phonetically or phonemically balance the materials. (However, the reading passage was initially designed so that all the consonants and vowels of Cantonese appeared with equal frequency.)

The materials are used for assessing the speech of Cantonese-speaking clients. They are appropriate for a wide range of age groups. The single words, for example, should be easily understood by children in Grade 3. They can also be used for assessing a wide range of speech disorders (for example, they were trialed with clients with dysarthria, cleft palate, and oral cancer).

The materials can be used to provide a detailed speech analysis. They are intended to be used for research and/or pre- and post-assessments (of speech therapy, surgery, or prosthetic intervention, for example).

They be can used in a variety of ways. For example,

1. The materials can be phonetically transcribed (narrow or broad transcription) by one or more speech therapists and later analyzed using any one of a number of analysis systems currently available.

2. A listening task can be set up, using a group of naive or experienced listeners, where the listeners write down orthographically what they have heard. This could provide, for example, a single-word intelligibility score.

It is strongly suggested that when the materials are used, the highest quality recording possible is used. Ideally, the client will be recorded in a sound-proof or sound-attenuated room using a good quality microphone and DAT tape recorder. The microphone should be held at a constant distance from the client's mouth (for example, 8 cm).

The Cantonese Speech Materials form part of a larger research project undertaken by Tara Whitehill. Modifications may be made in the future. It is strongly recommended that the materials be administered, analyzed, and interpreted by a speech therapist (speech-language pathologist).

REFERENCES

Kam, T. P. K. (1982). *Speech audiometric test material in Cantonese.* Unpublished master's thesis. University of Southampton, Southampton.

Whitehill, T. (1994). *Cantonese Speech Materials.* Hong Kong: Department of Speech and Hearing Sciences, University of Hong Kong.

Yiu, E. (1991). Barbra Streisand Passage [in Chinese]. Department of Speech and Hearing Sciences, University of Hong Kong.

SECTION 1: WORD LIST

Item No.	Chinese Character	Phonetic Transcription	English Translation	
1	樹	/sy$_6$/	TREE	
2	牙	/~a$_4$/	TEETH	
3	瓜	/kwa$_1$/	MELON	
4	野	/jΣ$_5$/	WILD	
5	鎖	/s$_2$/	LOCK	
6	父	/fu$_6$/	FATHER	
7	波	/p$_1$/	BALL	
8	魚	/jy$_2$/	FISH	
9	他	/t^{h}a$_1$/	HE	
10	車	/ts^{h}Σ$_1$/	CAR	
11	婦	/fu$_5$/	WOMAN	
12	茄	/k^{h}Σ$_2$/	TOMATO	
13	火	/f$_2$/	FIRE	
14	住	/tsy$_6$/	LIVE	
15	遮	/tsΣ$_1$/	UMBRELLA	
16	壽	/si$_6$/	MATTER	
17	鋸	/kœ$_3$/	SAW	
18	故	/ku$_3$/	PAST	
19	湖	/wu$_4$/	LAKE	
20	拿	/na$_4$/	PICK	

Item No.	Chinese Character	Phonetic Transcription	English Translation	
21	耳	/ji$_5$/	EAR	
22	市	/si$_5$/	MARKET	
23	麻	/ma$_4$/	GRANDMOM	
24	借	/tsΣ$_3$/	LEND	
25	怕	/pʰa$_3$/	FEAR	
26	和	/wø$_4$/	AND	
27	下	/ha$_6$/	DOWN	
28	可	/hø$_2$/	CAN	
29	多	/tø$_1$/	MANY	
30	靴	/hœ$_1$/	BOOT	
31	誇	/kʰwa$_1$/	SHOW OFF	
32	羅	/lø$_4$/	A SURNAME	
33	居	/kœy$_1$/	LIVE	
34	叫	/kiu$_3$/	CALL	
35	跑	/pʰau$_2$/	RUN	
36	老	/lou$_5$/	OLD	
37	牛	/~áu$_4$/	COW	
38	回	/wui$_4$/	COME BACK	
39	栽	/kʰwái$_4$/	(PLANT)	
40	菜	/tsʰøi$_3$/	VEGETABLES	

SECTION 1: WORD LIST *(continued)*

Item No.	Chinese Character	Phonetic Transcription	English Translation	
41	猫	/mau$_1$/	CAT	
42	蟻	/~ái$_5$/	ANT	
43	灰	/fui$_1$/	GREY	
44	蟹	/hai$_5$/	CRAB	
45	海	/høi$_2$/	SEA	
46	蕉	/tsiu$_1$/	BANANA	
47	酒	/tsáu$_2$/	WINE	
48	龜	/kwái$_1$/	TORTOISE	
49	流	/láu$_4$/	FLOW	
50	刀	/tou$_1$/	KNIFE	
51	腦	/nou$_5$/	BRAIN	
52	水	/sœy$_2$/	WATER	
53	油	/jáu$_4$/	OIL	
54	袋	/tøi$_2$/	BAG	
55	快	/fai$_3$/	FAST	
56	米	/mái$_5$/	RICE	
57	你	/nei$_5$/	YOU	
58	跳	/t^{h}iu$_3$/	JUMP	
59	手	/sáu$_2$/	HAND	
60	草	/ts^{h}ou$_2$/	GRASS	

SECTION 1: WORD LIST *(continued)*

Item No.	Chinese Character	Phonetic Transcription	English Translation	
61	企	/kʰei$_5$/	STAND UP	
62	兔	/tʰou$_3$/	RABBIT	
63	要	/jiu$_3$/	WANT	
64	球	/kʰ u$_4$/	BALL	
65	鼻	/pei$_6$/	NOSE	
66	銀	/~án$_4$/	SILVER	
67	釘	/tƩ~$_1$/	NAIL	
68	翼	/jikʰ$_6$/	WING	
69	哭	/hukʰ$_1$/	CRY	
70	劍	/kim$_3$/	SWORD	
71	域	/wikʰ$_6$/	REGION	
72	筆	/pátʰ$_1$/	PEN	
73	男	/nam$_4$/	MALE	
74	核	/wátʰ$_6$/	SEED	
75	籠	/lu~$_4$/	CAGE	
76	狂	/kʰwø~$_4$/	CRAZY	
77	文	/mán$_4$/	PASSAGE	
78	尺	/tsʰƩkʰ$_3$/	RULER	
79	平	/pʰi~$_4$/	SMOOTH	
80	山	/san$_1$/	MOUNTAIN	

Item No.	Chinese Character	Phonetic Transcription	English Translation	
81	裙	/k^{h}wán$_4$/	SKIRT	
82	鹿	/luk$^h_2$/	DEER	
83	咳	/k^{h}át$^h_1$/	COUGH	
84	針	/tsám$_1$/	NEEDLE	
85	力	/lik$^h_6$/	STRENGTH	
86	糖	/t^{h}ø~$_2$/	SWEET	
87	答	/tap$^h_3$/	ANSWER	
88	濕	/sáp$^h_1$/	WET	
89	隻	/tsap$^h_6$/	(CLASSIFIER)	
90	甲	/kap$^h_3$/	GRADE 'A'	
91	納	/hap$^h_6$/	ACCEPT	
92	塔	/t^{h}ap$^h_3$/	TOWER	
93	琴	/k^{h}ám$_4$/	PIANO	
94	潑	/p^{h}ut$^h_3$/	SPLASH	
95	出	/ts^{h}œt$^h_1$/	OUT	
96	飯	/fan$_6$/	RICE	
97	粉	/fán$_2$/	POWDER	
98	骨	/kwát$^h_1$/	BONE	
99	遠	/jyn$_5$/	FAR	
100	喊	/ham$_3$/	CRY	

Source: Adapted from Kam, T. P. K. (1982).

CHAPTER 9

LEP PARENTS AS RESOURCES: GENERATING OPPORTUNITY TO LEARN BEYOND SCHOOLS THROUGH PARENTAL INVOLVEMENT

JI-MEI CHANG, PH.D.
ANNA Y. LAI, M.A.
WARD SHIMIZU, M.A.

The eighth National Educational Goal promotes parental participation (National Education Goals Panel, 1994); this goal is specifically aiming at increasing parental involvement and participation in promoting the social, emotional, and academic growth of children. Based on 30 years of research, the crucial link in achieving a high-quality education and a safe and disciplined learning environment for all students is to have greater parental involvement and build solid teacher-parent partnerships (United States Department of Education, 1994). As a result, Secretary of Education Riley has led a nationwide endeavor to increase family involvement in children's learning (e.g., Goals 2000 Community Update, 1994).

Creating and promoting partnerships between parents and teachers is a means of linking students' home and school learning. A major feature of creating these partnerships is that they help increase students' opportunity to learn both in and beyond school. One of the objectives of the eighth National Educational Goal is that every state will assist local schools and local agencies in establishing programs that aim at increasing and sustaining parent-teacher partnerships, particularly among parents with children who are limited English proficient (LEP) and who are also learning disabled (LD), or LEP + LD. However, if schools are going to increase students' opportunity to learn by promoting parent-teacher partnerships, they must recognize the sociocultural differences between schools and families. Schools and families may not have similar expectations, especially nonmainstream, inner-city Chinese families. For example, the findings from Chang's (1993) field work and research suggested that many of these Chinese parents who are LEP, generally see teachers as the experts for school learning, and they could not see themselves as teachers' partners. Furthermore, these parents believed that they should leave the teaching to teachers and schools. Thus, recognizing sociocultural differences may help reduce the potential for misunderstandings between teachers and nonmainstream, inner-city Chinese or some Asian parents with LEP.

In addition, we must look closely at the extent to which sociocultural factors may influence the nature of parents' involvement in their children's education or school learning. For example, Asian and Asian American parents, in general, value school education and support their children's academic learning by generating various social capital to facilitate their school achievement (e.g., Chang, this book, Chapter 2; Coleman, 1987; Trueba, Cheng, & Ima, 1993). This type of parental involvement in some ways might have sustained the myth of Asian minority student syndrome which suggests that all Asian students will have home support to achieve academically in schools. However, not all of these types of support generated school success for their children (e.g., Chang, 1993; this book, Chapter 2).

Generating opportunity to learn is important for inner-city Asian students with LEP + LD because they are likely to encounter a series of missed learning opportunities under the current service delivery systems (Chang, this book, Chapter 2). Therefore, in order to generate more opportunity to learn in and beyond schools for such a student population, the purpose of this chapter is to use field research evidence to achieve the four interrelated goals as follows:

1. To heighten teachers' and specialists' awareness of varying literacy and language experiences inner-city Asian American students with LEP may have had beyond school, generated from home and extended to their community.
2. To demonstrate that nonmainstream, inner-city parents and children with LEP could generate valuable resources for their child's learning when teachers or specialists incorporate these resources in formal schooling.
3. To reveal the obstacles, perceived from parents' perspectives, in forging partnership with teachers and specialists.
4. To provide specific, often nontraditional, suggestions that may promote teacher-parent partnerships feasible for involving nonmainstream, inner-city Asian parents with LEP.

To achieve these four goals, this chapter is organized in two parts. In part one, we attempt to address the first three goals by presenting a descriptive study that examines the home language uses and literacy activities of a group of inner-city Chinese children who are LEP + LD. A brief summary of findings illustrates self-reported information regarding their home language use and native language literacy practices. In part two, we address the fourth goal by providing relevant rationale based on either research or field tests among similar groups of Asian parents. Once we have realized the four goals, we might increase teachers' ability to help poverty stricken, inner-city Asian parents with LEP who have less than a middle school education become productively and meaningfully involved in their children's education.

Before continuing, the following terms need clarification: literacy, multiple literacy, and native and home language. In reviewing Taylor's (1983) work on family literacy, we found the definition of literacy provided in Southgate (1972, p. 9) appropriate for our study as well. Literacy is defined as "the mastery of our native language in all its aspects, as a means of communication." Such a broad view of literacy was necessary while considering the complexities and facets of native language literacy activities within the sociocultural context of nonmainstream, inner-city homes of Chinese children who are LEP + LD and their closely linked community.

The concept of multiple literacy was adopted for Chang's (1993) study of inner-city Chinese American literacy practices in order to broaden the educational perspective. This broadened view includes a variety of activities commonly occurring within inner-city communities when the target students are involved in communicating or interacting with others beyond school. For example, as observed by Taylor (1983, p. 92), literacy of inner-city families is "deeply embedded in the social processes of family life and is not some specific list of activities added to the family agenda to explicitly teach reading." In other words, multiple literacy activities occur in natural daily environment without directly tying in with any identifiable books or paper-pencil activities. Hence, inner-city Chinese American children who are LEP + LD are likely to have varying types of literacy experiences beyond schools which may or may not directly link with school literacy learning that is directed by the school's core curriculum criteria.

These expanded views of literacy serve two specific functions in this discussion. First, it highlights why we need to respect native-language-speaking parents as resources for their children's learning since most of these multiple literacy activities involve parents through the use of home language(s). Second, it can provide a basis for teachers and specialists in linking the unique family practices to classroom literacy experiences for these LEP children. A more detailed discussion is presented in part two of this chapter.

The terms "native language" and "home language" are used interchangeably. They refer to the Asian LEP child's dominant language used at home as reported by the child and the parents. These terms were operationally defined as Cantonese language used outside of school in specifically designated time, space, events, and activities in which the children who are LEP + LD participating in the study were involved with their parents, adults, or peers. The term "native language literacy activities" was broadly defined to include any activity involving the use of home language occurring within the home or community and between the parent and a child across designated time, space, and events.

⎣⎡

MULTIPLE LITERACY PRACTICES OF INNER-CITY CHINESE AMERICAN FAMILIES: SELECTED LEP+LD CASE STUDIES

Data presented in this section are a part of the home-school-community-based study of the social, language, and literacy environment of

16 inner-city Chinese American children who are LEP + LD (Chang, 1993; this book, Chapter 2). This study provided a framework that allowed the researchers to gather information over a period of time from every possible aspect of the life of a child who is LEP + LD. The particular working model that guided the study of home language use and native language literacy activities beyond schools involving parents, family members, and other related individuals was developed by analyzing three interrelated sets of information. These are (1) data obtained from a survey of a typical day of children who are LEP + LD both in- and outside of school during a period of time; (2) field observations; and (3) interviews of children's parents, teachers, and community informants. The data were collected and analyzed in four components: time, space, event, and activities (Spradley, 1980) (see Figure 9–1). Information relevant to home language use and native language literacy activities was collected according to the following areas: (1) time—including before and after school and during holidays and weekends; (2) space—including home and its closely linked inner-city Chinese American community; and (3) events and activities—including specific events and activities occurring across school days, weekends, and special holidays, specifically whenever parents were involved. The events and activities items also included a variety of self-reported activities occurring as part of daily routines, as well as on birthdays and special holidays. Interview data were coded to examine the specific patterns that prevailed across the 16 cases.

Because of the limitations of descriptive methodology, various attempts were made to assure the representativeness of self-reported data. The interview items were constructed and field tested with feedback from parents, teachers, community informants, and research consultants. Two identical interview forms were constructed to collect information from parents and their children regarding home language uses and native language literacy activities when parents were involved. Parent interviews were conducted over the telephone by a trained school staff member who had frequent contact with these parents. Child interviews were conducted by the researcher and assistants within each school site during regular school hours. The two self-reported data sets obtained from parents and children were largely consistent across all 16 cases as revealed during the structured interview.

A SUMMARY OF RESULTS AND DISCUSSION

With the active participation of children and their parents, teachers, and community informants engaged in various research activities, the

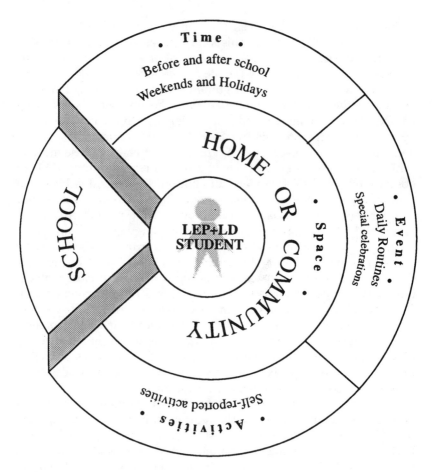

FIGURE 9–1
Components of the working model for the study of home language uses and
literacy activities beyond school.

native language literacy activities typically reported include: doing
homework or chores before or after school; shopping on weekends or
holidays; eating or dining out with family daily, or for special events,
such as celebrating birthdays or special holidays; and leisure time
activities on weekends and holidays. Most of the leisure time activities reported by this group were watching TV and Cantonese videotapes, playing video games, going to see Chinese movies, going on
outings such as shopping or visiting relatives and friends.

The profile of self-reported home language uses and native language literacy activities involving parents across designated time, space, events and activities is presented in Table 9–1. Through the composite profile, it is evident that among the group of 16 Chinese American children who are LEP + LD, Cantonese was frequently used to communicate with their parents. Given the high level of their English BICS (basic interpersonal communication skills) (see Chapter 2), it could be expected that they frequently use English as well, particularly during literacy activities involving school work and/or with their siblings in doing daily chores. From structured interviews, the data show that, collectively, this group of children has gained a variety of English and native language literacy experiences beyond school; furthermore, these activities are often supported by their LEP parent(s). Typical activities when parent(s) were involved, reported by this group of children, are presented in Table 9–2.

TABLE 9–1

A profile of self-reported home language uses and literacy activities involving parents across designated time, space, events, and activities.

Gender	Grade	Homework	Daily Chores	Eating	Shopping	Leisure Time	Celebrations*
M	3	E/C	E/C	E/C	E/C	E/C	E/C
M	3	E/C	C	C	C	C	C
F	3	E	E/C	C	C	C	C
M	3	C	C	C	C	C	C
M	3	E	E/C	E/C	E/C	E/C	E/C
M	4	E	E/C	E/C	E/C	E/C	E/C
M	4	E	E/C	E/C	E/C	E/C	E/C
M	4	E/C	C	C	C	C	C
M	4	E/C	E/C	E/C	E/C	E/C	E/C
F	5	E/C	E/C	E/C	E/C	E/C	E/C
F	5	E	E/C	C	C	C	C
F	5	E	E/C	C	C	C	C
F	5	E/C	E/C	C	C	C	C
M	5	E/C	E/C	C	C	C	C
M	5	E	E/C	C	C	C	C
M	5	E/C	E/C	E/C	E/C	E/C	E/C

Note. E = Use of English language, C= Use of Cantonese language.

*Celebrations represent literacy activities that occurred during holidays, such as Chinese moon festival, New Year, and other major holidays.

TABLE 9–2

Commonly reported native language literacy activities that involved parents among 16 inner-city Chinese American LEP + LD children.

---

1. Watching Cantonese videotapes or movies (12/16 or 75%).
2. Doing math homework (11/16 or 69%).
3. Visiting relatives or friends (10/16 or 63%).
4. Eating out (8/16 or 50%).
5. Reading newspapers general or sales ads (8/16 or 50%)
6. Shopping (5/16 or 31%).
7. Cooking (5/167 or 31%).
8. Doing chores (4/16 or 25%).
9. Playing video games (4/16 or 25%).

Reading with parents was not a common activity reported by this group of children and parents. Furthermore, as many of these children's parents worked late every day, often juggling two or more low-paying jobs in sewing factories or restaurants, reading bedtime stories with their parents did not seem to be an option or a natural act for many of the children who participated in the study. However, many of these children who are LEP + LD did scan English or Chinese newspapers for general and/or sales ads. Due to the lack of ethnographic data over time, the current findings did not address the quality of the home language uses and literacy activities that occurred between parents and children.

LIMITED LANGUAGE EXPERIENCES AND VOCABULARY DEVELOPMENT

Based on interview data, 50% (8 out of 16) of the children who are LEP + LD indicated that they preferred using English, while 31% (5 out of 16) indicated a preference for using both English and Cantonese. Only 13% (2 out of 16) of them reported that they preferred using Cantonese. Many of them indicated that they preferred speaking English with their peers; however, in inner city schools their peers were often non-standard English speakers. Many of these students were bused to schools that may not have been the closest one to their homes in order to achieve racial or ethnic balance among student populations. Typically, their English language models were often those who came from non-Anglo American groups and who were either LEP or speakers of non-standard English dialects.

All of them remained limited proficiency in either English or Chinese language. Even though some parents could only speak Cantonese when interacting with their children at home, they did not lobby to have their child enrolled in a Cantonese-English bilingual program. Furthermore, once these children were enrolled in a special education program, all of them abandoned their after-school or weekend Chinese language studies. The importance of a student's native language development in promoting overall language, particular English language, and literacy development (e.g., Snow, 1990; Wong-Fillmore, 1988, 1990, in press) was rarely mentioned by either resource specialists or parents.

It was common for regular and special education teachers to recommend to these parents who were LEP that they use English at home. Such a suggestion may inadvertently limit these students' opportunities to develop their Chinese cognitive/academic language proficiency through interactions with their parents and others beyond school context.

This is particularly important, because many children from low-income home environments are at-risk for low achievement in the areas of vocabulary and reading comprehension (e.g., Snow, Barnes, Chandler, Goodman, & Hemphill, 1991). Vocabulary and reading comprehension are critical to academic learning. In the case illustrated by Tim, it was apparent that he never acquired proficiency in reading comprehension even after he entered middle school. It seems obvious that for the groups of children who faced a triple challenge of being poor, LEP, and LD, teachers and parents need to be well-informed and trained to generate meaningful learning opportunities in order to facilitate vocabulary development in both home and English languages.

SOCIOCULTURAL ROLE OF HOMEWORK

Homework plays a significant role in the lives of low-income LEP Chinese American families in providing literacy and language experiences. Based on parents' responses, supervising homework is an important academic and social activity between themselves and their children, as presented in Table 9–3. Although this may be also true for Chinese/Asian American parents across a wide range of socioeconomic status and educational levels, it is a particularly meaningful activity for these parents. Out of necessity, many of these parents have had to become dependent on their children, in particular, relying on their children to translate for them from English into Cantonese in various public or private transactions. Supervising their children's homework helps reassure LEP parents of their place in their children's lives.

TABLE 9–3
Function of homework in Chinese parents' life.

Supervising homework is important to parents because:

■ This is the way they can communicate to the child the value that the education is important.

■ This is another way to assert their authority as an adult or parent for a task being carried through—as for many LEP parents, they have to reverse the traditional role of authority outside of their home because of a lack of a command of English. They often have to rely on their child to communicate with a clerk, police officer, or other person.

■ This is one way they can keep the child busy with something meaningful.

■ They can feel that they have contributed to their child's education on a daily basis.

■ They can actually see the child engaged in educational activities.

■ They are also able to supervise when assisting with math homework. This affirms their role as an authority figure, because they feel competent in their contribution in this subject area.

OBSTACLES FOR FORGING PARTNERSHIP WITH SCHOOLS

Traditionally, suggestions for encouraging parental involvement in their children's' education have focused on activities such as reading with their child on a regular basis, taking their child to the public library, or joining Boy or Girl Scouts. However, many of these parents have limited energy, skills, and time. Because of these limitations, they usually have an extremely difficult time acting on the traditional suggestions provided by teachers, such as reading to their child. They tended to feel inadequate as parents when they could not do what was suggested by teachers. Consequently, this reinforces their perception that schools and teachers do not really understand their situation.

In analyzing parents' responses, a major obstacle confronting some of these parents' involvement in school activities may have been their perceptions of their own limitations. First, these parents believe that school education is best left to teachers because teachers know best about how to educate their child, particularly in academic learning. Second, they reported that their involvement in their child's formal education in this country is limited by many factors. These factors can be summarized as (1) the need of both parents to work long hours, including weekends; (2) their own English language limitations or inability to use English language with their child at home as requested by his or her regular or special education teachers; (3) their inability to provide suggestions when they were asked by teachers about how or what teachers might do to help their child who is LEP + LD in school; and (4) their lack of understanding of the educational system in the United States. Finally, many of these parents came from traditions in which the only time parents received a summons from the school was when a child had done something wrong.

Traditionally, many Chinese/Asian parents strongly believe that teachers will make the best decisions regarding their children's education, particularly those whose children have special needs. These expectations are often unfulfilled by LD resource specialists and other school personnel as shown in Chapter 2. The gap between Chinese/ Asian American LEP parents' expectations and the reality of what many inner-city, low-income Chinese/Asian American children who are LEP with special needs have experienced through special education intervention has been illustrated previously in Chapter 2 (see Chapter 2, the scenario on Tim, pp. 31–35). Tim's case illustrates the sort of educational treatment that has limited Chinese/Asian American LEP children's access to school learning. Unfortunately, Tim's school experiences may not be an isolated case in the increasingly complex inner-city school context across the country.

In sum, many Chinese American parents with LEP who participated in the study had (a) no time, (b) no English communication skills, and (c) no experience or knowledge about helping their children in American schools. On the other hand, teachers or specialists (a) suggested that parents give more time in reading to their children, (b) suggested that they try using English when communicating with their children, and (c) provided parents with unfamiliar activities to try with their children such as reading American children's literature. Unfortunately, the gap between these parents and teachers and specialists has (a) reinforced parents feelings of powerlessness and that teachers do not understand them, their culture, or their situation, and (b) discouraged parents from getting involved in their children's education in ways in which the school suggests.

A WORD OF CAUTION

We acknowledge that within the inner-city Chinese/Asian American populations with LEP, family groupings are complex and diverse. The characteristics of each family differ, hence the profiles of home language uses and native language literacy activities vary accordingly. Data presented in this section were not intended to be generalized across a wide range of diverse inner-city Asian American groups with LEP. The research evidence of one group of Chinese American children serves to focus the discussion and rationale on the proposed recommendations.

Given the similarity of Asian cultural values toward school education and academic achievement (e.g., Peng & Wright, 1994; Trueba, Cheng, & Ima, 1993), some of the suggestions presented in the following sections that specifically consider unique situations of the inner-city working class environment may also promote parental involvement in children's learning for ethnically diverse groups of Asian American parents with LEP in a similar context.

⌐

IMPLICATIONS AND RECOMMENDATIONS

In part two of this chapter, the discussion focuses on (a) the resources that nonmainstream, inner-city Chinese/Asian American parents with LEP could generate for their child's learning and (b) the specific recommendations that may facilitate these parents' ability to meet the expectations of school educational practices.

LEP PARENTS AS RESOURCES

The research evidence further supports that home language is the medium that parents with LEP use to communicate with and supervise their child's school work. Providing support and demonstrating respect for a child's home language will likely generate more opportunity to learn for these groups of children who are largely confined to inner-city communities. By substantially supporting their home language, we provide both children and their parents the freedom to respect their own language and culture (e.g., Cummins, 1989) and allow them to function and grow in their own ways with words (Heath, 1983). Therefore, school administrators, policy makers, teachers and related specialists will need to carefully monitor their attitudes and school practices in order to maintain a positive view that these parents' unique langue and culture background will be conducive to their child's school learning (e.g., Delgado-Gaitan, 1993; Delgado-Gaitan & Trueba, 1991; Flores, Cousin, & Diaz, 1991; Ruiz,

1989). The research findings presented in part one suggested that these parents facilitate their child's learning by:

- Monitoring a child's attendance either in regular schools or in Saturday school-based English enrichment programs.
- Concern about their child's progress and achievement.
- Disciplining their child's home and school conduct.
- Encouraging their child to use English whenever possible.
- Watching movies or ethnic videotapes with their child.
- Helping with school work in mathematics.
- Arranging support for their child's homework, for example, using siblings or using private or public tutors in after-school programs.
- Supervising and signing the completion of their homework assignments.
- Supplying books and materials for school or home assignments.
- Searching ways that may enhance their child's academic performance.
- Applying for a public library card for their child.
- Engaging their child in various types of literacy activities after school, on weekends, or holidays that broaden their child's general information.
- Respecting school teachers as experts in their child's school learning.
- Attending school meetings.

GENERATING OPPORTUNITY TO LEARN BEYOND SCHOOLS

In order to generate more opportunities to learn among the specific groups of students who are poor, LEP, and with or without LD, at least three specific conditions must be addressed. These are adjusting for social-cultural differences, providing adequate planning and training, and modeling multiple literacy activities for home interventions.

ADJUSTING FOR SOCIAL-CULTURAL DIFFERENCES

Based on our findings, social-cultural differences in perceptions related to literacy practices exist between teaching professionals and nonmainstream, inner-city Chinese LEP parents. Many parents who participated in our studies admitted that they tended to shy away from school meetings. Essentially, at meetings, some of them felt pressured into taking responsibility for their child's school failures because of their inability to read or speak English to their child. For example, when teachers suggested that they try reading stories with their child, such as children's literature used in school, many of them were unable to meet this demand for various self-reported reasons, such as language differences and long work hours, often past their child's bedtime.

Many of these parents were LEP, and they also had little or no understanding of mainstream American culture and language. Form, content, use of language, and unfamiliar sociocultural contexts of the plots and characters inbedded in American children's literature often prevented their full understanding of the selected literature recommended by school teachers. In addition, it was rarely suggested to these parents nor supported by teachers that stories written in their native language be read to their child.

The main focus in this section is that a common act of parental involvement in their child's learning, such as asking parents to read to their children regularly, may or may not be generalizable across a wide range of nonmainstream, inner-city Asian students' families that are LEP. To illustrate the social-cultural differences, we selected Epstein's (1987) "16 Ways to Involve Parents" as a working framework to highlight specific modifications that may be necessary in order to promote and sustain parental involvement for their child's school learning (see Table 9–4).

Asian or Asian American parents from the middle or upper-middle class share similar values as teachers in American schools (e.g., Wong Fillmore, 1990); hence, the modifications to Epstein's (1987) recommendations might not be applicable to them. However, in the context of recently arrived immigrant parents from Southeast Asia or rural China, their prior educational experiences and current economic status might have a very different impact on their actual ability to become involved in their child's social and school learning. Hence, modifications may be meaningful for recently arrived rural immigrants who share similar daily life experiences as these inner-city, LEP, working class families.

The demographic changes in our general populations have definitely impacted the student populations. In many parts of the country, there are large numbers of new immigrants from different regions of Asian countries. According to a government report, many of them are

Table 9–4

Ways to involve parents in school learning.

16 Ways to Involve Parents Recommend by Epstein	Ways to Support Inner-City Asian LEP Parents' Further Involvement
1. Ask parents to read to their children regularly or to listen to the children read aloud.	■ Prepare books on tapes for them. ■ Videotape story telling/reading activity for family use. ■ Arrange for someone from the extended family or other literacy sites to read to children or listen to their reading.
2. Loan books, workbooks, and other materials to parents.	■ Contact community-based literacy sites to provide materials written in native language ■ Locate school related text that has been translated into their language.
3. Ask parents to take their children to the library.	■ Arrange field trips to a library for these parents, help them apply for a library card, and create a plan to prevent the loss of any library books. ■ Arrange for someone to take their child to library when necessary.
4. Ask parents to get their children to talk about what they did that day in class.	■ Model for parents how this can be done at home. ■ Suggest some specific questions or ideas that they can ask their children.
5. Give an assignment that requires the children to ask their parent questions.	■ Be sure parents can help their child with this particular assignment and provide them with strategies and realistic examples.
6. Ask parents to watch a specific television program with their children and to discuss the show afterward.	■ Model for parents how they might carry out a meaningful discussion in their native language. ■ Inform them of the importance of using native language during a child's concept development and learning.

continued

279

Table 9–4 *(continued)*

16 Ways to Involve Parents Recommend by Epstein	Ways to Support Inner-City Asian LEP Parents' Further Involvement
	■ Provide them with specific questions they can ask their children.
7. Suggest ways for parents to include their children in any of their own educationally enriching activities.	■ Provide parents with strategies and examples. For example, discuss with children what some of these parents are learning in adult education classes, or visiting different agencies.
8. Send home suggestions for games or group activities, related to the children's schoolwork, that can be played by either parent and child or by child and siblings.	■ Videotape recommended activities for these families. ■ Make it explicit that home language is highly valued and recommended in these activities.
9. Suggest how parents might use home materials and activities to stimulate their children's interest in reading, math, and other subjects.	■ Provide parents with strategies, e.g., to develop a child's interest in applying math skills, a parent can discuss grocery shopping, store sales, budgeting, and so on with their child.
10. Establish a formal agreement whereby parents supervise and assist children in completing homework tasks.	■ Most of these parents generally supervise their child's homework. ■ Inform them the possible community sources for supervising homework.
11. Establish a formal agreement whereby parents provide rewards and/or penalties based on the children's school performance or behavior.	■ Help LEP parents recognize their child's unique abilities and establish realistic expectations. ■ Inform parents of the characteristics of LEP + LD and that slow progress may not be from laziness or lack of effort.
12. Ask parents to come to *observe* the classroom (not to "help") for part of a day.	■ Videotape a part of the school day with narration in their native language to show to these parents. ■ Organize special Parents' Nights with interpreters to explain the cur-

Table 9–4 *continued*

16 Ways to Involve Parents Recommend by Epstein	Ways to Support Inner-City Asian LEP Parents' Further Involvement
	riculum, materials, ways of teaching, and school expectations of students and their parents.
13. Explain to parents certain techniques for teaching, for making learning materials, or for planning lessons.	■ Provide videotapes with narration in parents' native language to explain these activities.
14. Give a questionnaire to parents so they can evaluate their children's progress or provide some other form of feedback.	■ Use an interpreter to ask parents how they feel about their child's school progress. [Based on field research, these parents are often unable to evaluate their child's progress through formal survey tools.]
15. Ask parents to sign homework to ensure its completion.	■ Most of these parents supervise and sign off their child's homework. ■ Inform parents, when necessary, the types of after school tutorial programs that might be available for their child.
16. Ask parents to provide spelling practice, math drill, and practice activities, or to help with workbook assignments.	■ Most of these parents are able to fulfill these types of activities involving math drills and spelling practices. ■ Provide them with strategies and rationale for specific assignments.

living in poverty (United States General Accounting Office, 1994). Having a materially impoverished home environment, some children are less likely to do well in school as indicated in an extensive review of research on parent involvement and student achievement from the family perspective (Henderson & Berla, 1994). Furthermore, as discussed in Chapter 2 of this book, being poor, LEP, and LD, students were likely to face a series of missed learning opportunities in schools. This is why adjusting to social-cultural differences will likely enhance these students' equal access to school education.

PROVIDING ADEQUATE
PLANNING AND TRAINING

In this section we highlight the need for coordinating and making the best use of parents' and teachers' abilities through thorough planning and training in order to increase students' opportunity to learn. According to Leitch and Tangri's (1988) research on barriers to home-school collaboration, home-school problems did not always result from misperceptions between parents and teachers; rather, it was "the lack of specific planning, or, at a more basic level, the lack of knowledge about how each can use the other person more effectively that is a major barrier" (Leitch & Tangri, 1988, p. 74).

In our home-school-community-based research, we learned that many special education teachers had limited contact with the LEP parents because of the language barrier; hence, both parties were unlikely to use one another effectively to facilitate the learning of the child who is LEP + LD. Given the shortage of Asian American bilingual and biliterate school personnel and language specialists in school, communicating with these diverse Asian parents who are LEP will continue to be a challenge to many teachers and language specialists. In order to promote and sustain teacher- or specialist-parent partnership, the teachers, specialists, and parents will need training in order to provide ideas and strategies for one another to generate systematic support for these children's language, literacy, and cognitive development.

Many researchers working with low-income Hispanic groups of parents have devised language arts and math activities for family activities (Delgado-Gaitan, 1990; Delgado-Gaitan & Trueba, 1991; Gallimore & Goldenberg, in press; Simich-Dudgeon, 1986; Snow et al., 1991; Violand-Sanchez, Sutton, & Ware, 1991). However, there is very little published literature and school programs that address the unique needs of nonmainstream, inner-city Asian families that are LEP.

MODELING MULTIPLE LITERACY
ACTIVITIES FOR HOME INTERVENTION

In this section, we provide suggestions for teachers and specialists who are working with these inner-city Asian families. This set of multiple literacy activities was based on field work with the target group of parents. The first step in providing support and training toward a meaningful teacher-parent or special-parent partnerships is to respect these parents as valuable resources in their childrens' school learning and basic concept development. Only when we empower these parents as respected partners in their child's formal schooling are we likely to promote greater parental involvement conducive to their child's native and English language and literacy development.

Furthermore, the key elements for enhancing home multiple literacy activities in language and literacy development for these working families are that the activities need to be easily and naturally implemented within a daily routine. When parents are willing and able to follow through with activities that are relevant to their lifestyle and the environment in which they live, then we can expect desirable outcomes in their child's language and literacy development. In sum, the basic formula that empowers these parents is:

$$Ease + Consistency = Outcome.$$

Multiple literacy activities parents can and will do make a positive difference in their children's education. Moreover, multiple literacy activities can be carried out through activities that they are already doing with their children, so they are likely to be practiced consistently. However, the relationship between the suggested home activities and school work needs to be clearly illustrated so parents understand the purposes and value of their contributions. The activities provided here usually require little extra time for parents to perform within their daily routine.

HOME LANGUAGE USES. For many Chinese American families watching television and mealtime are the two times when most family members are doing the same activity. Activities that promote language stimulation for engaging children in elaborated open-ended verbal exchange as opposed to one-word query responses can be carried out while parents and children watch TV or video programs. Sample questions for discussion may include: Who are the main characters? What happened to them in the last episode? Why are these events happening? Why is it funny, scary, sad, and so on? How did one event lead to another? When did this event occur? Through discussion, parents help their children understand cause-and-effect relationship, develop memory skills, make inferences, solve problems, and promote oral expression in a more natural way.

HOME LANGUAGE LITERACY ACTIVITIES. Activities that promote literacy development can be carried out through parents' modeling of reading newspaper or magazines of their home language in the presence of their child. Discussion of topics of common interest or current events can expand a child's use of language beyond simple communicative purposes to more cognitive and academic use of their home language. For more ideas refer to Table 9–4, in particular, for ways that involve inner-city Asian parents who are LEP.

CONCEPT DEVELOPMENT. Activities that promote basic concept development serve as a foundation for academic learning. These activities can be carried out while doing household chores together and talking about how and why work is done in certain ways. For example, while doing laundry, parents can explain the choice of temperature of water (establish cause-and-effect relationship), amount of detergent used (establish elementary measurement concepts), sequence of steps, and counting money. In addition, folding clothes can be used as an opportunity to teach elementary matching and sorting concept, such as categories or sizes.

Another set of daily chores may include washing dishes. For example, sorting what is and is not breakable and sorting pots, pans, and dishes by size can be a tactic. Talking about the names of utensils and using a variety of descriptive words can expand a child's oral expression and use of elaborated syntax and vocabulary. Furthermore, a simple cooking activity would enhance their awareness of the basic sequence of steps for cooking and the exercise of basic safety precautions. Shopping together can also be valuable for reinforcing skills for classifying different kinds of food by color, taste, smell, and size. Literacy activities can also be expanded to include writing shopping lists, making change, budgeting, reading ads for sales, and learning about consumer education.

ᄂᄀ

CONCLUDING REMARKS

Promoting parental involvement is one of the national education goals (National Education Goals Panel, 1994). However, without adequate understanding and sensitivity, forging partnerships between nonmainstream, inner-city Asian American parents with LEP and teacher/specialists can be a difficult challenge. From field-based research, findings suggest that these parents respect teachers and value school education, and they have already involved themselves in their child's academic learning in their own ways. Furthermore, many LD resource specialists who participated in the study indicated that they have had limited contact with these Asian LEP parents. It seems that a large number of parents and specialists were unaware of the ways in which continued use of a home language along with native language literacy activities, are vital in the social, language, literacy, and cognitive development of children who are LEP + LD.

A few field-tested activities that enhance home language use for literacy and cognitive development have been provided for teachers and specialists to suggest to parents. The activities empower parents to realize that everything they do at home, especially the use of elaborated home language, can have a significant positive impact on their child's school learning. These activities may not be viewed by many parents or teachers with shared middle-class values as activities for education or quality time with children. However, for nonmainstream, inner-city Asian families with limited means and English proficiency and who may not be adequately educated or trained, the focus of the home activities recommended is to make parents feel comfortable and capable of being meaningful partners in their children's learning. Only when activities are perceived as easy, convenient, and natural and backed up by systematic support and training, can we expect results over time in forging meaningful partnerships with these parents. As these parents' native language is valued and reasonable and naturalistic activities are suggested for them to follow, the empowerment of these parents will inevitably generate much-needed social capital for the academic success of their children.

Most importantly, although these activities are suggested to encourage parents to become actively involved in their children's education for language and literacy development, the outcome of these naturally positive and constructive child-parent interactions will have a great impact on establishing long-lasting bonds between the parents and children. Many of these Chinese American parents are likely to experience some types of language, culture, and generation gaps as their Americanized children grow older. The early established quality time together through consistent communication of ideas, support, love, and understanding hopefully will also bridge these gaps.

Finally, in recognizing that inner-city Asian students who are LEP + LD have varying literacy experiences, in conjunction with the forging of partnerships between schools and home, we can facilitate these students' language, cognitive, and literacy development. However, partnerships can only be forged if the participants focus on these three key factors: respect for inner-city LEP parents as resources, an expanded view of multiple literacy, and provision of systematic modeling and training for inner-city LEP parents.

⊔

REFERENCES

Chang, J. M. (1993). *A school-home-community based conceptualization of LEP with learning disabilities: Implications from a Chinese-American study.* Proceedings of the Third Research Symposium on Limited English Proficient Students' Issues: Middle Schools (pp. 713–736). Washington, DC: Office of Bilingual Education & Minority Language Affairs, U.S. Department of Education.

Chang, J. M. (1995). LEP, LD, poor, and missed learning opportunities: A case of inner city Chinese children. In L. L. Cheng (Ed.), *Integrating language and learning for inclusive schools: An Asian/Pacific Islander focus.* San Diego, CA: Singular Publishing Group, Inc.

Coleman, J. S. (1987). Families and schools. *Educational Researcher, 16*(6), 32–38.

Cummins, J. (1989). A theoretical framework for bilingual special education. *Exceptional Children, 56,* 111–119.

Delgado-Gaitan, C. (1993). Research and policy in reconceptualizing family-school relationships. In P. Phelan & A. L. Davidson (Eds.), *Renegotiating cultural diversity in American schools* (pp. 139–158). New York: Teachers College Press.

Delgado-Gaitan, C. (1990). *Literacy for empowerment: The role of parents in children's education.* London: The Falmer Press.

Delgado-Gaitan, C., & Trueba, H. (1991). *Crossing cultural borders: Education for immigrant families in America.* London: The Falmer Press.

Epstein, J. L. (1987). What principals should know about parent involvement. *Principals, 66*(3), 6–9.

Flores, B., Cousin, P. T., & Diaz, E. (1991). Transforming deficit myths about learning, language, and culture. *Language Arts, 68,* 369–379.

Gallimore, R., & Goldenberg, C. (in press). Activity settings of early literacy: Home and school factors in children's emergent literacy. In E. Forman, N. Minick, & C. A. Stone (Eds.), *Education and mind: The integration of institutional, social, and developmental processes.* Oxford: Oxford University press.

Goals 2000 Community Update. (1994, October). *Riley urges families to get involved in children's learning,* No. 1, 4, 17. Washington, DC: United States Department of Education.

Heath, S. B. (1983). *Ways with words.* Cambridge, MA: Cambridge University Press.

Henderson, A. T., & Berla, N. (Eds.) (1994). *A new generation of evidence: The Family is critical to student achievement.* Washington, DC: National Committee for Citizens in Education.

Leitch, M. L., & Tangri, S. S. (1988). Barriers to home-school collaboration. *Educational Horizon, 66*(2), 70–74.

National Education Goals Panel (1994). *The national education goals report: Building a nation of learners.* Washington, DC: The United States Department of Education.

Peng, S. S., & Wright, D. (1994). Explanation of academic achievement of Asian American students. *Journal of Educational Research, 87*(6), 346–352.

Ruiz, R. (1989). Orientations in language planning. In S. L. Mckay & S. L. C. Wong (Eds.), *Language diversity: Problem or resource?* (pp. 3–25). New York: Newbury House Publishers.

Simich-Dudgeon, C. (1986, December). Parent involvement and the education of limited-English-proficient students. *ERIC Digest.* Washington, DC: Center for Applied Linguistics.

Snow, C. E. (1990). Rationales for native language instruction: Evidence from research. In A. M. Padilla, H. H. Fairchild, & C. M. Valdez (Eds.), *Bilingual education: Issues and strategies* (pp. 165–189). Newbury Park, CA: Sage.

Snow C. E., Barnes, W. S., Chandler, J., Goodman, I. F., & Hemphill, L. (1991). *Unfulfilled expectations: Home and school influences on literacy.* Cambridge, MA: Harvard University Press.

Southgate, V. (Ed.). (1972). *Literacy at all levels: Proceedings of the eighth annual study conference of the United Kingdom Reading Association.* London: Ward Lock Educational.

Spradley, J.P. (1980). *Participant observation.* New York: Holt, Rinehart and Winston.

Taylor, D. (1983). *Family literacy: Young children learning to read and write.* Exeter, NH: Heinemann.

Trueba, H. T., Cheng, L. L., & Ima, K. (1993). *Myth or reality: Adaptive strategies of Asian Americans in California.* Washington, DC: Falmer Press.

Violand-Sanchez, E., Sutton, C. P., & Ware, H. W. (1991). *Fostering home-school cooperation: Involving language minority families as partners in education.* Washington, DC: National Clearinghouse for Bilingual Education.

United States Department of Education. (1994). *Strong family, strong school: Building community partnership for learning.* Washington, DC: Author.

United States General Accounting Office. (1994). *Limited English proficiency: A growing and costly educational challenge facing many school districts.* (Report No. GAO/HEHS-94-38 Limited English Proficiency). Washington, DC: U.S. General Accounting Office.

Wong Fillmore, L. (1988). Myths and realities of the linguistic minority child. In K. Hakuta (Ed.), *Policy and research perspectives on linguistic minority education* (Vol IV, pp. 15–20). Sacramento: University of California.

Wong Fillmore, L. (1990). Now or later? Issues related to the early education of minority-group children. *In Early Childhood and family education: Analysis and recommendations of the council of Chief State School Officers* (pp. 122–145). New York: Harcourt Brace Jovanovich.

Wong Fillmore, L. (in press). Against our best interest: The attempt to sabotage bilingual education. In J. Crawford (Ed.), *Source book on U. S. English.* Chicago: University of Chicago Press.

ANNA Y. LAI, M.A.

Anna Y. Lai is a Licensed Educational Psychologist who is a school psychologist for the San Francisco Unified School District. She has been serving the needs of the limited and non-English proficient Chinese students in the district for the past 20 years. Her special interests are in parent education and the development of appropriate educational programs for this population.

WARD SHIMIZU, M.A.

Ward Shimizu is a research assistant at San Jose State University. He received his bachelor's degree in 1987 from Oregon State University and his master's degree in 1995 from San Jose State University. Among his special interests are reading comprehension strategies, teaching writing to ethnically and linguistically diverse students, and effective tutorial strategies.

CHAPTER 10

REFRAMING THE STRUCTURE

LI-RONG LILLY CHENG, Ph.D.

The increase in the number of language-minority students in the United States has caused repercussions that can no longer be ignored. As discussed in Chapter 1, ethnic minorities presently constitute more than-one third of the nation's student population, and these numbers are rising steadily. This situation calls for a major reexamination, reevaluation, and restructuring of our present educational curriculum and policy to fully encompass the social, cultural, economic, and linguistic characteristics of the diverse minority population. This chapter propose guidelines for shifting our patterns of relationship and intervention strategies with a new category of student in mind.

In recent years, working in public education has grown increasingly challenging—commensurate with the rising numbers of newly arrived immigrant students. However, these challenges—characteristic of the multicultural classroom setting—have, in fact, existed for decades.

丩

YESTERDAY

It was more than 30 years ago when the first major influx of Cuban refugees arrived in Miami. The following is a letter written by a young Cuban boy to a teacher who helped him with his transition to his new life.

An Ode to a Great Teacher

I hope that Mrs. Penley will read this. I would prefer to express my appreciation of her in a more personal manner and not in this very public way, but I have no idea where she is. I don't even know her first name. One never knows a teacher's first name.

I am referring to the Mrs. Penley who taught seventh grade at Miami Springs Junior High School during the 1960–61 school year. If you are Mrs. Penley, this column today is just for you.

An Exotic Sight

You may not remember me, Mrs. Penley, but I am the Cuban kid who walked into your classroom exactly 30 years ago. I was the only Cuban student in your homeroom class. In fact, for a while, I was the only Cuban in the whole school. Of course, things started to change pretty fast after that. That school must now be full of children from Latin America.

But back then I was a pretty exotic sight in Miami Spring Junior. That first day I was wearing my best clothes. First impressions count, I had always been told. My pleated gray dress pants were the same ones I had worn earlier that week on the plane. My mother had bought them for me at the fancy J. Valles store in Havana. The shirt was plain white and pressed, the shoes and the socks black. Not one dark hair was out of place.

As I took my seat in the second row, I could feel that all eyes in the class were on me. I was especially aware of the blue eyes and green eyes that stared at me from under blonde locks and blonde crew cuts. And I noticed my classmates' canvas sneakers, white athletic socks and plaid shirts, rolled-up sleeves.

I was definitely no longer in the Havana classroom I had been attending less than a week before. I yearned for the security of my old school, which I had attended since kindergarten. Where was the brown and khaki uniform that I had always worn to school? And where were the friends and teachers whom I had known all my life?

You understand immediately. "What are you all staring at?" you asked the class. "Perez is a new student and comes from Cuba which is not far away. Does anyone know why he is here?" And you went into a whole lecture about what was happening in Cuba. You almost made it sound as if the momentous changes taking place in the island were happening just so I could join your class.

Direct from Havana, complements of Fidel Castro: the new seventh grader.

You told the class that according to the Principal, I spoke English fairly well. Not only that, you said, "Perez speaks Spanish, too. How many of you can speak two languages, huh?"

It was a little embarrassing, but it also made me feel special. And all the kids treated me that way on my first day. It made me feel good and accepted. It helped me fit in and make friends.

Many of my contemporaries who left Cuba at about the same time can recite horror stories about their first days in the U.S. school. But thanks to you, that was not my experience. Throughout the year, you went out of your way to make me part of the class. I remember, for example, the time you asked me to help you put together lessons on Cuba. The students took their cue from your positive attitude.

It was not until the following year, Mrs. Penley, that I was able to appreciate fully what you had done for me.

In eighth grade, things were very different from your class. My home-room teacher was Mrs. X. I would tell you her name, but I don't remember it. I think that psychologists call it repression.

That year there were several of us from Cuba in the class, and more were coming. In the months after the Bay of Pigs there was the perception in Miami that a tidal wave of Cubans was about to hit. And Mrs. X didn't like it one bit. Throughout the year she let us Cuban kids know it in many ways.

I remember the time that she admonished us for speaking in Spanish among ourselves in the hallway before class. She would remind us that "We are now in America, and the language here is English." She said that she didn't want to hear any more Spanish from us.

Not Mrs. X, Please

It was a terrible year, but I was able to handle it much better than my compatriots in the class. I already had one year of positive experiences under my belt. It would have been a real trial if that eighth grade had been my first school year in the United States.

The new school year is just getting started in schools throughout South Florida. If the trend continues, this year there will be more than 12,000 students who will be entering public schools here directly from a foreign school, as I did 30 years ago.

I wonder, Mrs. Penley, how many students will have a teacher like you? And how many will have a teacher like Mrs. X?

Conversely, the following life story provides a glimpse of how a student struggled to succeed and an explanation as to why so many students feel alienated, defeated, and isolated, and eventually drop out.

I was born in Tijuana, Mexico, and we moved to the United States in 1971. My parents wanted to provide a better life for us. I started preschool in San Ysidro, California when I was four. I remember walking to school with my mom and three little sisters. She took us to a building and told us to stay. I began to cry because I thought that I was being given away. She spanked me and made me stay. From that day on I hated school. I felt scared every time I attended school. At that time, my father was learning English and he would teach me how to read English and Spanish. I felt a lot of pressure in learning.

I was a nervous wreck when I entered kindergarten. I remember my teachers using me as an interpreter for other children who did not understand English. I had a teacher who continuously mispronounced my name. She also scolded me often and put me facing the wall when she thought I was acting inappropriately. I usually did not know what I was doing wrong because she would not tell me. I remember a particular day when we had a new boy in our class, named Pedro from Mexico City. I was sitting with Pedro in the front. The teacher was reading a story when suddenly she asked Pedro to move. He did not understand and I translated what she said. When I turned back to the teacher, she slapped me. She accused me of imitating her and making fun of her. I was embarrassed, scared and very confused. I was fearful of school and learning. My second grade teacher was kind to me and my third grade teacher thought I should be jumped to the fourth grade. In the middle of my third grade, I jumped to the fourth grade and I felt dumb, terrified and out of place. I started fearing and hating school again. I finally asked my mom to move me back to the third grade. I missed important information with the change of grade. When I went into the fourth grade another teacher decided that that it would be a good idea for me to jump to the sixth grade. I started to go downhill in my grades. I had lost pertinent information by skipping the fifth grade. I detested school more than ever. The highest grade I could get was a "C."

The junior high was a disaster. The teachers did not teach much; they spent more of the time trying to manage the class. Some teachers were afraid of the students and they just showed movies. I hated school even more. For my birthday, I asked my mom if I could stay home.

In the seventh grade, I became interested in the "Literacy Club" and the teacher who was heading the club was the first teacher in junior high that made me feel smart. She knew that I was a poor speller and that I had trouble with grammar, but she thought that I had good ideas and she encouraged me to write. I entered a contest and won first place in the essay contest. I felt smart and that I had learned something. The next year, I had a wonderful teacher who was asked to resign. I felt lonely in the eighth grade and once again I had no ambition to learn and my grades reflected that.

I was never told that Mexican people who had no money could go to college and I never had counselors come to our school to invite us to their campuses. I decided that I wanted to be a cosmetologist or a bank teller. I enter Mar Vista High and was placed in remedial math and remedial English. I was kept after school practically everyday for talking too much during the ninth grade. In my junior year, I had a psychology class and I liked it so much. My teacher recommended that I enroll in a class called Cross-age tutoring. I would go to an elementary school and work with children with Downs syndrome, cerebral palsy and other handicapping conditions. One day I observed a lady working with children on their sounds. I asked her who she was and what she was doing. She told me that she was a speech therapist and that we need bilingual speech therapists. I told her that I did not have money and my grades were low. She told me that money should not be the issue and grades could be brought up. I worked hard and got As and Bs in my senior year. My hate of school changed to a love for school. I had new values in education and learning. Now I am in graduate school and I am proud of myself. I look back at all the hard school life I had and I realize that anyone can accomplish any goals if one is motivated to do so. My experience made me a stronger person (Angel, 1993).

⊐⊓

TODAY

20 years ago, we witnessed the flood of refugees from Southeast Asia; hundreds of thousands of Southeast Asians fled their homeland on boats, and many made their journey to the United States. The following is the story of two Amerasians:

Vietnam—14 Years Later

To the Vietnam I will never forget
Years have passed
Memories of you are dimmed
Happiness and fear
buried in my heart, head
remembrances of you
are of smiles through tears
Still I never thought
a day of my return
leaving you years before
in violence, hysterics
You've aged, my mother
You've dried and withered
you seem uncertain, sad
Your offsprings have uprooted
to find new soil—abandonment
I feel in your presence
Your charm and beauty you
still possess—your culture
carved in your soul as expressed
in your children's paintings
Your countryside green—endless
Oceans so blue—life swimming in
its vastness
Never will it erase
pain inflicted, heartbreaks
rejections, a denial
WE—AMERASIANS—your half children
had endured.
Now I am only a visitor
treated as foreigner
Do you not understand
Within my heart my love for you
Vietnam, I will always adore you
Miss you when I am far away
Vietnam, I am still your child . . .
(L. Parsons, 1994)

Crying Drops of Blood

If lyrics could be worded to spell out two lines
of blood, the kids who have never known love.

It could be written
With whiskey sours, this taste
of sadness, the truth in tears.
What possible version of poetry
Could be used to compare
Innocent souls? Smiles?
They come to our lips and
Burst with our tears, crying
Oh Mother, Where are you?
Oh Father, Are you
just a breeze?
Who poured these pains over us?
Who can understand orphaned
Children, the foreigners who fathered us,
Diluted our blood and divided us
In half. Never have we felt
fully human. Like wandering souls
Without relatives, we have
No temple, no offering.
Ghosts receive respect, we are greeted
With hate. People kick us
With pity back and forth.
Chi D. Pham [Translated by
Trong Nguyen and Janice Finney]
(Chuong & Van, 1994)

┞

TOMORROW—THE CHALLENGE: ESTABLISHING A PREMISE FOR CHANGE

The disintegration of the Soviet Republic resulted in the influx of immigrants from Russia to the United States. And, as we mentioned in Chapter 1, it is projected that there will be more immigrants from the Arab world; thus, more Muslims will enter our schools. It behooves us to prepare for a greater number of new immigrants and refugees who will arrive in decades to come. Our diverse student population demands and will increasingly demand that educators be aware of general cultural and linguistic values of global populations, if they are to be able to promote effective communication among diverse populations. To establish an atmosphere that might break down cultural and communication barriers, facilitate learning, promote integration and interaction, and enhance understanding, teachers must recognize and anticipate potential weaknesses in their own abilities to handle such a diverse student body and to remedy problems.

⌐┐

CULTURAL LITERACY TO MULTICULTURAL LITERACY

As we face a multicultural society, we are challenged by the need for more information about our diversity (Chapters 3 through 6 provide such much needed information). It is imperative that we understand that the essence of pluralism is not simply to tolerate differences but to embrace them. We need to come to grips with the fact that a multicultural concept of "American" promotes unity as well as diversity (Macedo, 1994). As the global community shrinks, it is increasingly apparent that citizen interdependence exists at national and worldwide levels. Our nation's citizens must acquire multicultural literacy be able to cope with the rapidly changing pace of world economics and politics.

In general, our educational curriculum should serve the practical needs of people who are diverse in terms of cultural orientation, socioeconomic standing, folk beliefs, personal life history, and academic preparation. Increased sensitivity on the part of educators will enable students to reach their highest potentials (Allen, 1987; Rueda, 1993). By the same token, student-teachers/clinicians will require preparation in dealing with the ever-increasing diverse populations. They must be equipped with knowledge about cultural pluralism and an orientation toward diverse modes of communication and interaction. It is therefore important for us to infuse multicultural and pluralistic perspectives into our course content, design, instruction, and evaluation processes (Cole, 1989; Erickson & Iglesias, 1986; Hakuta, 1986; Pang & Park, 1992; Taylor, 1986a, 1986b).

The notion of reforming educational practices requires not only informed awareness of linguistic and superficial cultural differences but also of fundamental, culture-based differences in cognitive style and belief systems. For example, many teachers in the U.S. encourage creativity, exploration, inquiries, discussion, and debate. Their students are expected to ask questions, state personal opinions, volunteer information, participate in discussions, and debate about issues of concern. On the other hand, some teachers, especially those from the native lands of many students, simply provide lectures and transmit knowledge. Students, in moving from culture to culture and teacher to teacher, must shift gears from being told what to do to being offered options and from being given directions to sharing in decision making. Students must make adjustments in the level of their class participation, from being *asked* to participate in discussion to being *expected* to participate, from memorization of facts to complex problem solving, and from dependence on teachers to self-reliance in finding information, and so on. Such shifts can cause conflict and may require serious adjustment by the student.

Educators have the responsibility of evaluating their own preferred teaching style and of understanding the potentially diverse learning styles of their students. They must also cope with difficult discourse with students, families, and potentially, even whole communities (Cheng, 1993; Pang, 1988; Rueda, 1993). Educators need to reexamine assumptions about what their students know and how to explicitly explain what is expected of students. Further, teachers and students should discuss together how to bridge linguistic and cultural gaps and how to improve the quality of understanding by both. And, teachers should consider incongruencies within their cultural and pedagogical expectations before entering into discourse/teaching.

⊔

DIFFICULT DISCOURSE

Individuals experience different levels of "difficult discourse," meaning the sociological and psychological difficulties arising from conflicts of culture, language, and ideology (Cheng, 1994, Ripich & Creaghead, 1994; Trueba, Cheng & Ima, 1993). Difficult discourse involves values, traditions, beliefs, religion, personal life history, and the process of acculturation. Furthermore, it implies an understanding of classroom and societal rules of discourse and contrasting influences of home and classroom, with confusion arising from cultural identity, society, and family. "Hidden curriculum" is the underlying values, behaviors, and ways of thinking demanded of students—in other words, the means by which they are judged as students. Hidden curriculum consists of unspoken understandings shared by the mainstream classroom population (Jackson, 1968). (For example, when a student receives praise, the child should say "Thank you.")

The following excerpt illustrates how hidden curriculum and difficult discourse may surface:

Mimi is an 11-year-old immigrant who, at age 8, arrived in Los Angeles from Hong Kong with her parents. She speaks Cantonese at home but has difficulty reading Chinese, as she received only 1 year of formal education in Hong Kong. Initially, her U.S. teachers observed her as absent-minded in class and attributed this to her new environment and lack of English language proficiency. After 2 years of English as a second language (ESL), Mimi had made some progress but was still inattentive in class and exhibited other problems as well. A referral was made to the Student Study Team (SST), which attempted to test her native language skills and found that she did not possess cognitive academic linguistic proficiency (CALP—a term used by Cummins [1984]) in her native language, although she could speak it to some extent.

After several months of observation and deliberation, a recommendation was made to send Mimi to a special education class. Her parents were informed and they agreed, saying that they were grateful that the school was so concerned about their only child. Mimi was then enrolled in special education and received help in Cantonese from the Cantonese-speaking aide. The SST also recommended that Mimi and her parents receive counseling. This suggestion was presented to Mr. and Mrs. Lee by Mimi's teacher. The Lees seemed offended by this, and, within a week, they withdrew Mimi from the school and had her transferred to a private school. This turn of events, of course, puzzled the principal and the teacher.

What made the Lees decide to transfer Mimi to another school? What caused this sudden decision? The answer is complex and requires in-depth understanding of the cultural implications of a referral for counseling. In hearing such a suggestion, the Lees inferred that they were being viewed as abnormal and in need of psychiatric treatment. This brought great shame to the family, and to not lose face or to show a lack of respect for the school, they chose school transfer as their way out. The school officials, on the other hand, felt frustrated that the parents had not understood what they considered to be constructive intentions. All parties perceived the situation through their limited understandings of cultural/social implications.

Clearly, service providers and educators make assumptions about what students and families should know about schooling. For example, children should wear clean clothes to school and address teachers when they see them. Parents should get involved in PTA activities, volunteer their service, participate in school nights, read to children, take them to the library, assist children in school projects, call the school when the child is sick, and so on. In school, forgetting to hand in assignments on time may imply that the student lacks discipline or that the parents may be negligent in raising their child. Such "hidden curricula" must be defined by teachers and students, specifically for students who have not had parental coaching and education (Iglesias, 1990). The following section discusses the concept of "hidden curriculum" in detail.

THE HIDDEN CURRICULUM

The concept of hidden curriculum is not a new one. In his book entitled *Life in Classrooms*, Jackson (1968) defines it as "the crowds, the praise, and the power that combine to give a distinctive flavor to classroom life . . . [that] each student (and teacher) must master if he is to make his way satisfactorily through the school" (p. 34). Its mastery is crucial for academic success and requires understanding and sharing of the same set of values and beliefs held by teachers.

Limited English proficient (LEP) students from diverse cultural and social backgrounds have the challenge of acquiring knowledge to become cross-culturally competent (Cheng, 1990, 1994). Teachers may not understand that some observed "aberrant" behavior may be considered appropriate in the home milieu. For example, a Korean girl may giggle to show embarrassment when praised. Unfortunately, this may be misinterpreted by her teacher as a sign of disrespect (Cheng, 1991). Similarly, lack of participation or verbalization may be interpreted by the faculty as a lack of interest or motivation (Philips, 1983), when, in fact, it is not.

It is of utmost importance for each educator to critically examine personal world views, values, beliefs, way of life, learning style, cognitive style, and personal/family life to adapt for and reduce potential misunderstanding in classroom discourse. The following excerpt illustrates a typical conflict scenario:

Linda, a 13-year-old Hmong girl, was born in the United States after her parents escaped from Thailand. She attended Buena Vista School and was a very obedient student. In class, she often helped students who could not understand English. She explained to them what the teacher was saying and helped them with their work. Her teacher often praised her for her help. One day, the whole class was given an examination and the new students looked to Linda for help. As usual, Linda gave them the answers. This infuriated the teacher. She asked Linda to stay after school, at which time she reprimanded Linda for sharing her answers. Linda was in tears and totally humiliated. Her teacher said: "Linda, I thought you were a good student and you would not cheat. You should know better than that. I am deeply disappointed in you." Linda went home and did not show up the following day. Her teacher found out later that the whole family had moved away.

What went wrong? What did Linda not understand? Is it possible that Linda had received contradicting messages about helping in the classroom? Are there two sets of rules operating here? What "should Linda have known"? Was it the "hidden curriculum" that students do not share information during competitive examinations that Linda did not know?

DIFFICULT DISCOURSE VERSUS EASY COMMUNICATION

Difficult discourse often occurs at home when two or three languages are spoken. Often "broken English" is the primary mode of communication. The following case study provides a glimpse of the multiple layers of language use and how they lead to emotional conflict in the Smith family.

Kim Smith is an 8-year-old Amerasian boy. His parents married in Korea, where his father had been stationed. His mother speaks very little English and communicates with the family in "broken English." In Korea, Kim spoke to his mother in Korean and his father in simple English. In his new preschool, children laughed at him because his hair was "mousy blonde" and his eyes "slanted." He often asked his mother why did he not look like the rest of his peers, and she explained that his father was American.

When they moved to Riverside, California, Kim again met the ridicule of classmates who taunted him "Chinese, Japanese, Dirty Knees." They did not want to play with him because he did not understand the rules of games they played and did not "follow instructions." Additionally, in the classroom, he often could not understand his teacher, sometimes failing to turn in homework because he neither understood the instructions nor received assistance from his parents. Kim's teacher requested a parent conference, which his mother rejected out of fear. And Kim, growing aware of his physical and cultural differences, did not know how to deal with these difficulties.

After 6 months in the United States, Kim began to forget the Korean language; communication between him and his mother became increasingly difficult. His parents often argued, his mother always conceding, unable to express herself in English. Loss of her social network and support caused severe loneliness and frustration and homesickness for her family and friends increased. She had no friends to talk to and limited social opportunities, as she could not speak much English. And she was in sole charge of Kim most of the time because her husband was often away on military assignment.

The erosion of mother-son and husband-wife communication grew so serious that Mrs. Smith became withdrawn and hopeless. This affected Kim greatly; he felt displaced and alienated. He did not want to go to school because he felt like an outcast and did not understand the school discourse—yet he did not want to stay home because his relationship with his mother was strained. He became isolated, or what Spindler might call the withdrawal strategy of adaptation.

In a case such as this, educators or service providers need to consider the student's affective domain and the child's need to maintain a cultural identity, which may be biracial/bicultural. They may even have to help the student sort out confusion about "mixed-up identity."

PHILIP: A CASE OF MISMANAGEMENT?

Philip Law was born in 1985. The pregnancy was normal, but delivery was complicated. Five days past the due date, Mrs. Law could not feel the baby move for 6 hours and called her doctor. Her doctor told her to wait, but a day later, Mrs. Law was very concerned and was taken by her husband to the hospital. As soon as she was seen by the doctor in the emergency room, she was rushed to the delivery room; an emergency Ceasarian-section was performed. Philip was born blue from lack of oxygen and needed additional oxygen for many days. After being diagnosed (with little explanation) as having cerebral palsy, Philip was discharged from the hospital.

For the first 2 years of Philip's life, the Laws fed him, changed him, and played with him. The pediatrician did not say much about him, even when at 4 years of age, he still could not walk and was extremely shy. He was unable to talk, to understand what his parents were saying, to feed himself, or to dress himself. Worried, his parents went to a regional center for help. Its specialists identified cerebral palsy as the cause of Philip's delayed development and stated that as Mandarin was Philip's home language, fair assessment of his language skills was difficult. Philip did not receive adequate service, and the Laws became increasingly concerned about his development and growth.

Mr. Law took time off from his accounting business to train Philip. Finally at the age of 7, Philip was able to let go of his father's hand and walk on his own. In the meantime, Mrs. Law routinely read Philip a picture book before putting him to bed. Finally, one day, they heard him say "ball" and "bird." They were thrilled, but when they asked Philip to say it again, he would not. Unable to conquer their son's learning problem, the Laws asked the school to help and Philip was placed in a special education class where, in their opinion, he received only limited help.

Mr. Law found a newspaper article about autism from which he gleaned information leading him to believe that Philip exhibited "autistic behaviors." He called the writer of the article, but was unable to learn much from the conversation. Out of sheer frustration, he consulted a friend who happened to know a Mandarin-speaking speech pathologist. The clinician examined and diagnosed Philip with autism, mild cerebral palsy, and moderate to severe mental retardation.

The Laws were shocked. They could not believe their son had so many handicaps. Mrs. Law wanted to return to Hong Kong to look for cures. Her in-laws blamed Philip's condition on her negligence. Mr. Law, on the other hand, blamed the *school* for not taking care of his son.

SCHOOL-HOME DIFFICULT DISCOURSE: A CULTURAL CONFLICT

Teachers, students, and parents inadvertently influence each other. Students are often torn between a school's implicit (culturally determined) values and those they learn at home. Disparities between those values create misunderstandings beyond the level of language difference, as illustrated by the following case:

Johnny, an American Samoan, arrived in Los Angeles at the age of 9 with his family. They reside together with numerous members of the extended family and visitors in a three-bedroom apartment. His father works in an auto shop.

Johnny is the youngest child in his family and extremely attached to his brothers and sisters; in Samoan culture, young children are cared for by an older sibling. Johnny often arrives at school with bruises. When asked about the bruises, his parents say that it is necessary to punish their children at times. Additionally, they say, if a child cries during a beating, he or she is commonly beaten until the youngster sits still and behaves.

Johnny, who once saw his 18-year-old brother beat his 13-year-old sister to the point of causing a cerebral hemorrhage, was told to not challenge authority and to adhere to a strict social hierarchy. Because Johnny fears punishment, he presents a socially amiable attitude in school by masking his real feelings. His teachers find him difficult to work with: He is frequently absent, late to turn in work, and nonparticipatory in class. His parents punish him severely, frequently using extreme humiliation as a mode of punishment.

Johnny's teacher referred him to speech/language evaluation, during which the speech pathologist learned from his parents that he suffers from "musu," a deep-seated depression. "Musu" also refers to an unwillingness to comply with the dictates of those in authority, and the "musu" child often refuses to work or speak and is stubborn and sulky. In the Samoan tradition, the authority figures would severely punish such an offending child, often utilizing extremely humiliating measures.

Johnny and his family are caught in a problematic cultural affirmation strategy in which their attachments to their beliefs and practices frustrate their attempts at assimilation. In such a situation, teachers, speech pathologists, and counselors should seek knowledge about the belief systems and child-rearing practices of the culture in question. Through communicating with families and community leaders of differing cultures in search of a better understanding of their needs and motives, many problems can be alleviated.

HIDDEN AGENDA:
THE BROKEN AMERICAN DREAM

Immigrants and refugees face numerous challenges. Choices they are forced to make entail serious consequences and these choices are often uninformed or made out of necessity. Immigrants and refugees come to the United States to fulfill their "American dream," unaware of sacrifices implicit in what might be called the dream's "hidden agenda." They want to assimilate, but find themselves rejected—feeling marginalized and alienated. They want to belong, yet may be excluded because they do not meet the American "requirements" of proper speech, appearance, and so on. They want to learn English, often at the expense of their home language—a loss that entails fragmentation, a disconnection from home culture and family members.

Fragmentation results in the type of dysfunctional family we will see in the following case study. What can we do to prepare people for transplantation and transformation? What lessons have we learned by working with dysfunctional families? What advice can we provide newcomers about language, school, literacy, and so on? This case study offers some insight into these questions and the search for the American "Dream" (Trueba et al., 1993).

Wang left China as a refugee more than 10 years ago, leaving behind his son, parents, and wife. He and his wife, Tang, had met in college. When they moved back to Beijing, Wang and Tang were assigned to two different cities to work, only seeing each other a few times a year. Wang was able to emigrate to the United States because of his job, and once in the United States, he applied for immigration status for his family. After 4 years of waiting, Wang was reunited with Tang and his son Yu.

Wang rented a tiny two-bedroom apartment with a common area that served as a family room, dining area, and living room. His wife had learned a little English when she was in China, but in general, could not understand the language well. She attended church and met Chinese-speaking friends. At first, when she could not find a job, she felt useless and depressed. She finally found a job washing dishes. Ten-year-old Yu, on the other hand, was not unhappy with the new living situation, even though he initially could not speak English. He was fascinated by sports, cartoons, and games. Yu became absorbed by the programs on TV and spent many hours watching them. He picked up the language quickly and was able to find friends in the apartment building, through his sports activities, and at school.

Wang and his family, like all new immigrants have a story or two to tell about the difficulties of making the transition to American life. Some immigrants are able to integrate their two cultures, while some choose to reject their own cultural heritage in favor of their new culture. In the process of searching for the "American dream," some immigrants may lose their identity, and many immigrants entirely fail to assimilate to American culture because of social, racial, linguistic, and cultural barriers (Takaki, 1989).

SUGGESTIONS

Had Wang arranged for Tang and Yu to study English together and encouraged Tang to go to Adult ESL school, he might have been able to establish a better fundamental linguistic, emotional, and pedagogical connection among the members of his family. As it happened, after many years of separation, they were thrown together in a completely new environment that demanded new linguistic and cultural codes. Extra effort of courtesy and understanding on everyone's part might have given them space needed to reflect on their experiences and plan adaptation strategies.

OVERALL SUGGESTIONS

The following are suggestions for those working with of ESL or language minority students:

- Do not base assumptions on professional records. Reliability of records is dubious at best, especially given that some children are too apprehensive or shy to answer questions in the context of an interview.
- Do not base assumptions on any single source. Teachers may not be able to elicit responses from their students because the students are not used to the interactional style of the teachers or the classroom.
- Provide time and space for family members to interact and respond. Share with them the concerns about the student and attempt to solicit feedback, reaction, or responses from them.
- Ask many questions about the family; elicit feelings. However, be sensitive not to place value judgments on the family. Their way of life and world view may be very different from those of the practitioners and may not be easily comprehensible.
- Be aware of shyness, fear, and apprehension. Many parents find the school context intimidating and school personnel threatening. They fear that they will be criticized for not taking care of their children and at the same time may fear to hear the truth from the professionals.
- Understand that "no" may be said indirectly. Instead of saying "No, I don't want to get a hearing aid," "No, my son doesn't have a hearing loss," or "No, I disagree with your findings," some parents or caretakers may inadvertently say something that seems irrelevant (e.g. talking about a child's misdiagnosis).

Many refugee families place a great deal of emphasis on the continuation of a home culture and language, ensuring a connection with "old" ways, even if it means their children may be misdiagnosed, misinterpreted, or misplaced. Most believe their children will learn English language and social skills in due time and assimilate naturally without losing their native culture.

⊔

THE NEW FRAME: A PARADIGM SHIFT

A shift in our educational paradigm to a multicultural world view will do more than minimize classroom problems and maximize efficiency (see Table 10–1). It will incite change in our perception of language-minority students and to our philosophical conception of how to receive, socialize, and teach our nation's ethnic populations. The sections below present suggestions in hope of providing equitable access to resources and chances for academic success to all students. Information has been extracted from the article "Facing Diversity: A need for paradigm shifts" (Cheng, 1990).

FROM COMPENSATORY TO ENHANCEMENT

Teaching in a multicultural university of the 21st century will require that we challenge our traditional approach to language and language

TABLE 10–1
Paradigm shifts.

Existing Model	Paradigm Shift
Compensatory	Enhancement
Deficit	Asset
LEP	PEP
Tolerance	Acceptance/Respect
Disenfranchisement	Empowerment
Discrete	Dynamic
Isolated	Holistic
Clinician/Therapy-centered	Child/Family-centered
Assimilation	Adaptation
Hidden Curriculum	Open Dialogue
Difficult Discourse	Accessible Interaction

use. Custred (1990) stresses the importance of standard English and urges institutions of higher education to provide compensatory education to individuals using "folk speech." Instead of compensating for "deficiency," we can take a constructive approach by enhancing and adding to existing repertoires. Faculty and students should be open to diverse styles of writing, speaking, learning, socializing, and communicating (Vaughn-Cooke, 1983).

Custred (1990) highlights the importance of teaching the standard form of English to our students. On the surface, his concern for our student's lack of command in standard English seems legitimate—we should provide every opportunity for our students to practice standard English. However, this should in no way imply that one's diverse social and regional dialect or one's native tongue is less desirable or valued.

For example, Hoover (1990) emphasizes need for recognition of ebonics' (Black English) role in higher education and identifies its linguistic and cultural strengths. The complexity of the ebonics' lexicon, as described by Hoover, requires careful linguistic study and research. Hence, exclusive use of standard English denies scholars the opportunity to conduct legitimate research and inhibits active participation by students using diverse social and regional dialects.

Language has evolved through human interaction and societal need. The following poem illustrates one woman's feeling about her dialect:

> I am a child of the Americas,
> a light-skinned mestiza of the Caribbean,
> a child of many diaspora, born into this continent
>   at a crossroads.
>
> I am a US Puerto Rican Jew,
> a product of the ghettos of New York I have never
>   known.
> An immigrant and the daughter and granddaughter of
>   immigrants
> I speak English with passion: it's the tongue of
>   my consciousness
> a flashing knife blade of crystal, my tool, my
>   craft.
>
> I am Caribenal[1], island grown. Spanish is in my
>   flesh,

---

[1] Caribenal: A Caribbean woman.

ripples from my tongue, lodges in my hips:
the language of garlic and mangoes,
the singing in my poetry, the flying gestures of
    my hands.
I am of Latinoamerica, rooted in the history of my
    continent:
I speak from that body.
I am not african. Africa is in me, but I cannot
    return.
I am not taina. Taino[2] is in me, but there is no
    way back.
I am not european. Europe lives in me, but I have
    no home there.
I am new. History made me. My first language was
    spanglish[3].
I was born at the crossroads and I am whole.
(By Aurora Morales, 1992)

Scholars have written about Taglish (a mixture of Tagalog and English) and many other language mixtures. In addition to these, researchers have proposed the notion of "Englishes"—that is, varying styles of English, influenced by various local cultures and indigenous languages. For example, Singaporean English will include words such as sataay and sarong. Meanwhile, local native languages will also adopt many English words. In Hong Kong, many Cantonese words have been adopted from British English: bus, store, taxi, tips, ball, and so on. Both appreciation of such language interaction and acceptance of dialectic speech are crucial.

FROM DEFICIT TO ASSET

The term "deficit" implies a lack, connotes something negative. In the field of communicative disorders, the word is still used, but as linked to the medical model. People labeled as "deficient" feel self-conscious, exhibit low self-esteem, and are less likely to have a fulfilling educational experience. If students utilize different forms of communication, the speech needs to be considered as an *asset*, not deficit.

---

[2] Tainos: An Indian tribe native to Puerto Rico.

[3] Spanglish: A mixture of Spanish and English, used mostly in speech.

Instead of regarding diverse patterns of discourse as deficient, we can enrich our concept of language and appreciation of human diversity through acceptance of this diversity (Heath, 1983) and thereby create a positive educational atmosphere for all students.

There are many forms of English and many variations on the actual production of words; for example the word "tomato" may be pronounced either to-may-toe/to-ma-toe. Individuals with different home language bases likewise will present differences in word production. These phonological differences may cause difficulty in communication; teachers may misunderstand their students. The following examples are taken from *Refugee Update* (March 1992), *Dear Diane* (Wong, 1983), and additional personal communications.

Student:	"I have three bugs."
Teacher:	"Do you keep them in a jar?"
Student:	"No, I use them to buy things."
Teacher:	"Fill the cup." (Student touches the cup.)
Teacher:	"I asked you to fill the cup." (Student looks puzzled.) "I feel the cup."
Teacher:	"Put some water in the cup." (Source: *Refugee Update*, 1992, p. 1).

Such incidents are quite common; however, with effort by the teacher to learn more about a student's home language linguistic system, communications can be vastly improved.

On a functional/pragmatic level, difficulties occur when messages are misunderstood:

Teacher	(calling a student's mother): "I want to set up an appointment with you to talk about your son."
Mother	(assuming the call must concern something very serious): "What's wrong?"
Teacher:	"Nothing is wrong. This is for the teacher-parent conference."

Mother	(thinking): She must be hiding something from me. My son is in deep trouble.
Hostess:	"You must try this piece of cheese."
Guest/Student	(perceiving the offer as an order): "Thank you." (Source: Author's personal experience)
Teacher:	"I like this box. It is very pretty."
Student	(thinking the teacher likes it and, therefore, should receive it as a gift): "Please accept this."
Student:	"My mother asked me to give this to you."
Teacher:	"I don't accept bribes from students." (Source: Wong, 1983, p. 45).
Teacher:	"I am talking to you, Tran, look at me." (Tran takes a quick peek at the teacher and then looks down.)
Teacher:	"I said 'Look at me.' Why are you looking down?"
Tran:	(still staring downward): "I look at you." (The student is too scared to look at the teacher.) (Source: Author's personal experience).

The above scenarios illustrate mutual breakdowns in language form and function and nonverbal communication caused by lack of familiarity with the school language, social nonverbal communication patterns and/or cultural contexts. Nonverbal expression is extremely important in the communication process. Leubitz (1973) identifies four functions of nonverbal communication: to relay messages, to augment verbal communication, to contradict verbal communication, and to replace verbal communication.

Knapp (1972) suggests that 35% of a message's social meaning is transmitted by words, 65% through nonverbal channels. Other features of nonverbal communication include proximity, social distance, facial expression, and so on. Breakdown in nonverbal communication is common and needs to be examined and understood.

FROM LEP TO PEP

Foreign born individuals and immigrant parents often seek to "reduce" their foreign accents to avoid being labeled as "foreigners" and for assurance that they will not be discriminated against when applying for jobs. Many minority students and their teachers impulsively wish to "clear up" or reduce accents. Teachers should instead urge these students to add another style of articulation to their existing linguistic repertoires and code-switch to meet communicative demands of various social and cultural situations (Grosjean, 1982). Linguistically and culturally diverse students need to add various forms of academic discourse to their lexicon, what Cummins (1981) refers to as Cognitive Academic Linguistic Proficiency (CALP). Our guiding principle needs to shift from a reductionist perspective to an expansion and constructivist perspective and from limited proficiency to potential English proficiency (PEP).

Many instructional programs have been designed to train nonnative English speakers in phonology and effective communication or accent reduction (Biederman, 1989; Compton, 1983). Many clients of such programs are there because they feel that their English sounds foreign and awkward and they have experienced feelings of social isolation and frustration in their inability to communicate well. Many join these programs also because they feel that their job advancement has been hampered by an invisible, accent-based barrier. The goals of such training programs are to improve intelligibility and polish content to improve overall quality of communication and thus alleviate these psychological and experiential problems.

FROM TOLERANCE TO ACCEPTANCE

The notion of *tolerance* of language and cultural difference connotes conscientious indifference and perhaps even hostility, with *acceptance* connoting approval and support. When social dialects are tolerated, they are considered "harmless" but not "useful"; accordingly, they are often discouraged. Powell and Collier (1990), along with many researchers (Cole & Deal, in press), further advocate the need for an accepting, pluralistic perspective in course content and instructional and evaluative processes.

"Folk" speech might be tolerated for its "charming" variance, yet disregarded as representative of a valued, but different world view and set of experiences. Attempts to modify such speech might, in some context, be perceived as a violation of the speaker's right to choose cultural/personal characteristics.

Language transmits more than literal content. It transmits culture. The term "pragmatics" refers to this social function served by language. Given the great number of aspects that must be taken into consideration in performing a speech act, the difficulty of choosing a strategy in a multicultural context is clear.

The distinction between literal and nonliteral context is often obscured by a cross-cultural setting, as participants must mutually understand both the language form and context for successful communication to take place. Failure to distinguish between the modes of literal and nonliteral meaning often results in misinterpretation and intolerance. Again, acceptance and conscientious effort is the key to eliminating these negative effects.

FROM DISENFRANCHISEMENT TO EMPOWERMENT

Educators need to redefine their classroom, community, and society roles in a course of action to empower rather than disenfranchise ESL students (Cummins, 1986; Pang, Colvin, Tran, & Barba, 1992; Sleeter, 1989, 1991). When dialect styles are not validated or approved by instructors, students may feel inadequate and thus perform poorly in the classroom, resulting in disenfranchisement and alienation. To be empowered, students need to feel confident in speaking and communicating. Hoover (1990) advocates the power of self-esteem and fearlessness in overcoming communication barriers.

FROM THE DISCRETE TO THE DYNAMIC

Practitioners are trained to employ standardized testing procedures from which they derive discrete points, scores, percentiles, stanines, and so on. These data are then used to make clinical impressions, judgments, and recommendations. When such procedures are not available, practitioners are at a loss. In general, they feel inadequate and uneasy about identifying problems on the basis of "screening" or "personal expertise." This faulty paradigm has rendered clinicians powerless in many instances; yet many practitioners refuse to let go of the quantifiable data approach and continue to complain of a shortage of standardized procedures and a consequent incapacity to assist culturally/linguistically diverse populations.

As an alternative to standardized testing, the dynamic assessment model (Feuerstein, 1979, Haywood & Tzuriel, 1992; Lidz, 1987, 1991; Pena & Iglesias, 1993) suggests a test-intervene-retest format. It monitors a child's response to intervention, process of attention, perception, memory, simultaneous and successive coding, reasoning, and metacognition. The dynamic assessment approach empowers both the teacher and the student during the assessment process. Instead of constraining progress by requiring that the teacher report test findings, this model allows the teacher to conduct intervention and retesting and to glean a truer picture of the student's performance level. Additionally, promoting students' freedom to try personal learning strategies invokes confidence.

FROM ISOLATED TO HOLISTIC

Eisman (1991) advocates a model based on a child's holistic performance and real-world experience rather than on isolated test results (Erickson & Omark, 1981; Nelson, 1993). Thorough understanding of the child and his or her family and community provides the educator clearer understanding and promotes fair and beneficial decisions.

FROM CLINICIAN/THERAPY-CENTERED TO FAMILY/CHILD-CENTERED

For decades, speech-hearing professionals, accountable for the outcome of therapeutic intervention, have been trying to improve their methods. Children are often placed in "pull-out" programs, seen two or three times a week, sometimes in groups. But parents and family members are seldom involved in such therapy. To improve students' communication, we need to adopt methods that include the variables of home discourse (Ripich & Creaghead, 1994).

FROM ASSIMILATION TO ADAPTATION

Gordon (1978) describes assimilation as having two parts: behavioral assimilation and structural assimilation. Behavioral assimilation is an immigrant's acquisition of habits, attitudes, and lifestyles of the "host" culture. Structural assimilation means initiation into the society's organizations and economic and civic lives. Individuals attempting to behaviorally assimilate often strive to speak "correctly" and without accent. Instructors advocating assimilation of this sort will demand adherence to Eurocentric rules.

Kaplan (1966) and Westby (in press) state that diverse cultural thought patterns are framed by one's oral and literary presentations. Providing our students opportunities to acculturate and learn the Eurocentric style of articulation can be beneficial. However, instructors must realize the potential harm of solely enforcing assimilation, because assimilation may be extremely difficult for some students and impossible for others (Gollnick & Chinn, 1986).

On the other hand, acculturation is essential for students of linguistic and cultural diversity in coping with academic discourse even while they work to maintain their own cultural identities. Gollnick and Chinn (1986) further indicate that many individuals of oppressed minority groups—those denied full access to the majority group's economic, political, and social spheres—can never assimilate. For more information read Freire (1986) Macedo (1994) and Takaki (1989).

FROM HIDDEN CURRICULUM TO OPEN DIALOGUE

Krashen (1981) discusses the need for "comprehensible input" in classroom interactions. Many students find classroom discourse and its oral/written and nonverbal rules incomprehensible or at least difficult. These rules exist tacitly both in and out of the classroom, in what might be called the "hidden curriculum." LEP students are not familiar with the American culture and may violate the rules in the hidden curriculum. Mastering the hidden agenda requires that they understand and share their teachers' educational values. They must incorporate these into their education to become cross-culturally competent (Cheng, 1990). Teachers can reverse the situation by turning the students from feeling disenfranchised, with a lowered sense of identity, to having a heightened sense of self-worth and motivation to participate and be engaged. Teachers' open dialogues invite active engagement in classrooms so that the students do not feel ignored during classroom verbal interaction.

DIFFICULT DISCOURSE TO ACCESSIBLE INTERACTION

Teachers need to get to know their students' social codes and home discourse rules, and they may also need to explicitly explain and model certain school discourse rules (Cheng, 1989, 1994). In general, students are encouraged to volunteer information in American classrooms. Asian/Pacific Islander students may appear indifferent, difficult, or uncooperative when they do not understand what is going on in the classroom or what is implicitly expected of them.

The term "difficult discourse" refers to conflict of language, ideology, and cultural identity occurring between students/families and the American mainstream educational system (Cheng, 1994). Many factors contribute to difficult discourse observed in the classroom; these include degrees of adjustment and conflicting cultural values. Difficult discourse is ubiquitous in American schools; for example, often immigrant students and parents speak a language unknown to the school and teachers. Inadequate communication between the school and students or parents follows. Additionally, parents may feel out of place in the school environment, because they define respect for teachers as choosing not to interfere with school-related issues. Meanwhile, the school interprets such a nonparticipatory stance as discourteous and evidence of disrespect and disinterest. Accessible interaction can be promoted by the hiring of interpreters and consulting with community facilitators to chart a path to an easier interaction and smoother discourse.

⊔

TOWARD MULTICULTURAL LITERACY

Literature and literacy cannot be over-emphasized. Teachers and students facing the twenty-first century need to be literate in a multicultural sense (Simonson & Walker, 1988) to function for the benefit of all students. America's labor force is projected to include increasing numbers of ethnically and culturally diverse populations; in fact, by the year 2000, only 15% of new workers will be Anglo males (Reynolds, 1989).

ꓷ

CONCLUDING SUGGESTIONS

Given the ethnic, cultural, and linguistic diversity of our student/client population, in-depth knowledge of every student's language, culture, and social background is difficult to come by. However, cross-cultural communicative competence, or the ability to communicate effectively across cultures, can be developed. Educators need to integrate this competence into educational practices and curriculum (Cheng, 1989), as detailed by the following suggestions.

FACULTY

Excellence in education will require a culturally heterogenous cadre of professionals who are knowledgeable and who understand related social, linguistic, cultural, educational, and economic issues. If faculty are to be motivated to infuse multicultural information into their everyday teaching, a system of rewards and appraisal may be necessary to help promote individual, personal, and professional growth (Accent, 1989). Multicultural and social literacy will be necessary across the educational continuum.

The following guidelines can be used to develop faculty training programs that aim at improving the communicative competence of students from diverse backgrounds:

1. *Nurture bicultural identity.* Infuse cultural literacy and training not only in phonology, morphology and syntax, but also in pragmatics, semantics and ritualized patterns.
2. *Provide experience working with clients of different age groups and disorders.* Also, expose them to different working environments, such as school, health care, social, and governmental systems.
3. *Provide information on different narrative styles and the written and unwritten rules that govern them.* Conduct discussions of style similarities and differences, and what is considered appropriate and inappropriate.

⌐

CONCLUSION

Educators need to examine their methods and endorse the foregoing paradigm shifts to embrace and further cultural pluralism in the educational system. Institutions must reaffirm themselves as multicultural—in keeping with the true fabric of the American tapestry—and commit themselves to improving the quality of education for diverse students.

In the words of Gabriela Milstral:

There are many things that can wait;
But children cannot wait;
Their bones are growing;
Their blood is flowing;
Their concepts are forming;
We cannot say to them "Let's wait until tomorrow."
For their name is spelled "Today."
(Milstral, Chilean poet, translated by Author from
Chinese language brochure: China Children's Fund)

Finally, the following rephrasing from Oliver and Johnson (1988) sums up our ideas beautifully:

As we approach an increasingly diverse multicultural 21st century, education must play an important role in educating this and future generations of American students—white and black, native-born or foreign-born, immigrant and nonimmigrant—competitive enough to meet the human resource needs that our technologically advanced society demands.

⌐

REFERENCES

Accent on Improving College Teaching and Learning. (1989). Ann Arbor: University of Michigan, National Center for Research to Improve Post Secondary Teaching and Learning.

Angel, L. (1993). *Personal life history.* Unpublished manuscript. San Diego State University.

Allen, W. R. (1987, May-June). Black colleges vs. white colleges: The fork in the road for Black students. *Change,* 25–34.

Biederman, P. W. (1989, November 23). Dialectician puts accent on the stars. *Los Angeles Times*, p. J10.

Cheng, L. (1989). Service delivery to Asian/Pacific LEP children. *Topics in Language Disorders, 9*(3), 1–14.

Cheng, L. (1990). Recognizing diversity: A need for paradigm shift. *American Behavioral Scientist, 34*(2), 263–278.

Cheng, L. (1991). *Assessing Asian language performance: Guidelines for evaluating LEP students.* Oceanside, CA: Academic Communication Associates.

Cheng, L. (1994). Difficult discourse: An untold Asian story. In D. N. Ripich & N. A. Creaghead (Eds.), *School discourse problems* (pp. 155–170). San Diego: Singular Publishing Group.

Cheng, L., & Ima, K. (1988). The California Basic Educational Skills Test (CBEST) and Indochinese teacher interns: A case of a cultural barrier to foreign-born Asian professionals? In G. Y. Okihiro, S. Hune, A. A. Hansen, & J. M. Liu (Eds.), *Reflections on shattered windows: Promises and prospects for Asian American studies* (pp. 67–79). Pullman: Washington State University Press.

Chuong, C. H., & Van, L. (1994). *The Amerasians from Vietnam: A California study.* Sacramento: Bilingual Education Office, California Department of Education.

Clark, L. W., & Cheng, L. (1993). Faculty challenges in facing diversity. In L. W. Clark (Ed.), *Faculty and student challenges in facing cultural and linguistic diversity.* Springfield, IL: Charles C. Thomas.

Cole, L. (1989). E pluribus pluribus: Multicultural imperative for the 1990s and beyond. *ASHA, 22*(4), 317–318.

Cole, L., & Deal, V. (in press). *Communicative disorders in multicultural populations.* Rockville, MD: American Speech-Language-Hearing Association.

Compton, A. J. (1983). *Compton Phonological Assessment of Foreign Accents.* San Francisco: Carousel.

Cummins, J. (1981). The role of primary language development in promoting educational success for language minority students. In California State Department of Education, Office of Bilingual/Bicultural Education. *Schooling and language minority students: A theoretical framework* (pp. 3–49). Los Angeles, CA: Evaluation, Dissemination and Assessment Center, California State University.

Cummins, J. (1984). *Bilingualism and special education: Issues in assessment and pedagogy.* Clevedon, England: Multilingual Matters.

Cummins, J. (1986). Empowering minority students: A framework for intervention. *Harvard Education Review, 56*, 18–36.

Custred, G. (1990). The primacy of standard language in modern education. *American Behavioral Scientist, 34*(2), 232–239.

Eisman, K. (1991). *Restructuring.* California Center for School Restructuring. San Diego: Patrick Henry High School.

Erickson, J., & Omark, D. (Eds.). (1981). *Communication assessment of the bilingual bicultural child.* Baltimore: University Park Press.

Erickson, J., & Iglesias, A. (1986). Assessment of communicative disorder in non-English proficient children. In O. L. Taylor (Ed), *Nature of communication disorders in culturally and linguistically diverse populations* (pp. 181–218). San Diego: College-Hill Press.

Feuerstein, R. (1979). *The dynamic assessment of retarded performers*. Baltimore: University Park Press.

Freire, P. (1986). *Pedagogy of the oppressed*. New York: Continuum.

Gollick, D. M., & Chinn, P. C. (1986). *Multicultural education in a pluralistic society*. Columbus, OH: Charles,E. Merrill.

Gordon, M. (1978). *Human nature, class and ethnicity*. New York: Oxford University Press.

Grosjean, F. (1982). *Life with two languages: An introduction to bilingualism*. Cambridge, MA: Harvard University Press.

Hakuta, K. (1986). *Mirror of language: Debate on bilingualism*. Rowley, MA: Newbury House

Hale-Benson, J. E. (1982). *Black children: Their roots, culture, and learning styles*. Baltimore: Johns Hopkins University Press.

Haywood, H. C., & Tzuriel, D. (Eds.). (1992). *Interactive assessment*. New York: Springer-Verlag.

Heath, S. B. (1983). *Ways with words: Language, life and work in communities and classrooms*. New York: Cambridge University Press.

Hoover, M. R.(1990). A vindicationist perspective on the role of Ebonics (Black Language) and other aspects of ethnic studies in the University. *American Behavioral Scientist, 34*(2), 251–262.

Iglesias, A. (1990). *Sharing parenting*. (Videotape for parents and teachers dealing with child socialization practices and/or child development). Philadelphia: Temple University.

Jackson, P. W. (1968). *Life in classrooms*. New York: Holt, Rinehart & Winston.

Kaplan, R. (1966). Cultural thought patterns in intercultural education. *Language Learning, 16*, 1–20.

Knapp, L. (1972). *Nonverbal communication in human interaction*. New York: Holt, Rinehart & Winston.

Krashen, S. (1981). Bilingual education and second language acquisition theory. In California State Department of Education, Office of Bilingual Education (Ed.,) *Schooling and Language Minority Students: A theoretical framework* (pp. 51–79). Los Angeles: California State University, Evaluation, Dissemination and Assessment Center.

Leubitz, L. (1973). *Nonverbal communication: A guide for teachers*. Skokie, IL: National Textbook.

Lidz, C. S. (1987). *Dynamic assessment: An interactional approach to evaluating learning potential*. New York: Guilford.

Lidz, C. S. (1991). *Practitioner's guide to dynamic assessment*. New York: Guilford.

Macedo, D. (1994). *Literacies of power*. Boulder, CO: Westview Press.

Morales, A. (1992). *Heath English* (J. A. Senn & C. A. Skinner, Eds.). Lexington, MA: D.C. Heath.

Nelson, N. W. (1993). *Childhood language disorders in context: Infancy through adolescence.* New York: Macmillan/Merrill.

Oliver, M. L., & Johnson, J. H., Jr. (1988). The challenge of diversity in higher education. *The Urban Review, 20*(3), 139–145.

Pang, V. (1988, August). Ethnic prejudice: Still alive and hurtful. *Harvard Education Review, 58*(3), 375–379.

Pang, V., Colvin, C., Tran, M., & Barba, R. (1992). Beyond chopsticks and dragons: Asian-American literature for children. *The Reading Teacher, 46*(3), 216–224.

Pang, V., & Park, C. (1992). Issues-centered approaches to multicultural education in the middle grade. *The Social Studies, 83*(9), 108–112.

Pena, E., & Iglesias, A. (1993, November). *Dynamic assessment: The model and its application to language assessment.* Short course presented at the American Speech-Language-Hearing Association Convention, Anaheim, CA.

Philips, S. (1983). *The invisible culture.* New York: Longman.

Powell, R., & Collier, M. J. (1990). Public speaking instruction and cultural bias: The future of the basic course. *American Behavioral Scientist, 34*(2), 240–250.

Refugee Update. (1992, March). Folsom-Cordova, CA: Folsom-Cordova School District.

Reynolds, A. (1989, November). *A new look at old models: Getting higher education out of the 14th century to the multicultural university of the 21st century.* Speech delivered to the Conference on Celebrating Diversity, Oakland, CA.

Ripich, D. N., & Creaghead, N. A. (Eds.). (1994). *School discourse problems.* San Diego: Singular Publishing Group.

Rueda, R. (1993, June 23). *Language acquisition theory.* Multicultural Education Infusion Summer Institute. San Diego: San Diego State University.

Sleeter, C. (1989). Multicultural education as a form of resistence to oppression. *Journal of Education, 171,* 51–72.

Sleeter, C. (1991). *Empowerment through multicultural education.* Albany: State University of New York.

Simonson, R., & Walker, S. (Eds.). (1988). *Multicultural literacy.* St. Paul, MN: Graywolf Press.

Stateline. (1990, February). Los Angeles: The California State University.

Takaki, R. (1989) *Strangers from a different shore.* Boston: Little, Brown & Co.

Taylor, O. L. (1986a). A cultural and communicative approach to teaching standard English as a second dialect. In O. L. Taylor (Ed.), *Treatment of communication disorders in culturally and linguistically diverse populations.* San Diego: College-Hill Press.

Taylor, O. L. (1986b). *Nature of communication disorders in culturally and linguistically diverse populations.* San Diego: College-Hill Press.

Trueba, H., Cheng, L., & Ima, K. (1993). *Myth & reality: Adaptive strategies of Asian newcomers in California.* London: Falmer Press.

Vaughn-Cooke, F. (1983). Improving language assessment in minority children. *ASHA, 25,* 29–34.

Westby, C. (In press). Cross-cultural differences in adult-child interaction. In L. Cole & V. Deal (Eds.), *Communication disorders in multicultural populations.* Rockville, MD: American Speech-Language-Hearing Association.

Wong, Y. M. (1983). *Dear Diane: Letters from our daughters.* Oakland, CA: Asian Women United of California.

APPENDIX

HAWAII DEMOGRAPHICS

Hawaii State Population By Race and Ethnicity.

Race/Ethnicity	1990 Population	Percent of Total
White	369,616	33.4
Black	27,195	2.5
American Indian	5,099	0.5
Asian	522,967	47.2
Chinese	*68,804*	*6.2*
Filipino	*168,682*	*15.2*
Japanese	*247,486*	*22.3*
Asian Indian	*1,015*	*0.1*
Korean	*24,454*	*2.2*
Cambodian	*119*	*0.0*
Vietnamese	*5,468*	*0.5*
Hmong	*6*	*0.0*
Laotian	*1,677*	*0.2*
Thai	*1,220*	*0.1*
Other Asian	*4,036*	*0.4*
Pacific Islander	162,269	14.6
Polynesian	***157,749***	***14.2***
Hawaiian	*138,742*	*12.5*
Samoan	*15,034*	*1.4*
Tongan	*3,088*	*0.3*
Other Polynesian	*885*	*0.1*
Micronesian	***3,968***	***0.4***
Guamanian	*2,120*	*0.2*
Other Micronesian	*1,848*	*0.2*
Melanesian`	***291***	***0.0***
Other Pacific Islander	*261*	*0.0*
Other Ethnicities	21,083	1.9
Total Population	**1,108,229**	**100.0%**

Source: US Census Bureau, 1990 Census, Summary Tape file 1A.

INDEX

A

Acculturation, 13–16, 117, 154–158, 201. *See also* Cultural expectations
adjustment requirements, 233–238
Asian Americans-Pacific Islanders (API), 19–20
communicative competencies, 227–228
and families, 13–14, 154–158, 302–303
Hmong, 244–245
integrating cultures, 305–306
language
content, 226
culture/communication interplay, 227–230
form, 224–226
styles, 228–229
use, 226
language-culture gap, 17–18
and mainstream peers, 13–14, 98
multicultural competencies, 227–228. 317
and pluralism, U.S., 228
Agenda
"hidden" curriculum, 11, 189–190, 299–300, 301–302, 316
Asian Americans-Pacific Islanders (API). *See also* Cultural expectations; English as second language (ESL); Indian subcontinent; individual nations; Pacific Islanders
acculturation, 13–16
language
form, 224–226
assumptions of Asian students, 12, 50
at-risk factors, 12–16
collaborative inquiry language process, 97–98

Asian American-Pacific Islanders
(*continued*)
communication
interpersonal confusion features,
222–223
nonverbal, 191–192, 221–224
cultural expectations
adjustment with, 277–281
family continuity, 232
folk beliefs, 91, 232, 244–245
health attitudes, 91, 226
language
use and culture, 226
variation among groups, 224–226
language-culture gap, 17–18
languages, 216–218
multicultural competencies, 227–228
oral tradition (collective stories),
97, 242–243
Poetry, 296–297
religions, 78–79, 91, 127, 229–230,
231–232
self-image, 14
speech-language-hearing
specialists, 21
Assessment, 200, 201. *See also*
Preassessment
bilingual, 118–119, 121, 161–164,
168–172
Cantonese, 258–264
dynamic model, 315
and families, 19, 118, 166–170,
303–304
Hmong, 238–249
Native Hawaiian Assessment
Project, 67–69
paradigm shift, 314–315
special education, 118–119,
161–164, 168–172
standardized, 314–315
At-risk factors, 12–16, 93, 151, 155,
165, 167

B

Basic interpersonal communication
skills (BICS)

limited English proficient (LEP),
194
limited English proficient (LEP) +
learning disability (LD), 34
Southeast Asians, 116
Bilingual certified teachers (Asian
Americans-Pacific Islanders
[API]), California, 116–117
Bilingual education, 117. *See also*
Educational system; English
as second language (ESL);
Special education
assessment, special education,
118–119, 121, 161–164
and Pacific Islanders, 95–96
"Sheltered English," 117
Specially Designed Academic
Instruction in English
(SDAIE), 117
staff needs, 119–121, 159–164,
200, 248
Bilingual Education Act 1968/1974,
3, 117

C

Cambodian language/Khmer, 21,
109–110, 111, 116, 117
lexicon, 113
naming system, 110
phonology, 112
speech-language-hearing
specialists, 21
writing, 113–114
Cambodians, 116, 151
Cantonese. *See* under Chinese/
language groups
Chamorros (Guam), 73–74, 225
hospitalization, attitudes
toward, 91
language, 225
Chinese, 191, 223–224, 275
cultural interactions, 191, 225–226
English as second language (ESL),
184–187

family and language, 225
language groups, 9–10, 225–226
  Cantonese, 31–35, 258–264, 272,
      300, 310
    cognitive linguistic proficiency
        (CALP), 194
    proficiency, limited English
        proficient (LEP) + learning
        disability (LD), 47–49
  Mandarin, 303–304
    cognitive linguistic proficiency
        (CALP), 194
  speech-language-hearing
      specialists, 21
learning disability (LD)
  in Taiwan, 38–39
limited English proficient (LEP) +
    learning disability (LD),
    31–56. *See also* Special
    education
  ethnic community view, 39–40
  reading processes analysis, 39
  speech-language-hearing
      specialists, 21
  study of limited English proficient
      (LEP) + learning disability
      (LD), 40–56
    Cantonese proficiency, 47–48
    cognitive profiles, 49
    comparison, Cantonese/English
        performance, 48–49
    English oral language profiles,
        45–47
    social emotional aspects, 49–50
    special education referral
        factors, 44
    status referral factors, 42–44
Cognitive linguistic proficiency
    (CALP), 11, 313
  English as second language (ESL),
      192–193, 194
  limited English proficient (LEP) +
      learning disability (LD), 34,
      47, 53, 55
  Southeast Asians, 116

and writing mastery, 194
Counseling, 154–158
Cultural expectations, 151–154, 166,
    172–174, 190–193, 234,
    274–275, 276, 304–305. *See
    also* Acculturation
  adjustment with, 277–281
Curriculum
  agenda, "hidden," 11, 189–190,
      299–300, 301–302, 316

D

Demographics
  Filipinos, 83
  general
    distribution, 4–5, 7–10, 241
    diversity, population, 8–10
    families, 7–8
    history, 4
    nationality information, 5–6, 143
    in U.S., 4–8, 108–109, 125–126,
        143
  Hawaiians, 65–67, 69, 326
  Indian subcontinent, 127–130
  Samoans, 74–77
  Southeast Asians, 107–109
Drop-out factors, 12. *See also* At-risk
    factors

E

Educational system. *See also* Bilingual
    education; English as
    second language (ESL);
    Families; Paradigm shift;
    Special education
  and acculturation, 14–16, 19–20,
      117, 141–175, 154–158
  adjustment requirements,
      233–238
  Asian written discourse style,
      229–230
  assessment. *See also* Assessment;
      Preassessment

Educational system *(continued)*
 special needs, 118–119, 161–164,
  168–172
 assumptions about Asian students,
  12, 37
 barriers
  challenges, 50–53, 159–164,
   245–246
  self-perceived, 234–235
 bilingual certified teachers (Asian
  Americans-Pacific Islanders
  [API]), California, 116–117
 classroom issues, 116, 190, 199, 229
 code-switching, linguistic/
  cultural, 191
 collaboration, socially constructed
  teaching, 97–98
 collaboration with families,
  202–204
 collaborative model, professional,
  254, 256–257
 contextualized learning provision,
  97–98
 counseling, 154–158
 and cultural expectations, 151–154,
  166–168, 172–174, 190–193,
  304–305
  adjustment with, 277–281
 cultural/linguistic awareness,
  191–192, 210
 curriculum needs, 234
 discourse styles, classroom, 116,
  190, 299–301, 311–312, 317
 drop-out factors, 12
 employment needs, students, 19–20
 English as second language (ESL)
  guidelines, 307–308
  strategies, 181–208
 experience-based teaching, 192
 families
  collaboration with, 72–73, 200,
   246–248, 274–275, 277–281
  checklist, 279–281
  concept development, 284

 language uses, home, 283
 literacy activities, home, 283–284
 as resource, 55–56, 276–277
 state partnerships with, 266
 training of, 282
 first language-English cognitive
  linguistic proficiency
  (CALP) support need, 53
 gap, theory-practice, 10–11
 gifted program, 162–163
 Hawaiian public, 69–72
 hidden agenda/curriculum, 11,
  189–190
 Hmong learning styles, 243–244
 homework role, 273–274
 instructional program connection
  need, 51–53, 55–56
 learning beyond schooling,
  277–284
 literacy
  multicultural, 298–299, 317, 318
  multiple
   modeling, 282–284
 mainstream placement
  considerations, 233–234
 misunderstanding, cultural,
  164–174
 multidisciplinary need, 22
 multisensory teaching approach,
  116
 and Pacific Islanders, 95–96
 personnel recruitment, 21–22,
  119–121
 resource issues, 200
 "Sheltered English," 117
 social support need, 53–54, 55
 Southeast Asians
  basic interpersonal
   communication skills
   (BICS) needs, 116
  cognitive linguistic proficiency
   (CALP) needs, 116
  content mastery, 116–117
  needs, 115–117

and teaching style, typical
American, 116
special education exclusion, 183
staff awareness issues, 200
staff development/training, 21
support needs, 18, 50
teaching, first-person stories,
192–295
translators, 151–152, 159–161, 167,
200
viewed by culturally diverse
families, 98
Employment
barriers/challenges, 13–16
educational needs, 19–20
English as second language (ESL).
See also Educational system;
Paradigm shift; Potential
English proficient (PEP)
adult, 306–307
affective filter, 188
agenda/curriculum, hidden,
189–190
basic interpersonal communication
skills (BICS), 194
characteristics, shared, 182
Chinese, 184–187
classroom case study, 184–187
classroom issues, 199
code-switching, linguistic/
cultural, 181
cognitive linguistic proficiency
(CALP), 192–193, 194
community activities, 203, 234
conflict, intragroup, 185
cultural/linguistic awareness,
191–192, 210
culture adjustment, 192
discourse incongruencies,
classroom, 190, 229
English practice needs, 192–193
experience-based teaching, 192
families, 188, 199–200, 265–285,
307–308

collaboration with, 199–200,
202–204
suggestions for, 204, 206
guidelines, 307–308
high-context orientation, 189
homework role, 273–274
language loss, 188
learning style adaptation, 189
limited English proficient (LEP)
strategies, 181–208
and limited English proficient
(LEP), 10, 159–154
literacy acquisition, 193–194
memorization, rote, 185–186
methods/theories, successful,
186–187
nonverbal communication,
191–192
optimal language learning
environment and
experiences for English
(OLLEEE), 202–203
optimal language learning
environments (OLLE), 182,
202–203
optimal learning environments
(OLE), 182, 201–203
optimal learning environments
(OLE) optimal language
learning environments
(OLLE), 182
paradigm shift
empowerment from
disenfranchisement, 314
preschool English training, 200
resource issues, 200
and special education, 159–164,
167–168
and specific learning disability
(SLD), 33–35
staff awareness issues, 200
staff needs, 200
success case history, 207
unaccompanied minors, 195–199

English as second language (ESL)
(*continued*)
writing mastery, 194

F

Families, 200, 201
and acculturation, 13–14, 154–158,
302–303
adjustment with, 277–281
and assessment, 19, 118, 166–170,
303–304
and code-switching,
linguistic/cultural, 191
collaboration with, 18–19, 72–73,
199–200, 200, 202–204
checklist, 279–281
obstacles to, 274–275
concept development, 284
cultural expectations, 151–154,
166–168, 173–174, 274–275,
276
and educational success, 194–199
and English as second language
(ESL), 188, 199–200, 265–285
English as second language (ESL)
guidelines, 307–308
and "hidden agenda," 300–301
homework role, 273–274
and language socialization, 188
language uses, home, 283
and limited English proficient
(LEP) + learning disability
(LD), 39–40, 266–285
and literacy acquisition, 193–194
literacy activities, home, 283–284
non-English-speaking, primarily,
7–8, 31–35
and overcoming barriers, 246
and preassessment, 235–236, 237
as resource, limited English
proficient (LEP) + learning
disability (LD), 55–56,
276–277
and special education, 118, 120,

149–159. *See also*
Acculturation; Special
education
state partnerships with, 266
suggestions for, 204, 206
and therapy model, 315
training of, 282
view of U.S. educational system, 98
Filipinos. *See also* Pilipino/Tagalog
education, homeland, 87–88
family system/obligations, 84
history/demographics, 83
immigration to U.S., 86–87
language, 84–86
as U.S. students, 88–90

G

Gifted program, 162–163
Guam. *See* Chamorros (Guam)

H

Hawaiians, 202
culture revival, 67
educational collaboration, families,
72–73
Hawaiian/Caucasian value
comparison, 70
history/demographics, 65–67,
69, 326
hospitalization, attitudes toward,
91
intervention strategies, educational,
71–72
Native Hawaiian Assessment
Project, 67–69
native language skills, 68
Pihana Na Mamo Native Hawaiian
Special Education Project,
69, 71
special education, 68, 69, 71
Hindi language, 132–142. *See also*
Indian subcontinent,
languages/linguistics

Hmong, 116, 151. *See also* Southeast
        Asians
    acculturation, 244–245
    alphabetic writing system, 114
    assessment, 238–249
    cultural expectations, 234
    current U.S. situation, 248–249
    curriculum, "hidden," 301–302
    distribution in U.S., 241
    diversity among, 240
    family collaboration with
            educational system, 246–248
    folk beliefs, 244–245
    history/demographics, 239–241
    learning styles, 243–244
    naming system, 110
    oral tradition (collective stories),
            242–243
    school system, homeland, 243
    speech-language-hearing
            specialists, 21
    trauma before immigration, 239–240
    in U.S classrooms, 245–246
Hmong language, 111, 116, 117
    oral, 241–242
    stress/intonation, 242
Homecoming Act of 1988, 108

I

Immigration
    adjustment in U.S., 182–183
Immigration law, 1965
    and Filipinos, 87
Indian subcontinent, 126–146. *See also*
            Hindi language; Kannada
            language
    communicative disorders clinical
            aspects, 145–146
    culture/language, 141–143
    history/demographics, 127–130
    immigrants in U.S., 143–145
    Indo-Europeans (Indo-Aryans,
            Indic people), 128
    kinship terms/family
            communication, 142–143

language/culture, 141–143
languages/linguistics, 130–140
    consonant system, 134–135
    determiner system, 140
    Dravidians, 127–128, 130–141.
            See also Kannada language
    Indo-European (Indo-Aryan,
            Indic), 131–141. *See also*
            Hindi; Sanskrit
    morphology, 136–37
    overview, 130–133
    phonetics/phonology, 133–140
    postpositions, 140
    subject-verb agreement, 139–140
    syntax, 138–139
    vowel system, 133–134
religions, 127
social language use, 141–142
writing/measurment, 128
Interpreters/translation, 151–152,
        159–161, 167, 224, 236–237,
        238
Iu-Mien, 116, 151
    alphabetic writing systems, 114

K

Kannada language, 132–140, 142–143.
        See also Indian subcontinent,
        languages/linguistics
Khmer/Cambodian language, 21,
        111, 116, 117
    lexicon, 113
    naming system, 110
    phonology, 112
    speech-language-hearing
            specialists, 21
    writing, 113–114

L

Lahu, 116
Language. *See also* individual
        listings; Preassessment;
        Speech-language
        pathology (SLP)

Language *(continued)*
California State Bilingual Education
Office (BEO) Asian
Americans-Pacific Islanders
handbooks, 11
Cantonese, 310
Chamorros (Guam), 225
Chinese, 9–10, 21, 31–35, 112,
184–187, 225–226
collaborative inquiry process, 97–98
cultural interactions, 224–230
and form, language, 224–226
Hmong, 21, 111
imperative markers, Southeast
Asian, 112
Indian subcontinent
language/culture, 141–143
languages/linguistics, 130–140
Khmer/Cambodian, 21, 111, 112,
113–114
Laotian, 11, 21, 111, 112
lexicon, Southeast Asian, 113
literacy
multiple, 268, 282–284
primary, 10, 35, 51, 53, 55, 246,
283–284
morphology, syntax, Southeast
Asian, 112
naming systems, Southeast
Asian, 110
Pilipino/Tagalog, 21, 84–86, 310
Samoan, 81–82
Southeast Asian, 111–114, 112
communication
nonverbal, 110–111, 114–115
Thai, 21
Vietnamese, 21, 112, 113, 226
word order, Southeast Asian, 112
Laotian language, 109–110, 111, 116.
See also Laotians
Handbook for Teaching
Laotian-Speaking Students, 11
phonology, 112
speech-language-hearing
specialists, 21
writing, 113–114

Laotiâns, 116, 117, 151. *See also* Lao
language; Southeast Asians
naming system, 110
school system, homeland, 243
Lau vs Nichols (1974), 3, 117, 181
Learning disability (LD). *See also*
Limited English proficient
(LEP) + learning disability
(LD)
in Taiwan, 38–39
Life in Classrooms, 11, 190, 301
Limited English proficient (LEP), 313.
See also Educational system;
English as second language
(ESL); Potential English
proficient (PEP); Special
education
and assessment, special education,
119, 161–164
bilingual special education, 16–17
characteristics, shared, 182
collaboration with families, 202–204
curriculum, "hidden," 301, 316
English as second language (ESL)
strategies, 181–298
and English as second language
(ESL), 10, 159–164
English practice needs, 192–193
experience-based teaching, 192
homework role, 273–274
language-culture gap, 17–18
learning beyond schooling, 277–284
literacy acquisition, 193–194
primary language emphasis, 3,
283–284
social-cultural differences
adjustment for, 277–281
Southeast Asian communication
styles, 115–116
special education exclusion, 183
writing mastery, 194
Limited English proficient (LEP) +
learning disability (LD),
31–56. *See also* Learning
disability (LD); Specific
learning disability (SLD)

basic interpersonal communication
skills (BICS), 34
cognitive linguistic proficiency
(CALP), 34, 47
contributing factors, 42–45
first language-English cognitive
linguistic proficiency (CALP)
support need, 51, 53, 55
language experience limitations,
272–273
social support need, 53–54, 55
vocabulary development, 272–273
Literacy
concept development, 284
multicultural, 298–299, 317, 318
multiple, 268, 282–284
primary language, 10, 35, 51, 53, 55
246, 283–284
stories, first-person, 192–295

M

Map, Pacific, 2
Mien. *See* Iu-Mien

O

Optimal language learning
environment and
experiences for English
(OLLEEE), 202–203
Optimal language learning
environments (OLLE), 182,
202–203
Optimal learning environments
(OLE), 182, 201–203

P

Pacific Islanders, 63–98. *See also*
Asian Americans-Pacific
Islanders (API); Chamorros
(Guam); Filipinos;
Hawaiians; Samoans
at-risk populations in U.S.,
hidden, 93

challenges in U.S. educational
system, 94
Chamorros (Guam), 73–74
Filipinos, 83–90
Hawaiians, 65–73
hospitalization, attitudes toward,
91–92
kinship patterns, 92–93
limited English proficient (LEP)
students, 92, 93
overview, 63–65
religious/philosophical
viewpoints, 91
Samoans, 74–83
and U.S. Classrooms, 90–91
Pacific map, 2
Paradigm shift
acceptance from tolerance, 313–314
adaptation from assimilation,
315–316
asset from deficit view, 310–312
empowerment from
disenfranchisement, 314
enhancement from compensation,
308–310
potential English proficiency (PEP)
from limited English
proficient (LEP), 313
Parents. *See* Families
Pilipino/Tagalog, 84–86, 310. *See also*
Filipinos
speech-language pathology (SLP)
specialists, 21
Poetry, 296–297, 309–310, 319
Potential English proficient (PEP),
207, 213–215. *See also*
English as second language
(ESL); Limited English
proficient (LEP)
Poverty, 31–35, 152, 157, 165,
167–168, 232, 281
Preassessment. *See also* Assessment;
Language
adjustment requirements, 233–238
Asian written discourse style,
229–230

Preassessment *(continued)*
auditory processing/discrimination, 237
checklist, 255
classroom discourse, 229, 311–312
cognitive delay, 236
collaborative model, professional, 254, 256–257
communication
nonverbal, 221–224
verbal, 218–219
communicative competencies, 227–228
culture, 215–216
communication, 224–230
grammar, 219
histories
cognitive skills, 237
cultural-linguistic, 235–236
developmental/health, 235
family, 235–236
home country experiences, 235
language development, 236–237
social/emotional, 237–238
Hmong language
oral, 241–242
stress/intonation, 242
language
content, 226
culture/communication interplay, 227–230
styles, 228–229
use, 226
mainstream placement considerations, 233–234
multicultural competencies, 227–228
phonology, 219–220
pragmatics, 220–221, 222–223, 314
religions, 229–232
semantics, 220

R

Research needs, 16–17, 21–22
special education, 118

S

Samoans, 74–83, 304–305
aggression, 80–81
child rearing, 79–80
education, homeland, 82
history/demographics, 74–77
American Samoa, 77
Western Samoa, 75–76
language, 81–82
lifestyle, 77–78
as limited English proficient (LEP) students, 82–83
religion, 78–79
Sanskrit, 110, 111, 112. *See also* Indian subcontinent,languages/ liguistics, Indo-European (Indo-Aryan, Indic)
Panini, 130–131
Social-cultural differences
adjustment for, 277–281
Southeast Asians, 107–121. *See also* Hmong; Iu-Mien; Laotians; Vietnamese
acculturation, 117, 154–158
bilingual education, 117
communication
nonverbal, 110–111, 114–115
content mastery U.S. educational, 116–117
cultural expectations, 151–154, 166, 172–174
difficulties, English communication, 112, 114–115
education needs in U.S., 115–117
and English as second language (ESL), 159–164, 167–168
families and special education, 118, 120, 141–175
Homecoming Act of 1988, 108
immigration to U.S., history, 108–109, 240–241
interpersonal relationships, 110–111
language diversity, 111–112

language variations from English,
109–111
lexicon, 113
mastery English-taught content,
116–117
misunderstanding, cultural,
164–174
morphology, syntax, 112
naming system, 110
needs, basic interpersonal
communication skills
(BICS), 116
needs, cognitive linguistic
proficiency (CALP), 116
needs, social/cultural adjustment,
117
phonology, 112
religious beliefs, 118
respectful relationships, 110–111
Sanskrit, 110, 111, 112
Sino-Tibetan language family, 111
special education, 118–121,
149–175
assessment, 118–119, 161–164,
168–172
cultural view, 118
and special education. *See also*
Special education
speech-language-hearing
specialists, 21
students with mild disabilities,
118–121
translation, 151–152, 159–161, 167
trauma before immigration, 108,
239
writing, 113–114
Special education, 31–56
assessment, 118–119, 161–164,
168–172
bilingual
assessment, 118–119, 121, 161–164
limited English proficient (LEP),
16–17, 119
personnel needs, 119–121,
159–164

cultural expectations, 151–154,
166–168, 172–174
cultural needs, 149–175
cultural view, Southeast Asians,
118
determining etiology, 150–151
and English as second language
(ESL), 159–164, 167–168
gifted program, 162–163
Hawaiians, 68, 69, 71
misunderstanding, cultural,
164–174
parent training, 282
personnel, monolingual, 119–121
Pihana Na Mamo Native Hawaiian
Special Education Project,
69, 71
referral factors
study of limited English
proficient (LEP) + learning
disability (LD), 42–45
and religious beliefs, 118, 155–156
Southeast Asians, 149–175
Specific learning disability (SLD),
31–35. *See also* Limited
English proficient (LEP) +
learning disability (LD)
Speech-language-hearing, 18, 21, 315
Asian Americans-Pacific Islanders
(API), 21–22
multidisciplinary need, 22
Speech-language pathology (SLP),
32–35, 145–146. *See also*
Language
Asian Americans-Pacific Island
(API) specialists, 21
assessment, standardized, 314–315
classroom discourse, 229, 299–301,
311–312
collaborative model, professional,
254, 256–257
communicative competencies,
227–228
English as second language (ESL)
guidelines, 307–308

Speech-language pathology
(continued)
families
concept development, 284
language uses, home, 283
literacy activities, home, 283–284
histories
assessment, 303–304
Indian subcontinent, 145–146
language
culture/communication
interplay, 227–230, 303–304
styles, 228–229
literacy, multiple
modeling, 282–284
morphology
Indian subcontinent, 136–137
Southeast Asians, 112
multicultural competencies,
227–228, 318
phonology, 112, 133, 219–220
Cambodian language/Khmer,
112
differences, 311–312
Indian subcontinent, 133–140
Southeast Asian, 112
preassessment, 213–259
auditory processing/
discrimination, 237
communication
nonverbal, 221–224
verbal, 218–219
culture, 215–216
grammar, 219
histories
cognitive skills, 237
developmental/health, 235
family, 235–236
language development,
236–237
linguistic-cultural, 235–236
social/emotional, 237–238
Hmong language
oral, 241–242
stress/intonation, 242

phonology, 219–220
pragmatics, 220–221, 222–223, 314
semantics, 220
primary language therapy lack,
200
referral and limited English
proficient (LEP), 37
syntax
Indian subcontinent, 138–139
Southeast Asians, 112
therapy, family, 315

T

Tagalog/Pilipino, 84–86, 310. See also
Filipinos
speech-language-hearing
specialists, 21
Tamil language, 132, 135
Thai, 21
speech-language-hearing
specialists, 21
Translation/interpreters, 151–152,
159–161, 167, 224, 236–237,
238
Trauma
before immigration, 108, 239

V

Vietnamese, 116
acculturation, 154–158
cultural expectations, 151–154, 166,
172–174
English as second language (ESL),
184–187
and English as second language
(ESL), 159–164, 167–168
misunderstanding, cultural, 164–174
special education, 141–175. See also
Special education
assessment, 161–164
translation, 151–152, 159–161, 167
Vietnamese language, 113, 117. See
also Southeast Asians

cognitive linguistic proficiency
     (CALP), 194
lexicon, 113, 226
naming system, 110
speech-language-hearing
     specialists, 21
Vygotskian paradigm, 97–98

W

Writing
     Asian written discourse style,
          229–230
     Hindus, 128
     Southeast Asians, 113–114